A YEAR OF FESTIVALS IN
IRELAND

D1609796

A YEAR
OF FESTIVALS
IN IRELAND

AN EPIC TALE OF MEANDERING MISADVENTURE
AND ANTI-ECONOMICS

MARK GRAHAM

NEW ISLAND

A YEAR OF FESTIVALS IN IRELAND
First published 2014
by New Island
2 Brookside
Dundrum Road
Dublin 14

www.newisland.ie

PRINT ISBN: 978-1-84840-333-8
EPUB ISBN: 978-1-84840-334-5
MOBI ISBN: 978-1-84840-335-2

British Library Cataloguing Data. A CIP catalogue record for this book is available from the British Library.

Cover image: Forbidden Fruit, in the grounds of The Royal Hospital, Kilmainham, 2012, © Mark Graham.

Typeset by JVR Creative India
Cover design by XXXXXXX
Printed by ScandBook AB, Sweden

10 9 8 7 6 5 4 3 2 1

To all the people who give their time, energy and imagination to create and curate the festivals that make Ireland a better place – Big Love!

Contents

Acknowledgements

*A*fter playing a gig with guys who I've been knocking around with for years, I finally worked up the courage to tell them that I was taking a break from playing for a while – a year's break to be exact – to go to three festivals in Ireland every week.

They were confused, and didn't believe me at first, but like so many other people I know, they offered cautious, bemused encouragement and gave me the leeway to hit the road. My mother and sister suffered me being even more flakey than usual, but fair play to them, they're still there, haven't disowned me and are always on hand to offer help and advice. I missed birthdays, stag nights, weddings, trips away and a host of other things that I should've been at with friends, but thankfully most of them are still talking to me. Cheers for that.

Anthea from *The Irish Times* somehow gave me her support and a patch of real estate in The Ticket; as surprising as it was appreciated. It's hard to gauge just how much this helped my year of festivals, but it helped a lot. She also continues to support Aston Villa, so it's likely that her judgement is questionable. Eoin Purcell from New Island Books may also have dodgy judgement, but thanks to him for his patience and for taking a punt on a chancer in a van. The financial institutions that refused me a mortgage gave me a new lease of life, but an unfortunate side effect is they've also made me question the existence of unappreciated wisdom in Garth Brooks' lyrics.

Festivals wouldn't be worth the effort if it weren't for the fab and freaky folk who populate them. These people have taken years off my life, but in the best way possible. It's their stories that I've stolen for this book. The crew that have been entertaining and educating me through Facebook and Twitter have had much of their festival wisdom nicked too and reproduced in these pages. I'll get ye all a pint or something. Those who read and engaged with my blog can take the blame for encouraging me to write about my festival adventures; they have my thanks, if no one else's. More than anyone else, I've been leeching off the hard work and goodwill of the legions of troopers who organise and run Ireland's festivals. Without these decent *daoine*, I'd be collecting stamps and writing about Inverted Jennys.

God bless ye, every one!

Introduction

*O*n a sharp November evening, after three nights spent sleeping in a van at the side of a road in Tullamore, the door of Wanderly Wagon, my camper van home from home, slid back and I emerged in a neat tux and black tie. Suited and booted, I imagined myself cutting a figure somewhere between Daniel Craig's Bond and Johnny Depp's Roux from *Chocolat*. In reality, I was styling it somewhere between Ricky Gervais and Pecker Dunne. To be fair, I'd found the boots in a skip in Ballinasloe, so I was working 'skip-diving chic' as best I could. It was night three of *Macra na Feirme's* Queen of the Land Festival, and I'd been invited along to act as escort for one of the unlucky Lovely Girls. I stank of baby-wipes with an underlying hint of diesel fumes, but I was ready to party.

This shindig was three months into my quest to attend three festivals in Ireland every week for a year. Let me run that by you again – three festivals EVERY week, for a whole year. 'Impossible!' I hear you cry. Impossible? Maybe. Difficult? Definitely. Spending three nights sessioning with a rabble of wild, young, rural types from all over Ireland at a Lovely Girls competition in Co. Offaly is more fun than a bag of mushrooms on a ghost train, but it can knock a couple of years off your life expectancy.

In May 2011, having scraped together a 10 per cent deposit for a house, I applied for a mortgage. One financial institution told me to call back to them in three months with a tidier ledger; another said that they would give me a mortgage if I anted up 20 per cent of the cost of the bubbled-up price tag. I prepared myself for some serious scrimping and saving, repetitive weekends shackled to the couch, getting sucked in by some reality television programme or other. Thankfully, a little voice in the back of my head yelled 'Stall the Digger! This crowd has a worse credit rating than you, and you're going to kowtow to them? Cop yerself on!' So I did. Using the savings I'd squirreled away, I bought a fifth-hand VW camper van and decided to seek out the festive pueblos, parishes and páirceanna of Ireland to load up on some positivity. I was tired of being told how we lost the run of ourselves in a bubble bath of bad banking decisions. I certainly hadn't lost the run of myself, and I had a Ronnie Whelan that I wasn't on my own. My suspicion was that not only were there a number of people out there who were innocent of bankrupting our country, they were more than likely the same people who were still volunteering to create fun and festivals in the places where they lived, making the country a better place to live in and giving the rest of us something to look forward to. I was so sure of this that I was willing to bet a year of my life and my dwindling deposit on it. I wanted to meet these people, and to be free from negativity. The plan was to become something of a positivity vampire.

Taking to the road meant making some sacrifices. Quiet weekends at home by the fire, spare time, hobbies and any flimsy chance that existed for a stable relationship were all non-runners. To participate fully in the spirit of a few of these festivals, I'd need to put my physical health, sanity and general well-being on the line. *Supersize Me* is only in the ha'penny place compared to throwing yourself consistently into the middle of some of the sessions out on the festival trail of Ireland. The flip side was that lots of responsibilities were shed to go and live in a van and be part of the best parties Ireland had to offer for a whole year. I don't know why I didn't think of it sooner.

Even during the preliminary stages of partially planning my adventures, I had a feeling that my quest was going to lead to festival experiences of epic proportions. I decided to give the folk at the *Guinness Book of Records* a shout to check what it might take for me to qualify for their yearly catalogue of obsessives. They weren't keen on my idea, and reckoned that if you had two lads on a street corner in Wexford banging pots together, a few other heads would turn up with bags of cans and we'd call it a pot-banging festival, i.e., we have loose criteria for what constitutes a festival in Ireland. When you encounter something like the Cow Dung Festival in Castleconnor, Co. Sligo, you'd have to concede that they might have a point.

In order to put some structure on my trundling around the country, I decided to come up with my own festival definition. It's a loose-fitting description at best. I like to think of it as a telescopic yardstick, capable of being altered slightly to fit different situations, but it certainly helped to steer a course through the festival-infested fields of Ireland. I took a festival to be:

An event, usually and ordinarily staged by a local com-munity or interest group, which centres on and celebrates some unique aspect of that community, interest group and/ or festival itself. It can be a day or period of celebration, a religious commemoration, an annual celebration or anniver-sary or an organised series of events, concerts, plays, films or activities, typically held annually in the same place.

The adventure hadn't even started and already the spontaneity and joy was being sucked out of it by trying

3

to define it. Jaysus, get the Guinness crowd on the phone again, I think I just broke the wet blanket land speed record.

My festival definition was spurious at best, but at least it was a little clearer than that offered by Indian mystic and guru Bhagwan Shree Rajneesh, who said: 'The truth is that existence wants your life to become a festival.' I have absolutely no idea what he meant by that, but I do know that trying to capture or define something as ephemeral as the landscape of Irish festivals is problematic, impractical and idiotic.

And so we begin.

1 | *On a Mission from God*

Something special was needed to get the festival wagon rolling. The idea of an ancient religious festival of sacrifice seemed appropriate. There is a rich historical tradition where those about to undertake a quest begin their journey with a pilgrimage for spiritual cleansing, enlightenment and guidance. God knows that I could always do with a hefty dose of all three. Declarations to deities aside, I'd have to consider myself agnostic, which can seem like a cop-out. Professing a lack of knowledge as a belief is a bit wishy-washy, but it's the best I can do. Even though I'm unsure of His/Her existence, I do hope that God/Allah/Vishnu/Gaia won't hold that against me. Even with a gaping hole where my spirituality should be, the annual holy happenings on Lough Derg in Co. Donegal had been on my radar for many years for a number of reasons.

The three-day retreats that take place on the remote lake island during the summer months are reputed to be the most severe and challenging Christian pilgrimages in the world, and Krishna knows I've always been easily egged on by a dare. On rare trips to exotic locations I've often found myself in a temple of some description, tangled up with some strand of the spiritual culture of the place. Witches, sadhus, monks, gurus, shamans, medicine men and acid casualties always manage to find a way of adding some colour to my foreign travels. In recent years it began to seem negligent; having experienced what some interesting places around the world have to offer in extremist spirituality, I'd neglected to explore what similar homegrown adventures might lay out on the altar. The pilgrimage to Santiago de Compostela sees thousands of people traipsing through the Spanish countryside each year, but compared to St Patrick's Purgatory on Lough Derg, it's just a stroll in the sunshine. A bit of hardship and penance while exploring one of the oldest festivals in Ireland actually seemed appealing to me. Little did I know....

When it comes to festivals, the Catholics have been at it for a looooong time. There's a feast day for some saint or other celebrated on almost every day of the week on the Roman Catholic Calendar; Christmas and Easter are just feast day festivals that have gone viral. One of the things that early Christians did in this part of the world was to figure out that, as they got rid of the pagans, it would be advantageous to keep the pagan feast days, but attach a new significance to them in an effort to secure the permanence of the usurping Christian festival. The proximity of Christmas to the Winter Solstice is no coincidence. There is a large cohort of pagans in Ireland still celebrating the pre-Christian festivals and, speaking from personal experience, pagans throw a good session (you can be sure that some of them will be sampled in these pages, just for the sake of completeness, don't you know). Not only were dates reallocated, but the Christian party planners also rezoned sites of significance to pagans, and it would seem that the islands in Lough Derg can be counted among these places.

The lake and islands turn up in fairy tales and folklore, with stories of Fionn mac Cumhaill swinging his mother around the place by the ankles in an effort to keep her safe. Happy Mothers' Day! But it's the stories that associate the place with the Godfather of Irish saints, St Paddy himself, that have blurred the border between folklore and religion. Some legends tell that the islands in Lough Derg were the last strongholds of the Celtic Druids, and Big Pat came to town to wipe out the last of them. There are also stories that suggest that around AD 700 the bold Patsy landed up on Saint's Island for a spot of prayer and penance while he was in the neighbourhood, where a cave provided him with some shelter. This cave became the focus of original pilgrimages to the area. Evidence would suggest that the Godfather was in Donegal at some stage, and he left a capo in charge in the shape of a disciple by the name of Davog. Davog's name crops up a lot in the area, and he seems to have been responsible for establishing a number of churches and religious settlements here, but it is through association with St Patrick that the place became irresistible to pilgrims, who have continued to visit the island for well over a thousand years. The area has become even more associated with St Patrick than a beer-soaked Temple Bar on 17 March.

The prep for this pilgrimage craic begins at midnight the night before hitting the road for Lough Derg. This is when your fasting begins, yep – fasting! The fasting will last for seventy-two hours, with one meal allowed each day. The term 'meal' in this instance is to real food what Jedward are to singers. You are allowed dry toast and/or dry oatcakes accompanied by black tea once a day. That's it. Now I don't know if you're as fond of your grub as I am, but eating only dry toast once a day for three days was a challenge for me, and not something that was undertaken lightly. Jumping into the car early on Tuesday morning, with a stomach doing more grumbling than Simon Cowell at the regional heats of *Scór na nÓg*, the journey began. Pettigo in Co. Donegal is the nearest village to the island ferry, and the fastest way to get to Donegal from south-east Ireland is through Northern Ireland.

One of the interesting places that you might end up passing through to get to Lough Derg is the town of Kesh. Kesh is a Unionist stronghold, and a place that has seen its share of 'The Troubles'. During the Eighties, two IRA members and one British soldier were killed during a gun battle in the area. One of the things that is noticeable in recent trips to Northern Ireland is that, as the efforts towards a unified Irish Republic have become more peaceful and politically mainstream, there seem to be fewer Republican banners and flags. The amounts of Unionist trappings are not only steadfast, but have been changing in design and appearance in recent years. There seem to be some graphic designers at work amongst the Unionist ranks, but it is the Union Flag and the Red Hand/George's Cross/Crown combination that still seems to be most popular in some areas. Examples of all these trappings flap in the wind in Kesh. This was the first time that I'd been in an area so blatantly anti-Catholic whilst actually being on what could loosely be described as Catholic business.

It provided an interesting juxtaposition, and the usually unsettling sight of a Union Flag whilst on the island of Ireland had deeper resonances when travelling under the imagined auspices of the Papist regime. My stomach grumbled with an apt and eerily accurate impression of an ill-tempered Ian Paisley.

Eventually arriving at the island, stomach emptier than a politician's promise, one of the first things I was asked to do was hand over my shoes and socks. I hadn't been prepared for that. The pilgrimage is carried out barefoot. The shoes and socks are stowed under the bed – a bed that is used more for storage than it is for sleeping. This being the first day of the pilgrimage, no sleep would be allowed until about 10.00 p.m. on day two. By now you should be building up a picture of the demands of the pilgrimage: fasting, abstinence from sleep and cold feet – a picture I was beginning to wish I'd had figuratively the day before. These were only some of the preparations for what was to come. Every pilgrim is required to complete nine 'stations' while on the island. A station consists of kneeling on the stone flags at the foot of St Patrick's Cross and reciting prayers, kneeling on the stone flags at the foot of St Brigid's Cross and reciting prayers, standing with outstretched arms and reciting a renunciation, three laps of the outside of St Patrick's Basilica, walking around the outside of each of the six exposed stone circles (known as 'Beds') while saying prayers, kneeling on the stone entrances to the six Beds while saying prayers, walking around the inside of each of the six exposed stone Beds while saying prayers, kneeling on the exposed stones while reciting prayers at the foot of each of the six crosses inside the Beds, standing at the water's edge reciting prayers, kneeling on a stone block at the water's edge while still lashing out the prayers, back to St Patrick's cross for another assault on the knees, and finally into the chapel for another spot of kneeling and a sprinkling of prayer. That's one 'station'. Repeat all of it another eight times for a full dose of old-school penitential kicks. It turns out that kneecapping has been a form of torture in Northern Ireland long before gunpowder found its way here. All of this takes place on an empty stomach, with no sleep, and your bare feet exposed to the vagaries of a Donegal summer; weather that usually has all the warmth of Twink with a hangover.

All the while you're getting hungrier, increasingly tired, and your knees are doing more complaining than B. A. Baracus on a transatlantic Ryanair flight. The good news is that you only have to do the first three stations outside (each station takes just under an hour). The four stations carried out communally between midnight and 6.00 a.m. are conducted inside the basilica, but with all the walking and kneeling still included. It's difficult to give you an impression of how difficult the whole process becomes, and you may be asking yourself why anyone would do this. I was asking myself that very question at about 6.00 a.m. on day two. I nearly gave up, and I was seriously considering getting the boat back to the mainland and heading for the hills. Between hallucinations, I had an argument with my selves, and we all decided to stick with it.

My reasons for being there were weak. Cultural curiosity, a sense of wanting to tap into the spiritual roots of my own place and an interesting way to start a festival quest will only get you so far when hunger and sleep deprivation are driving you demented.

The weird thing is that after the sun starts to warm you on day two, you actually start getting into it. There are lots of opportunities to talk to the other pilgrims between stations, and the camaraderie of adversity creates a bond that makes the whole thing bearable. Austerity had become a well-established economic buzzword round about this time, but the experience of Lough Derg lent the idea of belt tightening an interesting perspective. There were people here from all walks of life, all age groups, and from the four corners of Ireland. I asked one lady in her early forties why she had returned to the island for a seventh time. She immediately replied 'Guilt!' I asked if she had single-handedly brought down the banks, perhaps explaining why she would feel enough guilt to make her come and torture herself. She laughed, and went on to explain that when she sees the suffering of others and looks at all that she has, she can't help but feel that three days a year of hardship is not a lot to give up in order to put her in touch with her spiritual core and give her a renewed sense of appreciation.

A 21-year-old student, between telling me in detail what she was going to do to a curry chip once her fast was over and she'd returned home, said that her sister was coming to the island and that she felt that she'd lost all contact with God, so tagging along with sis was her way of trying to re-establish the connection. As if to underline the Pagan/Catholic heritage of the place, a 60-year-old lady who had been there many times told me that she dabbled in Tarot card reading and matchmaking, but I wasn't allowed tell the priests this. She was a great character and, no matter how bad I felt, she managed to draw a smile and a laugh from me.

I chatted to one man who had been on a pilgrimage to Lough Derg seventeen times. When I expressed how impressed I was, he brushed it off by saying that he met a lady on one pilgrimage who had been there 203 times. 203 times! Why? Most p Leaving Cert ilgrims go as an offering, but stories abound of people who use their pilgrimage as a petition for a sick family member, or to help with some problem in their lives. When the prayers are answered, they come back. Two young girls were there because their Leaving Cert results were due out the next week. As they walked away, a somewhat cynical schoolteacher took a drag of her cigarette, and as she exhaled she acerbically commented into the smoke: ''Tis a bit late trying to fatten a pig after 'tis slaughtered.' In some strange, religious twist, you are allowed to smoke whenever you want on the island. For some, the nicotine offers comfort and relief from the pangs of hunger. Some people even took up smoking for the duration, me included. You can buy fags in the gift shop, which also sells rosary beads, funky PDF bibles on brightly coloured memory sticks and Lough Derg yo-yos. Twenty Bensons, a litre of holy water and a set of rosary beads please.

The place itself is impressive, and the setting is postcard perfect, even if the sun doesn't shine. It's like Disneyland for Catholics. One of the things that I was delighted to discover was that the windows in the basilica were made by Harry Clarke. Harry could capture a unique mix of the Celtic, Gothic and Nouveau, leading him to be regarded as one of the finest illustrators of the work of Edgar Allen Poe. Not surprisingly, I didn't take note of his work until after being allowed sleep at the end of day two's vigil, when some degree of sanity finally began to return.

It wouldn't be a festival without some music, and there was plenty of singing on offer at the many ceremonies during the days on the island. We even got a bit of harp thrown into the mix. But it was one *Taizé* chant that seemed to catch hold of me in particular.

Now I have no doubt that the influence of sleep deprivation, starvation and pain helped carry me away, but just before we were allowed go to bed at the end of day two, the young girls who had sung so sweetly in the church all day just seemed to hit the right groove with one particular chant. The nature of the *Taizé* is that it is extremely repetitive, and it builds to a crescendo over a long time and then fades out. The trance-inducing quality of the chant was experienced to a degree that I hadn't immersed myself in since Underworld lashed into 'Born Slippy' at the end of Homelands 1999. It seems that abstinence is a recession-busting way of getting out of your bin. Austerity might actually catch on as an underground club-culture movement.

We were eventually allowed into bed at 10.00 p.m. on day two. I slept the sleep of the innocent, which is not surprising as I'd been to confession that morning for the first time in an awfully long time:

'How long has it been since your last confession, my son?'

'So long that I've forgotten how this works, Father.'

'Well, is there anything you'd like to tell me?'

'Nope, I haven't pulled my sister's hair in years.'

'Are you a good person?'

'I do my best, like.'

'Okay, go over and say a decade of the rosary and an act of contrition.'

'How does that one start again, Father?'

When a blustery and rainy day three rolled around, I was surprisingly upbeat and strangely more alert travelling back home than I had been travelling up. Still on fast, I wasn't allowed to eat until after midnight. However difficult it is to keep fasting whilst on an island policed by priests in bright, shiny shoes and woolly socks, I might add, stopping for petrol at a garage that also stocks hot rashers and sausages is a temptation that I didn't think I'd be strong enough to resist. I can report that I didn't eat until after 1.00 a.m. on day four. How holy am I? I did, though, consider 'taking the soup' in Kesh.

Lough Derg is an amazing experience, and a facet of Irish culture that can often go ignored. It's easy to write off Catholicism as something that's dying out, only for the elderly and the dull, and I've probably been guilty of this on more than one occasion in the past.

It is impossible to deny how deeply religion has wound its roots into our culture. You should go and try it for yourself. I have no doubt that you will not enjoy all of it, and there will be times when you will want to give up, but you will not experience anything else like it in your lifetime. If you're visiting Ireland and want to experience something unique, wholly Irish and more hardcore than naked blindfolded bungee jumping in New Zealand, get thee to Lough Derg. Whilst on the island, a few people asked me if I would come back again. At the time, to be diplomatic whilst amongst the devoted, I said that I would need to reflect on the experience in order to decide, but secretly I was thinking 'No fecking way, are you mental?!' Before I left, though, I made a little promise, and I don't know if He was listening, but I will return to Lough Derg … after Waterford lift the Liam McCarthy Cup. Safe enough for a while yet.

Suitably cleansed and enlightened, I felt ready to begin my quest. I'd bought a St Christopher's Medal while on Lough Derg when I popped into the shop for twenty fags and a holy yo-yo. It was huge medal, and specially designed to clip onto car sun visors. Although sketchy in my beliefs, I didn't think having it blessed and sticking it up in Wanderly Wagon would do any harm. I was going to need all the help I could get.

2 | *September – Bog Warriors and The Runs*

*A*fter particularly epic bouts of nocturnal socialising, I can sometimes find myself lying in bed, mid morning/ late afternoon, suffering from what I endearingly refer to as a dose of the 'Oh Nos'. The Oh Nos are induced by a series of images that flash before your mind's eye; images that provide a brief glimpse of the most embarrassing and cringeworthy behaviour that you managed to get up to on the night before; the mental equivalent of the blush-inducing childhood photos that get blown up and stuck to walls at twenty-firsts. So there I was, lying in a tent on a Saturday morning, on an island off the coast of Cork, enjoying my little slideshow of shame, my brain trying to escape from my skull by swelling, whilst all around my tent the noisiest children in Christendom were having a game of 'Let's run around the tent and drive the sleepy man crazy'. You may not have much sympathy for self-induced torment, but technically it wasn't really my fault.

I landed on Cape Clear on a Friday evening, and hightailed it to the campsite to throw up the tent, hoping to pitch it quickly enough so as to catch the end of an Ireland international soccer match in Ciarán Danny Mike's (local watering hole and the backdrop for many an 'Oh No' flashback). I pulled the tent out of the bag, only to find that there were no pegs. This was not a good start to the very first festival on my year-long quest. I blame the pair of flakes who'd previously borrowed my tent for this facet of my descent into madness. It was now dark, and I began trying to fashion pegs from spit, clay and grass. I'd decided while packing that I wouldn't need a torch, using the logic that one's natural night vision should be sufficient for navigating the roads around the island after sundown. Night vision is Tom Gaul use on cloudy, rainy nights.

It turns out that I'm more Squirrel Simmers than Bear Grylls. I eventually got the tent pitched, the bed inflated and everything cushy, but only through grim determination; the kind of determination that is usually followed by a declaration in a low, manly voice: 'I'm going for a pint.' There are two problems with this. First of all, pints are social creatures, and they travel in herds; you will never find one or 'a' pint existing in total isolation in the wild. The idea of a singular pint is more far-fetched than the existence of unicorns and TV3 celebrities. The second problem is that grim determination has the potential to provide enough imbibing energy to power Las Vegas on New Year's Eve during the annual Immersion Tank Expo.

There was one overriding moral arrived at from my Oh No Slideshow of Shame the following day: when sailors ask if you would like to continue the singsong back on the boat where they keep their bottles of rum, logic will always get beaten down by grim, determination-fueled drinking. But it could be worse; at least I didn't have to watch a nil-nil draw being dragged out over ninety minutes. I did, though, nearly set a yacht on fire. Whoops!

The island in question was Cape Clear, off the coast of Co. Cork – an island with a population of about 120 people. For the first weekend in September, the number of people on the island increases significantly. They've been coming in their droves to attend the Cape Clear International Storytelling Festival for more than twenty years. They come from all over Ireland, and beyond, specifically to attend this event, which features storytellers from all around the world. Storytelling festivals do pretty much exactly what it says on the tin.

The festival features 'Tellers', who are gifted in the art of transporting listeners to different times and places through their words. But there's more than the stories going on here. More music than you shake a stick at, set-dancing, guided walks of the island, workshops and *Après Scéal* of proportions that would have kept Keith Moon happy. I was at a session on the Saturday night that saw locals, mainlanders, tourists and in-betweeners taking turns in singing songs and playing tunes. There were guitars, banjos, accordions, whistles of all shapes and sizes, saxophones, and a girl called Abigail who had a voice that could hush a group of unruly kids playing 'Let's run around the tent and drive the sleepy man crazy'. This wasn't a Temple Bar, lash-it-out-for-the-tourists kind of thing. This was people sharing songs and tunes, having a buzz. The pure drop. Much better than the carry-on from the sailors and me the night before. Mind you, one of the biggest of the sailors did a version of Erasure's 'A Little Respect' that was particularly haunting. Not good, just haunting.

The atmosphere and sense of celebration that was evident on the island was exactly what I was hoping to find out on the festival trail. Most people at the festival were camping for the weekend, with one Scottish girl glamping it up in a spacious yurt. Yurts are something of a leftover from our period of extravagance, but the tourists do seem to enjoy the camping equivalent of an episode of *Grand Designs*. I was happy in the tent I've had for nearly ten years now. Pegs would have been a bonus. The singing sailors were a group of lads from Cork who were staying on a yacht for the weekend. 'That must be very expensive?' I asked one of them as he drew breath between ballads. 'Not at all. There's nine of us, and we all chip in to rent a boat for a couple of weeks every year. Only a few of the lads can sail, and none of us have our own boat, so this is a great way to spend a holiday and it works out really cheap for a bunch of lads who enjoy a bit of craic and some sailing.' He flicked through pictures of their days sailing on his phone, showing blue skies, smiling faces and schools of dolphins. 'Travelling around our coast is a wonderful way to see the country, and we always manage to enjoy ourselves.' I didn't doubt him.

The best approach to the Storytelling Festival is to get a list of the events and pick out whichever ones you think you might like. If you're at a bit of a loss, refer to:

Irish Festival Rule No.9: *When stuck for information at a festival, pick out someone in the most unusual hat you can see. They'll know, or at least steer you in an interesting direction.*

During evenings at the festival there is a concert where the guest tellers from around the world each have a slot. The evening concert is a highlight of each day's events, and it's worth the jaunt up the biggest hill on the island to get an early seat near the front.

One of the guest tellers was Sheila Stewart, a Scottish travelling woman, whose family is steeped in folk music. Her grandfather was Jock Stewart, who had the song of the same name written about him ('Be easy and free when you're drinking with me, I'm a man you don't meet every day'.) Sheila's style is unpolished and natural as she talks about songs and stories like friends or family members, where she met them, who introduced her to them and what they mean to her.

Sheila is part of a tradition of stories and music that the Travellers managed to keep alive through their oral tradition. She told of a song that was passed down through countless generations of her family. A folklorist from a Scottish university managed to date their song back to the twelfth century. I'm something of a nerd, so I was lapping this shit up. At nearly 80 years old, you have to worry that the musical traditions of the travelling people may be something that is going to disappear with Sheila's generation. As the likes of Christy Moore, Pecker Dunne and others noted on a number of occasions, the world would be a poorer place without these songs and stories.

On a weekend when most of the festival's focus was on the rock 'n' roll circus that is Electric Picnic, a festival that has run up cumulative losses of millions and featured a public legal bust-up concerning who's holding the reins, it was nice to go down and attend a homely and wholesome festival that has become an important element of island life off the south-west coast. Cape Clear is an enchantingly beautiful place, and we were lucky enough to have the sunshine all day on Saturday, and a swim in the south harbour blew out the last of the cobwebs from the night before. If you get a chance, even when the storytelling isn't on, visit the island. You won't regret it.

The island is its own microcosm of economic woes. The population is just about big enough to keep the shop and the pub open; unfortunately, the post office has closed. Although there are other economic activities on the island, tourism and the Irish college are the key elements to the business life of the place, as they are in many Gaeltacht areas. A visit to the island is a worthwhile experience, and the Storytelling Festival is a wonderful way to spend a weekend in one of the most beautiful places the country has to offer. It sweetens the pot to know that you might also be positively contributing to the economy of a community that has been on the brink of being bust for much longer than the mainland. Beware of waylaying seafarers though.

In contrast to quiet island life, it would seem that Dublin is constantly hopping, especially in early September. The Theatre Festival, Fringe Festival, Dublin Contemporary and various film and book festivals had Das Kapital even busier than usual. When it comes to getting a shot of high-culture, you can usually count on the Dubs. So much so that autumn in Dublin has become known as Festival Season. It seemed like a good place to aim for next.

In my typical lowbrow approach to high culture, when seeking out a play for the evening, I choose *The Year of Magical Wanking*. This was absolutely because it had wanking in the title. From someone who once brought a first date to *Puppetry of the Penis*, this is no shocker. This was a play about homosexuality, Catholic guilt, drugs and much masturbation. Imagine everything that Dana (Rosemary Scallon, not the Transvestite Eurovision one) is opposed to. Got it? That's what this play was about. There was an immediacy, honesty and edge to this piece of theatre that impressed, made me squirm, think, laugh and, God forbid, even identify with. It wasn't for the faint-hearted or easily offended. A fella who thinks he's Jesus getting up to the shenanigans outlined in this play? If Dana catches a hold of him, he'll never wank again!

After a shot of culture, it was high time to get the hands dirty again. I headed for Monaghan early on a Saturday morning, having spent the night tucked up in Wanderly Wagon outside an Esso station in Palmerstown; not the most glamorous digs, but at least I didn't need pegs to stop it blowing away. It was fitting, in that the event I had my sights set on wasn't the most glitzy of affairs either. I was heading for Co. Monaghan to take part in the ancient Irish ritual of bog-snorkelling.

The brave souls gathered beside the murky bog-water to do battle. Masks down, neoprene body armour donned, an army of eejits waddling through the fields of Monaghan in their flippers, ready to vie for the title of Bog-Snorkelling Champion. Any event that requires people to wear flippers is going to be good craic. Nobody can look elegant, composed or graceful in flippers. Get Megan Fox to don a mask and snorkel and parade around a field in flippers, and she too would look like a tit. Bog-snorkelling is one of the last great levellers. The surreal nature of what lay ahead of me was hinted at as I drove through Cootehill and spotted the poster for the pig racing that was taking place there later that afternoon. Baby pigs 'race', complete with knitted jockeys strapped to their backs. I imagined the scene while Paul 'Uh Ahh' McGrath sang his latest single, 'Sunday Morning Coming Down', on Wanderly Wagon's wireless. It was becoming clear that Pat McCabe was scripting my day.

The Irish Bog-Snorkelling Championships take place in a bog-water-filled channel, at the bottom of a field in the wonderfully named townland of Doohamlet (it sounds even better when said in the Monaghan brogue). There is no doubt that the main purpose of this event is to have fun, whether you're young, old, local or a blow-in. Besides the main event, there's a barbecue, a fine selection of liquid refreshments, the ubiquitous bouncy castle and a selection of weird and wonderful bog-snorkellers to mingle with. The good-natured spirit of the event is evident from the moment you arrive, with upbeat banter flowing like bog-water released from a sluice. The mob in the bog call this 'Good, clane fun!' – the irony being that you'll be covered in peat, weeds, creepy crawlies, and God only knows what else, as soon as you finish your efforts in the bog-water.

The *chef d'équipe* of the Tullamore ladies' bog-snorkelling team told me that her team had been preparing by massaging their calves. I'm not sure how rubbing young cattle might help to prepare for paddling in bogs, but it must have worked, because one of the Offaly lasses took the ladies' crown. It was twenty quid to have a pop at the title, and you got two baby bottles of whiskey, a T-shirt, a certificate and tiny pieces of turf in most orifices of your body to take home with you. The proceeds of the event went towards raising funds for St Mary's hospital in Castleblaney; how can you not take your swimming hat off to that? A community coming together to have fun and attract some visitors, raise some funds and laugh all day long. This was exactly the kind of thing I was hoping to find.

The objective is to swim two lengths of the channel, up and back, faster than Phelps being chased by Sharknado. You can't use your arms for conventional swimming strokes. Underwater doggy paddling is permitted, but it soon became apparent that the best approach is to stretch your arms out in front of you to cut through the water like a torpedo or tugboat, whatever shape you're closer to. As you make your way along the channel, the master of ceremonies for the day's events follows you along the bank with a microphone, giving you both encouragement and abuse in equal measures. This fella is funny.

Addressing a snorkeler from Cavan (allegedly the meanest people in Ireland): 'G'wan ya hoor ya, there's a fiver down at the other end.'

Encouraging a folically challenged competitor from Altlanta, Georgia: 'This bog-water can cure baldness John, is chayper than fake tan, but unfortunately it can't cure being American!'

Egging on a young girl who was finding the challenge a bit much: 'I'd say the world record is safe, I'm after growing a feckin' beard!'

As a spaniel leapt into the bog after a competitor: 'G'wan ya dog ya!'

When my turn came, I tore into it with gusto and didn't do too badly. I was topping the leaderboard for a while, but a US Marine, a Duracell Bunny-like German and a series of experienced boggers knocked me down into sixth place. I thought that was a respectable enough showing for my first stab at doing lengths in a bog. Before you ask, as more than one cynic has, there were far more than six people competing. The cheek! When it was all wrapped up, it was off to the local in Castleblaney for the prize-giving and liberal administering of liquid refreshments, only to take the take the taste of bog-water out of our mouths you understand. Music on the night was provided by 'The Cheesy Bitches'. Perfect! I'm hoping to do much better next year. Some people run with the bulls in Pamplona, some swim with sharks in South Africa, but, lads, ye haven't lived until you've snorkelled with a dog in a bog in Monaghan.

After all the fluid in the bog, it was time to set my sights on something I could sink my teeth into. Up until I started my festival quest, I was not a fan of food festivals. Didn't really see the point of them. I'd been at a few, and had found them dull and drab.

Looking through the programme of the Harvest Food Festival in Waterford, I was torn between a few different events that looked like they might be fun. There was an introduction to whiskey that grabbed my attention – why wouldn't it? – but I thought that might get out of hand, seeing as myself and whiskey have agreed to avoid each other whenever possible. It's not like we have restraining orders out or anything; we just steer clear of each other to avoid trouble. I spotted that there was a night out where you got to go to three different restaurants in Waterford City over the course of five hours and sample the best that each restaurant had to offer. That sounded interesting enough, but what really caught my eye was that it was an event for single people. Unsurprisingly, I qualified.

I arrived in L'Atmosphere, and was like a goose looking into a barrel, trying to find the right table to sit at. Eventually, I figured it out. I was the second last person to arrive out of a group of eight. There were twenty-four people altogether, broken into three groups of eight for the grub crawl, and all came together for music and gargle at the last venue. Introductions were made, and small talk began about the usual kind of stuff. Then, the last member of our group arrived. She took my breath away. Literally, because I worked with her. She's in the office next to the studio in which I usually work. With all hope of imagined anonymity dashed, at least we had plenty to talk about. Understandably, everybody was a little nervous and apprehensive.

The waitress came round to take orders for drinks, starting at the opposite end of the table to me. Everybody before me ordered water. Shit! I'd left the Wanderly Wagon at home. Not to appear like a scumbag, I ordered water too. Damn you, peer pressure.

I'm not sure how advisable it is to eat in front of someone you've never met before whilst trying to make a good first impression, but I'm certain that trying to eat a starter of snails and beetroot mousse definitely isn't a good idea. It's difficult to maintain eye contact and small talk whilst poking at your starter trying to keep the quizzical look from your face. Peer pressure or not, I ordered a beer straight off when the waitress enquired next time round; 'twas badly needed at this stage. Low and behold, there were bottles of wine ordered for the table; the chances of being taken advantage of were looking up.

Desserts were eventually finished, without anyone losing an eye, and we all adjourned to the bar. As we chatted, everyone agreed that it was a really enjoyable evening, surprisingly so for most, who hadn't done anything like it before. Food festivals definitely have their moments.

Following the food and flirting fête, I needed some exercise to work off the snails, so I hopped into Wanderly Wagon on a glorious September afternoon to bomb up the road to Connemara. Connquest Connemara, stretching to breaking point my already elastic festival definition, was an event that required competitors to run/trek for 10K over a number of mountain ranges, while also completing a number of challenges along the way. A particular favourite of mine was a challenge called 'Shoot The Gimp'; a lesser-known popular pastime of Connemara farmers. If you failed to complete any challenge, you had to do an extra 0.5K loop on top of the 10K.

I'm all for a stroll through the mountains, especially when the scenery is as spectacular as it is in the Twelve Bens up around Renvyle, but why would you race through the mountains throwing javelins through hoops along the way? That has a distinct ring of torture about it to me, and I felt that I'd already built up enough penance credit in Lough Derg. Around about midday on Saturday, as the wind howled and the rain washed over Wanderly Wagon, you can be sure that I was asking myself some serious and soul-searching questions along the lines of: 'What kind of a Dope are you?!'

You may be as shocked as I was to find out that the whole running through the mountains *Krypton Factor* buzz was fun. You get all the scenery and the usual 'Isn't this wonderful?' experience, but there's a bit a of a challenge too, and lobbing shoes at George Bush cut-outs up a mountain in Galway, whilst enjoying amazing views of Inishboffin and Killary Harbour, is a cultural experience for which I find hard to find a parallel.

Now don't think for one minute that I wasn't in bits; I was heavy breathing like an asthmatic pervert on the phone to a hard of hearing supermodel, but the challenges broke up the course nicely, and thankfully I didn't have to complete any penalty laps. I nailed a gimp in the mountains of Connemara (never thought I'd ever get to say a sentence like that) with a paintball gun.

After running around the mountains, it was down the road for a well-deserved pint in Clifden at their Arts Festival. The weather wasn't great, but it did nothing to spoil the wonderful drive through Connemara. It's breathtaking, and even in the lashing rain, you'd have to ask yourself why we ever go abroad at all. The stone, moss, clouds, occasional snatches of sky and shadows are constantly changing the hue and blend of unspoiled scenery into a slow-moving tapestry of muted colours that have a wonderfully calming effect. I could happily sit on a rock in the Connemara countryside for extended periods of time just watching the clouds pass by. I'd bring a raincoat though.

It wasn't that the altitude and lack of oxygen had made me appreciative of cloudy rainy days; it was just that driving the van through some of the most wonderful scenery the country has to offer was becoming as enjoyable as the festivals themselves, and the west and north-west coasts of Ireland do that rugged, wild splendor thing so well. Being alone in the van, travelling through some beautiful Irish countryside that I'd never actually seen before, was taking on a meditative quality. Sometimes I'd listen to the radio. I regularly borrowed audiobooks from the library for long loops around the country, but on days like this in Connemara, silence was what worked best. Sometimes things just feel right, and as I made my way towards Clifden, I thanked my lucky stars for broken banks.

As soon as you arrive in Clifden at Arts Festival time, you get the feeling of a nice country town with a creative community buzz going on. The first person I came in contact with was Mary Donohue, who was manning the festival box-office/caravan. She couldn't have been friendlier, and her garrulous *geansaí* brightened up the otherwise dull day. After getting a programme and a bit of insight, it was off to Tom King's for the annual Arts Week Trad Session. There was a clatter of young musicians giving it sparks in the back of the bar. This event was free, and was also part of the Trad for Trócaire nationwide campaign. The bucket was passed around while the lads knocked out the tunes. Yet another community coming together, not just to enjoy themselves, but also to raise funds for a good cause. There was almost a pattern being established. It was a shame to have to hit and run, but a spot of trad in Tuam was planned for later that evening.

The contrast between Clifden and Tuam couldn't have been greater. The Trad Festival was good craic, and the crowd at the *céilí* couldn't have been more welcoming, even slipping me extra tickets on the sly for the raffle. It was the general atmosphere abroad on the streets in Tuam that wouldn't have me rushing back in a hurry.

Some odd characters, an arrest or two and a general feeling of unease permeated the night, all of which would ordinarily have me feeling right at home, but unfortunately I had to sleep in Wanderly Wagon at the side of these streets. The unsettling atmosphere in Tuam was a cross between *Bad Boy Bubby*, *The League of Gentlemen* and *Romper Stomper*. The best course of action was to stay indoors. Not a problem. After the *céilí*, I headed into Reapy's for a few bottles. Sean Keane was sitting up at the counter, where there was a bagpiper blowing up a storm between the tunes. When the concertina player sidled up to the bar looking for a phase tester, one of the punters nearly choked on his pint. 'What kind of a feckin' instrument is he playin'?!' I don't think that anything with a plug was allowed to make noise there. They needn't have worried: judging by the bulb on the box player, he probably wanted it to pick his teeth. As I made my way back to Wanderly Wagon, I saw a sign on a gentleman's outfitters: 'In 1951 during the filming of "The Quiet Man" John Wayne purchased a tweed cap in this shop'. Not much of interest has happened in Tuam since, methinks.

It was back on the road on Sunday morning, for a book festival in yet another little picturesque town, Graiguenamanagh, Co. Kilkenny. Graig is a beautiful spot, and the peaceful quayside belies what might wait for you on a night out in the likes of Gahan's Bar. It's been known to get pretty wild on this part of the Carlow–Kilkenny border. A sunny Sunday afternoon at a book fair in Graig is as chilled as Walt Disney's head though.

I took a stroll around the canal and fantasised about living on one of the houseboats while browsing the various pop-up bookshops that sprung up all around the pretty town for the festival. There was some clowning for the kids in the square, a bit of jazz outside the boathouse, a country market where I purchased buns, apples and fed my addiction for mixed olive tapenade. This addiction is not something I usually talk about, it's my secret shame. Having been bred from stock who were reared on skirt stew, beef chucks, tripe, pudding, cow's tongue, pigs' feet and pigs' heads, the middle-class predilection for a Mediterranean olive goo is not something of which I am proud. I imagine that every time I succumb to this most fancy foodie affectation, legions of offal-loving ancestors do enough spinning in their assembled resting places to supply ample energy for Funderland on St Stephen's Day. It was only a small jar, and I offset the purchase with an earthy rough Bukowski novel to add to Wanderly Wagon's growing library. The town had a nice autumnal vibe going on, and after a hectic weekend it was nice to have a relaxed goof around Graig, laze by the riverbank to bask in the unseasonal sunshine and wallow in my gastro-guilt.

Thankfully, the vast majority of festivals happen at weekends, which meant that I had time to regroup and lick my wounds between the epic bouts of festivalling that were usually being condensed into three days. The next leg of adventures saw me heading to Longford for a banjo beano. Getting there wasn't as straightforward as one might presume. On the festival website, where the directions to Longford should be, it helpfully informs you that: 'All roads lead to Longford'. Eh … no they bloody don't! But it was worth a little detour just to learn that Rathgar was host town to Afghanistan during the 2003 Special Olympics. My life is now complete.

Upon arriving in Longford, it was obvious what was happening. The streets were crawling with banjo slingers.

In flight cases, gig bags, hardboard boxes, plywood coffins and in the nude, banjos were being hauled around the place left, right and centre.

I have never seen so many banjos in all my life, and it seems that you are nobody at a banjo festival unless you are sporting a leather cowboy hat. It struck me that a well-organized cull at this festival would be considered, by some, to be a humanitarian act worthy of a Nobel Peace Prize nomination. But if you think that a banjo is merely a dull sitar, then you have no business being in Longford during Johnny Keenan weekend.

I managed to catch G-Runs and Roses, who are the real bluegrass deal. For a bunch of lads from the Czech and Slovak republics, they cannot only pull off the tunes, but also the close harmonies. The vocals on a Merle Haggard song had me wondering if there was a Bakersfield somewhere outside Prague.

On the same night, just down the road, was Spanish group Barcelona, who had an amazing harmonica player, chewing the harp and spitting out the tunes. The Dobro player was outstanding too. To cut a long story short, they were fairly savage all round. The assembled visitors to Ireland were well worth catching, but if it was a bit of life and atmosphere you were looking for, a pub called Tally Ho had a swinging session on the go, and it was here that things started to take a turn for the worst/best, depending on how you look at it.

I fell into the company of a *bodhrán* player from Laois. Around about closing time, he suggested we head to a session that was due to take place after hours in a pub up the road. A tap on the door, a twitch of a curtain, he flashed his weapon and in we went. Now the fella I was with was a lovely chap, but turning up to a session at a banjo festival with a *bodhrán* player is similar to turning up to a skincare convention with a leper. If you arrive with a particularly impressively deformed leper, chances are, the beauticians will be intrigued enough to study the antithesis of everything they represent. That's kind of what happened. By half past three in the morning we were all the best of long-lost buddies. I enjoyed the Banjo Festival a little too much. The plan had been to get to Galway at 11.00 a.m. the next morning. I couldn't have hit a cow's arse with a banjo at 11.00 a.m. the next morning.

I arrived in Galway the next afternoon ... late the next afternoon. To give myself a bit of a kick-start, I headed out to Blackrock in Salthill for a swim. The tide was full in, so I took this as a sign that my adjusted schedule was exactly as it should be. A couple of dives and an adventurous leap later, I was heading into town in search of oysters.

I was a little worried that my delicate condition wouldn't exactly be conducive to sucking and chewing on slimy oysters. What if I couldn't keep them down? Oysters are expensive y'know? It'd be an awful waste of money. I eased my way into the proceedings. On a sunny Saturday afternoon, there may be no city in Europe as pleasant as Galway. There is something about the atmosphere of this place that sits well with me. As you stroll up Quay Street and onto Shop Street, you have to think that this is as close as we'll ever get to the café culture that Micky Martin was on about when he banned the fags from pubs.

Buskers, crusties, boozers, Galwegians, the Saturday Market, well-dressed ladies on their way to the festival tent, scobies, tourists from all over the world, students and oddballs all mix to create a wonderful and vibrant atmosphere. In a small slice of street life from the city, a young girl was singing 'Peggy Gordon' while she played the guitar outside what used to be Una Taffe's jumper shop. Beside her was a table where Islam Ireland was signing up converts and arguing over their faith with non-believers. Across from this vignette was an anti-abortion group, doing similar but different things to Islam Ireland. Welcome to Galway.

There were many events you could have attended at the marquee in the harbour (it's in the docks, but the harbour sounds fancier). On Saturday there were two events: the first, from noon till evening, was €80 for a ticket, and the second was a ball later that evening asking €110 a ticket. This had the ring of a bygone economic era to me, the oyster-opening championship sponsored by Bollinger. The tickets were steep, and well out of my range. I had a feeling that some of the people who were actually responsible for losing the run of themselves might still be at it in the marquee at Galway's Oyster Festival. I ruled it out; I was looking forward to the mayhem of the Matchmaking Festival in Lisdoon that night, much more at my level. In fairness, the family event at the Oyster Festival on Sunday had a €15 entrance fee for adults, with under-12s free, so it wasn't all frocks and dicky bows. I headed for The Quays Bar, and settled in for half a dozen oysters and some Guinness to get my oyster festival fix. Have I mentioned that I don't like oysters?

There was a cruel prank that spread around the yard like wildfire when I was in primary school. You'd be told that there was something on your tongue, and to open your mouth so the concerned contemporary could get a better look. Once your mouth was open, the helpful client would phlegm into your gob. Brother Cornelius could be a right cruel bastard sometimes, but I suppose Christian Brothers needed something in their lives to cheer them up too.

That's what I think oysters are like: a bored Christian Brother phlegming into your mouth. I'm more than willing to accept that I'm a culinary philistine. I've tried them on a number of occasions. They're not for me. If it wasn't for the Guinness and brown bread, I wouldn't have gotten through it at all; I was still more than a little delicate from over exposure to banjos.

I'd worked in a pub in Galway during oyster season, and I'd been well schooled in the correct way to eat these things. You swallow one and have some stout. You chew the next and have some stout. So it continues. I'm not going to delve into the whole sexual/aphrodisiac quality of oysters; suffice to say that I think the reason that they have this reputation is that people would be delighted to get anything into their mouth, including someone else's tongue, if only to block the entry of another oyster.

After the selfless sucking of shellfish, I was back in the van heading south along the west coast, and had just about reached Clarinbridge, when I thought that the engine was making a strange sound. It wasn't the engine. I hope you'll indulge me while I take part in that wonderful Irish tradition of shifting blame to something we ate when we have something go wrong with us physically that is more than likely the result of too much drinking.

Usually, we somehow manage to shift the entire fault of feeling poorly onto a foodstuff, or that other most heinous offender, 'The Bad Pint'. It is due to this tradition that you'll invariably discover that the chipper with the worst reputation in any town in Ireland is the one closest to the most popular local hop or late-night bolthole. The reason for this is not that the food is the dodgiest in the village; it's because these establishments, due to their proximity to the scene of many drinking crimes, get the most accusations, generally from people who've drunk ten bottles of Bulmers, eight vodka and Red Bulls and three Jägerbombs, causing them to opine that 'I shouldn't have had that burger last night, I think I have Ebola. I think my kidneys are trying to escape and my head shouldn't be this colour, should it?' Pity the owners of these late-night conveniences; not only do they have to put up with serving the assembled wildlife every weekend, they then have to suffer the indignation of being slandered for their troubles, and if you throw enough shite....

The prediction of my mate Louise the night before, that I'd have an 'arse like a Japanese flag', turned out to be true. I made my way to Lisdoon with a dose of the scutters. If I had a tail, it would have been between my legs, purely to avoid possible follow through. Fecking oysters! I soldiered on to Lisdoon, with a couple of pit stops, chewing bananas whilst singing 'Bind us together, Lord'. Am I sharing too much?

After what seemed like an age, I eventually hit Ooooooh Lisdoonvarna. 'Welcome to Europe's biggest singles event' is what the sign says on the way into town. A whole month of deranged debauchery is what's on offer at this wonderfully wild get-together. A cross between the Ploughing Championships and Ayia Napa. *Bienvenido* to the Balearics for boggers. One night in Lisdoon would be enough for most, but if you have the stamina/prescription drugs, the festival lasts for the whole month of September. Bachelor farmers are hardcore.

I landed into the Matchmaker Bar early enough in the evening, and the place was already heaving. The dancing was in full swing, and the bachelors were on the prowl. I'm not going to be able to describe to you fully what the atmosphere in Lisdoon is like during the matchmaking festival. The closest I can probably get is to have you imagine your Debs ... got it? Now, what would it have been like if The Pogues, Charlie Sheen, Jackie Healy-Rae, Hugh

Hefner, Big Tom, Effin' Eddy and Paddy Doherty had all been on the organising committee, and they decided to have it in Kilnascully? Well, Lisdoon is wilder than that. I sat in beside the actual Matchmaker (and horse whisperer) himself, Willie Daly, to have a chat, and no sooner had my arse hit the seat than he was off:

'What would you think of that fine girl there?'

'I'm just looking, Willy, I'm not buying.'

'Well you could do worse than her, there's a lot of her in it to get a grip on. She's a Ban Garda.'

'I don't think a policewoman would suit me, Willy.'

'Jaysus, why not? Wouldn't you be the stupid fella to refuse a schteady income coming into the house ... What good is a hen if she can't put a few eggs into the basket? There's a lot to be said for a laying hen...'.

As this conversation was going on, there was a 60-something-year-old lady playing extremely suggestive charades in the window at the two of us. Two words ... first word, four letters, second word, three, rhymes with gob. It didn't faze Willy, so I pretended it didn't faze me either, but I've had bad dreams since.

To say that the atmosphere was anarchic is like saying that there was a spell there in the late '80s when Terry Waite didn't get out much. It was mental! But in a very good-humoured, we're-all-here-to-have-a-craic, kind of a way. I thought that it may have been intimidating for girls to be in an environment where fellas are so blatantly on the pull, but they seemed fine with it, one girl even suggesting that the fellas could do with being a little bit more forward. She amended that opinion later, when the drink had loosened them up a bit. I talked to a table-load of girls from Limerick who were there to primarily enjoy themselves, but if anything else happened along the way, that would be a bonus.

That seemed to be the consensus. Not many would admit to being there purely to find romance, except for one 60-year-old farmer, who informed me that this was his third weekend in a row in Lisdoon, and he hadn't paid for a B&B yet (nudge, nudge). He'd pleasured three different women in three weeks. 'I'm made of some stuff!' he informed me. I later saw another elderly gentleman, who must also have been made of 'some stuff', getting arrested for trying to fight a bouncer. He must have been holding up his pants with his hands, because no sooner were the cuffs on him than his pants fell down. The comic timing was immaculate, but it may also have been some quick-release mechanism that the scuffle inadvertently triggered.

I made it back to Wanderly Wagon for 1:30 a.m., which I thought was fairly good going when you consider what was happening around me. I would be lying to you if I said that there weren't a couple of offers that came my way. A Scottish lady, who had traveled to Co. Clare especially for these shenanigans, told me that I could park my van in her drive anytime I was in Inverness. I'm not sure if she meant that in a Grace Jones kind of way, but I took it at face value and thanked her. For some reason, most of the offers were coming from ladies who had been around for about long enough to have seen the Titanic stop off in Cobh. I thought I was cock of the walk, strolling down the main street with a mature lady on either arm, right until I was spotted by two girls I know from home. 'I'm only helping them across the street', I said. I don't think I got away with it.

This festival goes back over 150 years, originally based around a fair-day, when matchmaking would have been part of the fabric of a large gathering in the village. The matchmaking element taking prominence is a relatively recent phenomenon that has grown wonderfully out of hand. Whatever the economic situation in the country, Lisdoon has always been a fun place to be in September. Even if you don't drink, dancing is a huge part of the festival. Some of the best Country and Irish bands set up camp in Co. Clare for the month, and hot-steppers arrive in their droves to jive the night away in the spa town.

1:30 a.m. seemed early to be hitting blanket street in comparison to the carry-on the night before, but I did have a mountain-walking festival to attend at 10.00 a.m. When my alarm went off, shortly after 7.00 a.m. the next morning, I realised how much better I should have been. The rain was hammering off the side of the van, and it was doing nothing for the pulsing of the blood vessels in my head that had all the percussive effect of John Mullane beating an empty oil tank with a hurley. Snooze was engaged at least five times whilst I argued with myself. 'Sure I've already done three festivals this weekend. Another little snooze and I could be home 'n all, dry as a bone by lunchtime.' But the same tit-head who decided to take on this venture in the first place spoke up: 'Sure what's the point of doing it at all if you're going to give up when you feel a little bit tired and it's a bit wet?' I hate him. There was no sign of that bastard when I was sitting in my oilskins watching the rain dilute my tea at the top of a mountain in the Burren four hours later.

You may find this hard to believe, but after the initial shock to the system, I really enjoyed the Burren Peaks

Festival. If there is any place more suitable for blowing the cobwebs out than up on top of the highest points of one of Ireland's most unique landscapes, with the breeze howling in from the Atlantic, I haven't found it yet. Over the two days of the walking festival, the Ballyvaughan and Fanore Walking Club took over 400 people across the peaks of Ireland's protected limestone region.

The scenery and landscape are without comparison, and even on a blustery and occasionally damp day it was a wonderful place to be. Thankfully, John eventually put down the hurley.

There was a nice mix of people on the walk, and the atmosphere was worlds away from the mayhem of the night before. One of the ladies on the walk was from Ballyvaughan, only ten miles down the road from Lisdoon. She had been to the matchmaking once in her lifetime, and that had been more than enough for her. 'Were there any normal people at it?' she asked me.... Eh ... hello? She's originally from Dublin, and when she started dating her husband, he took her to Lisdoon for the matchmaking. It was nearly the end of their relationship. She thought that if this was how they behaved in the country, she wanted nothing to do with them. I got the feeling that he's not allowed to go out to play in Lisdoon any more.

The guy leading our walk was called Joe. He had a whole Gandalf buzz going on with his white beard and walking staff. Every now and then he'd stop and launch into some sagacious banter about something visible in the distance, a tiny plant particular to the area, or point out some Orc prints.

One of the things that caught Joe's eye was a stone structure called a 'Turf Slate', used for drying out cow shite to use as fuel for fires. There was no turf available up here, where the herders brought the cattle up to winter in the peaks that still offered fodder through bleak months, because the limestone slowly emitted the heat gathered during the summer months. I'm glad that someone could get the hang of those bloomin' storage heaters, I could never figure them out. Joe made the notion of the cow-shite fires sound rustic and somewhat romantic, but I know from experience that there is nothing to make you long for the peaty aroma of a turf fire while you snuggle into a hot toddy in your favourite country pub with John Sheehan playing 'The Marino Waltz' in your mind's ear more than getting a face and nose full of smoke from a fire that's burning cow shite. But the structures and stories were impressive.

Walking clubs don't get enough praise and credit for what they do. For forty Euros a year you can join the Ballyvaughan and Fanore Walking Club, and go walking in one of the most interesting and diverse landscapes in Ireland all year round. Recession-proof. Twenty quid for this festival walk, and I got two T-shirts, the walk, an education, all the tea I could drink and all the brack I could eat. Beat that, missus! I was wet and tired, but glad I crawled out of the van. I was hoping that this enthusiasm and joy would last for another eleven months. Gulp....

Festivals Attended in September

1. Cape Clear Storytelling – Cape Clear, Co. Cork
2. From the Mountains to the Sea Book Festival – Dún Laoghaire, Co. Dublin
3. Dublin Theatre Festival – Dublin
4. Dublin Fringe Festival – Dublin
5. Dublin Contemporary – Dublin
6. Bog-Snorkelling Championships – Doohamlet, Co. Monaghan
7. Harvest Food Festival – Waterford City
8. Town of Books Festival – Griaguenamanagh – Co. Kilkenny
9. Diamond Challenge, Connquest Connemara – Renvyle, Galway
10. Clifden Arts Festival – Clifden, Co. Galway
11. Arthur's Day – Nationwide Events
12. Tuam Trad Festival – Tuam, Co. Galway
13. Johnny Keenan Banjo Festival – Longford
14. Galway Oyster Festival – Galway City
15. Lisdoonvarna Matchmaking Festival – Lisdoonvarna, Co. Clare
16. Burren Peaks Walking Festival – Fanore, Co. Clare
17. Storytelling Southeast – Dungarvan, Co. Waterford

Other Recommended Festivals in September

Electric Picnic – Stradbally, Co. Laois
Harvest Time Blues Festival – Monaghan Town
Spirit of Folk Festival – Dunderry, Meath

3 | *October – All Hail the Conkering Hero*

The original plan for the first weekend in October was to head for Monaghan and Sligo for some high culture at the Patrick Kavanagh and Baroque Music Festivals; the perfect foil to some of September's excesses. But when an invitation came through to attend a Pagan and Irish Magic Festival, I was more than a little torn. Stony Grey Soil versus a Pagan hooley? Previous experience had taught me that Pagans know how to party, and investigating the day-to-day of those practising alternative lifestyles was much more carrot than Kavanagh's schtick. A day exploring the lesser-seen spiritual beliefs of Ireland, with the added incentive of an unholy session afterwards? I hit the Raglan Road (no offence, Paddy, but you would probably have done the same thing).

Féile Draíochta is the official name of a festival that features guest speakers, workshops, healers, readers, dancers, books, pagan bits and bobs and a gallery of odd objects to fulfil all your necromantic needs. I was en route to the affair, passing through the bowels of Co. Laois, when I spotted a poster announcing a 'Solemn Novena'. Now I don't really know what happens at a Solemn Novena, but I could have a good stab at it. I found it quite poor marketing; the Pagans were offering belly dancers and a sex-toy stall at their festival; the Catholics had lots and lots of prayers. No matter what your spiritual persuasion, you'd guess that a novena isn't going to be a place for glow sticks and whistles. Is there any need for pouring the grey cloying custard of the word 'solemn' over the event too? I decided that if I ever saw a poster announcing 'Novena of Hilarity' or even 'Jolly Novena', I'd be there with bells on. One of the noticeable things about *Féile Draíochta* was that the people for whom Paganism or Wicca is a spiritual way of life, while taking their spirituality very seriously, can still have a laugh and take the piss out of themselves. As proof, they decided to have a 'Cackling Competition'. Real life, bona fide witches, cackling. *Macbeth* never caught this mood.

The polished convention-esque arrangement of the event was something of a surprise. Name badges, reception area, lecture rooms, trade area and green room. Where were the cauldrons and mangy cats? I had to re-evaluate all of my preconceptions. I pencilled in attending two talks, and in the meantime I decided to slip in a healing or reading of some description. I sat down with a spiritualist and fortune teller called Melodi, and I was blown away when she knew all about my quest. She told me that she thought what I was doing was going to be a very interesting journey, and how she imagined it being lots of fun. I was stunned; I hadn't told her what I was doing! This was spooky. I was impressed and surprised by this lady actually being the genuine article; I didn't think they existed. Could she actually read my fortune? Could she read my mind? No. It turned out that she could read my blog. It's a small country. To be honest, I was just as impressed that a stranger was reading my blog; up until then I had presumed it had been just me and occasionally my mother.

By far the most interesting and informative of the events was a talk delivered by Janet Farrar and Gavin Bone on 'The Evolution of Modern Witchcraft'; this couple are practising Wiccans, and prodigious authors in the field.

There was lots of talk about the history of Witchcraft, initiations and progression through levels and the ins and outs of training that have developed over the years. A lot of this stuff went over my head faster than Griselda on a broom. Gavin made some jokes that everyone else found hilarious. As I tried to fit in, laughing uncomfortably late, too loud and for too long, I couldn't help but think that if this crowd needed to single out a non-believer for some nefarious purpose, they wouldn't have much bother. Thankfully, they didn't.

One aspect of the talk was a discussion focusing on the role that the Wicca Priest/Priestess could take in serving their community. Gavin explained that if those present were to take their 'vocations' seriously, this would mean finding a way to use their practices to serve the community, out in the open, in public. Recently, the town of Athboy had been twinned with a town in France. The coven of which Janet and Gavin are members was asked to perform a druidic rite at the twinning event for the assembled dignitaries and the populace of the town. Following on from that, the county council called on them for an annual gig in the area, where they do their thing on a local hill of spiritual and traditional significance beside a sacred/holy well. Gavin suggested that, as the dominance of the Catholic Church in Ireland recedes, people are becoming more open to spirituality of a kind that has an ancient relevance, as well as a sense of place and history that makes it accessible. A group of people who would have been burned at the stake 100 years ago, and who would have been pariahs and figures of ridicule relatively recently, were sitting discussing how they engage with the communities where they lived to enhance the areas. It seems that new fairytales may have to seek their villains elsewhere; the times are indeed a-changin'.

I was confused. The friendly, welcoming, good-humoured nature of this pack of Pagans is what's meant to be at the centre of Christianity. They weren't a bunch of mascaraed Goths. Similar to the crew I'd met on Pilgrimage in Lough Derg, they were just decent people. Lora and her partner John both work in the area of heritage, archeology, history and tourism. John gave a talk on respecting ancient sites and how to enjoy them (also touching on how to carry out al fresco rituals in an ecologically responsible way) whilst keeping them intact for future generations. I was warming to these people so much that I was worried they might be casting some sort of spell on me. *Féile Draíochta* had some belly-dancing gypsies too; just the thing to pull me out of the spiritual quagmire into which I had managed to navigate. Does Halfords stock spiritual satnavs? The jangling and gyrating of members of 'The Zoryana' took me to another place altogether, and a fine place it was too. Ladies like that could convince a man to convert.

I managed to break the spell of the hypnotic gyrations and janglings and get my mind back on the business at hand, and for the next couple of days that business was horses. Every October, Ballinasloe, Co. Galway, the usually bustling county town, turns into the rural Irish equivalent of Marrakech. They come from far and wide to ride, jump, race, sulk, buy and sell horses. I'd always wanted to visit this festival, which has the reputation of being a pretty rough and ready affair. I had barely pulled up the handbrake when I got a shout in the window of Wanderly Wagon from a fella to give him a hand getting his horse out of the trailer. Not two minutes in the town, and I was already in the thick of it.

You are no one at a horse fair without a stick, a length of wavin, a rod or a whip of some description to give any unsuspecting animal that happens across your path a good crack on the arse to gee it up. Down at the heart of the horse-trading, there were bucking horses, kicking mares, ponies being moved hither and thither, lads riding bareback bereft of regard straight through the throngs, threats being shouted, deals being struck and more shite than a pre-election debate on TV3. There isn't much health and safety in operation here. I saw one young fella getting a good kick from a mare, but it was fine – he kicked it back.

I've been to an ancient, bewildering souk in North Africa, and at frenzied religious festivals on the banks of the Ganges – shit, I've even been to a Lidl warehouse clearance sale – but nothing that I've ever experienced could have prepared me for the carry-on at the Horse Fair in Ballinasloe. It was deadly! This was the wildest of wests.

There's no way of writing about the event without homing in on Traveller culture; it's not the be all and end all of the fair, but it's a big part of what the whole thing is about. There are all walks of life here though, from gymkhana types with hard velvet helmets at one end of the spectrum, to fag-in-the-side-of-the-mouth Traveller young fellas riding roughshod through the crowds at the other. The common denominator is horses, and, more than anything else in Irish society, it seems to be the thing that can bridge the gap between the settled and travelling communities. My own neighbour, Catherine, told me that it was the first year she could remember not being at the fair. Her Dad was in the horse business, and loved the rough and tumble of the yearly event. She has wonderful memories of attending the fair and watching the business between her father and the other traders. She told me that: 'It's all about the horses, but drinking is a big part of it, and it can seem rough enough if you don't know some of the Travellers who are at it.'

Yeah, it's rough, but it can be friendly too, in a slightly threatening way. I went to take a photo of a 'three-card trick' man, who had attracted a big crowd as he challenged them to 'find the lucky lady'. There were fifties being handed over, before the punters (more than likely in cahoots with the dealer) got to guess at where they thought the queen lay among the three cards. He didn't like me having a camera in the vicinity, and made a go for me, but then stopped, saying 'Ah Jaysus don't be takin' pictures. The wife doesn't know where I am!' We struck a deal. I bet a fiver on finding the lucky lady, and I got to take a picture of the table and the wellies of the gathered gamblers underneath it, which were suitably shite-encrusted so as to disguise the identity of their owners. Did I find the right card? I did in me arse like.

As well as the horses, there were all manner of hucksters, sideshows, market stalls and fortune tellers to choose from. Oddly enough I didn't manage to find any mixed olive tapenade on sale anywhere among the many stalls. Sales and prices of horses have been down, year on year, for the last few years as a result of the recession. That year was the lowest ebb in horse-trading for a long time. A combination of lack of funds and an increase in supply led to a subsequent devaluation of the livestock. There was trading being done, but not to the same degree or with the same amount of money changing hands as there had been in previous years. But the mood was positive, and the huge crowds assembled for the fair were determined to enjoy themselves regardless. If the carry-on in the daytime was wild, then as the sun began to set and people began to retire to the local pubs, things were cranked up a notch or twelve.

Threatening joviality might be the best way to describe the evening atmosphere in Ballinasloe. It proved difficult to relax fully with Thom Yorke whining in the back of my mind, 'What the hell are you doing here, you don't belong here.'

It was interesting to explore my own prejudices, and maybe part of the reason I couldn't fully relax, enjoy a pint and throw myself into it entirely was because of hang-ups I have about Travellers. There were a few scuffles, and I saw a young fella pull a screwdriver out of his pocket and threaten to 'stick this through your throat and into your fuckin' brain, ya faggot ya' to an elderly man who had just told him to cop himself on. The volatility in the air wasn't totally imagined.

It's somewhat difficult to talk about the atmosphere around the town without maybe scaring people off a little, but I can't speak highly enough of the experience of being in Ballinasloe for the Horse Fair. Go and stand outside the busiest chipper in your town at 2.30 a.m. on a Saturday night/Sunday morning; the atmosphere was no more intimidating than that would be, although a bit more spread out and with a larger cast. I spotted one person who looked like they might be a foreign tourist in the middle of the melee, and I can only imagine the stories that she will have to tell when she goes home.

It's a side of our culture that I haven't explored before, and have possibly chosen to ignore, but if the cousins from overseas ever come knocking at the beginning of October, they are going to get a slice of Ireland for which they may not have been prepared, and won't they be the better for it? I don't have kids, but I'd like to think that, if I did, I'd try to offset their increasingly American inflections by bringing them to experience a real, traditional fair; well, my neighbour used to love it, and horse shite is the second least offensive member of the manure family. In my continuing search to find all those people who didn't lose the run of themselves during the fiscal frenzy, I couldn't help but feel that there were a good few of them here. Although the vast majority of them lost the run of themselves every evening during the Horse Fair, it was in a different way altogether.

There's a festival programme based around the fair itself, and it's plain to see that there is an effort to have family events that attract a more 'settled' crowd to the town for the week of the fair. There was a tug-of-war, a 'Queen of The Fair', street entertainment and music. It seems that there is something of an effort to repackage the event, and I can't help but feel that if you revamp this event and make it like any other run-of-the-mill festival in the country, we'll have lost the point, and something probably much more important besides. Sheila Stewart was talking about the dying traditions of the travelling people at the storytelling on Cape Clear in September. Luke Kelly was singing goodbye to the same traditions forty years ago. I can imagine how residents and the Chamber of Commerce feel the need to broaden the scope and profile of what happens in Ballinasloe at the start of October, but it seems to me that their time, money and effort might be better spent running a new festival at a different time of the year. Is this the world's only fringe festival where the programme sets out to raise the tone?

I watched one of the street entertainers down by a sparsely attended main stage in the town square. He was one of those fellas who paints himself silver and stands still for long periods of time – an artistic endeavour that always seemed futile to me, as it also would seem to be judged by a group of unruly kids in attendance on the day. The hapless mime's troubles began when one young fella started shooting him with a pellet gun. Seeing the sport in this, another couple of junior gun club members arrived, and it was open season on the mime's genitals. Another young fella, feeling left out as he didn't have a gun, decided to just give the silver fella a smack. Am I a bad person for finding this whole tableau highly amusing? Ah, come on! It was more entertaining than watching a shiny sham doing nothing. He eventually retreated. One mime down, but so many left to go.

To get the smell of horse manure out of my nostrils and off the soles of my boots, I headed for the Comeragh Mountains in Co. Waterford. I landed up in the Nire Valley near Ballymacarbry, on a morning that showed some positive signs of clearing up. This was the Nire Valley Walking Festival. I got out of the van to tie up the dirty boots and get the gear together, when a lady shouted over at me, 'Howya, weren't you walking up in the Burren two weeks ago?' Jaysus, I was becoming a regular at walking festivals. Sssshhhhh! Don't tell anyone, it's not very rock 'n' roll. To tell you the truth, though, I was really starting to enjoy these jaunts at the various parties of perambulation. Sunday mornings were pretty much designed for walking in the mountains, and, fittingly, we were bound for the summit of Cnoc an Aifrinn, a spot where the population of the area went every Sunday in penal times to celebrate the outlawed Mass. Upon reaching the summit that day, I sincerely hoped that none of them ever left their rosary beads up there and had to take the long slog back up the mountain to retrieve them. The mix of people on these jaunts is always great. You're looking at a range of late twenties to early sixties. The walk leader on the day told me that he's 63 years old. He tackles the hills with the assurance and agility of a young horny goat, and such is his humour that he wouldn't mind me saying so. Fellas like this make the prospect of the years that lie ahead a rosier proposition. Good man, Michael.

As always, the banter and chat on the trek was great. Two lads travelled all the way down from Mullingar for the weekend's walking. There was a lady from Carlow, who, despite her grey hair, would put the best of us to shame; she practically skipped to the summit. There was a pair of girls from Kilkenny who enjoyed themselves despite the fact that, for the bulk of our walk, we were in the clouds and couldn't see anything but the moisture in the air. Not much scenery, damp and misty, but invigorating, and if we let the weather stop us getting out and enjoying ourselves, we'd never leave the house.

When the wind picked up near the top of the mountain, the hoods went up and the chat wasn't as free flowing, but the dam broke when we came back below the clouds and into the clear on the descent.

The sun decided to pop out for a brief moment, and when it did, it actually got a spontaneous cheer. I bet it doesn't ever get that kind of response in the Bahamas. I chatted with an inspirational character who had been made redundant the previous year, but Martin refused to let this bring him down. He had been a skilled labourer all his life, learning the trade on building sites in England as a young fella and coming back to Co. Tipperary to build a home and family life when he'd saved a few bob. When the building work dried up after 2009, he knew there was trouble brewing, so he bought a bicycle just before he was laid off. He now goes hillwalking three times a week, goes for long spins on the bike about four times a week, and has his motorbike to fill the gaps in between. Whenever he hears of someone he knows becoming unemployed, he invites them out to join him on his jaunts around the countryside.

He had recently been called into the dole office for one of their periodical grillings. Martin is well into his fifties now, and he'd love to be working still, but the work just isn't there. When the young lady from Social Welfare started her interrogation, Martin stopped her and laid his cards on the table, finishing by telling her: 'If you ever have anyone in here that looks depressed, feel free to give them my number. I'll bring them out for a walk in the mountains, for a cycle round the coast or even for a spin on the back of the motorbike. There's far too much out there for us to enjoy to be getting bogged down by this shite.' She smiled, and Martin was dismissed. I know what she was feeling as she listened to him. No matter how bad things might ever get, as long as there are still a few Martins around, there's still some glimmer of hope. Listening to his stories and beliefs, told with passion, openness, honesty and lack of self-consciousness, I felt humbled. It made what I was up to seem childish and churlish, but it did lend me some perspective. People had begun asking me if I was getting tired of going to all these festivals; I'd never get tired of meeting people like Martin.

There is a walking club somewhere near you. Go out for a ramble with them at least once, just to see what it's like. Be warned, though: a lot of these weirdos actually prefer walking in winter. The Nire Valley club brought close to 200 people over the mountains during the festival that weekend, and the festival has been running for sixteen years now. If you happen to go out for a stroll with the club, tell Michael I was asking for him. This festival is in a beautiful part of west Waterford, and Hanora's Cottage comes highly recommended for a getaway and an evening meal in splendid solitude. I think that they might occasionally have some mixed olive tapenade on the menu.

I was starting to establish a nice balance between the wholesome and hedonistic. The jaunt in The Comeragh Mountains had certainly put a pep in my step, and while buzzing up through the midlands on the way to my next festival appointment, I had some time to kill, so I took a spin down to Moneygall to have a pint of stout by the Obama homestead. Like millions of other people, I watched as the Obamas made their way through the street (purposely singular) of Moneygall, so I was curious to see what effect it had on the village long after the dust settled. For a start, the village looked great, the window boxes were still flowering, the paint was still bright, the flags still flying, and Moneygall picked up a prize in the Tidy Towns awards. Whatever effect finding out about Falmouth Kearney had on Obama's subsequent presidential campaigns, the benefit to Moneygall has been huge.

I chatted to the girl behind the counter in *An Siopa Beag*, an establishment into which the bold Obamas bounded during their visit. The young girl told me that the summers have been nuts, with busloads of tourists every day visiting the village of the American President's great-great-great-grandfather. It was quiet enough on a Saturday afternoon in October, but I saw a couple taking a picture of the 'Obama Café', and four girls taking pictures in Ollie Hayes' pub. Even without the coachloads of eager snap-happy summer tourists, it seems that Irish people are stopping off too, where before they would have driven straight past on their way from Roscrea to Toomevara. You've got to love that place name. Say it with me, out loud: 'Too-me-vara'. Deadly!

At a time when most small rural towns have more of their Minor Football panel in Australia than at training, the industry that has sprung up here around their buddy Barack is impressive: Barack-embossed sliotars, bobblehead Baracks, plates, plaques, postcards, commemorative car-fresheners (I had to get one of those), roll-of-honour hurleys, and more T-shirts than the garage of the former president of Gary Glitter's fan club. My favorite shop has to be Mossy Hayes' Traditional Irish T-Shirt Shop. Liam Clancy is turning in his *báinín*. More power to the whole lot of them, and long may it last. I remember watching the footage from Moneygall on the big day, and being struck first of all by the swallow that your man had on him, like a sucky calf with a hangover, but also by the smaller pub directly across the road from all the fanfare. This pub also had the name 'Hayes' over the door. I grew up in a town where two sisters had pubs on the same street as each other. The atmosphere between the two of them was like Christmas Dinner in the Scallons' house with Dana and ALL the relatives. They didn't get on.

I couldn't help but imagine that, as Frankie Gavin played his fiddle by the fire like something from a Bord na Móna ad, and Barack pulled on the pint like Brendan Behan after Lent, J. Hayes was across the road looking out his window with a head on him like a bulldog, thinking to himself, 'Bastards!' It was with this in mind that I decided I would go into the smaller, more traditional and overshadowed Hayes' for a pint. It was closed. I supped on my pint in Ollie's, and I couldn't help but notice that there were no black people in Moneygall, not even a few Brazilian lads from a local chicken farm, when lo and behold … no, false alarm, 'twas a life-size cardboard cut-out of himself.

One of the pleasures of travelling around Ireland can often be the simple act of getting lost. Even the always-confident voice of Tom (my satnav) can often be bamboozled by the places I'd been trying to get to. Doohamlet was one that silenced him. It would seem that Leap Castle in Co. Offaly is yet another one of those places. Getting lost yet again, I found myself in what is known in Offaly as 'The Mystic Triangle'. Sure no wonder I was lost. This triangle isn't something that your one, Meg, uses for geometry; it's an area of Ireland associated with paranormal activity, similar to the Bermuda triangle, but the ghosts here are paler. The first sign that things were a little different was St Kieran's Bush and its odd decorations.

The idea of the rag bush is that it has some history associated with the mystic, more often than not its history features in some miraculous event or story, like St Patrick stopping there for a piss after holding it in for forty days. It could be just that the bush is near a holy well, which is much more likely than the miracle of the burning bladder. The tradition is that you place a piece of clothing belonging to someone who is ill or requires some type of intervention on the tree, and as the cloth rots, the person begins to receive some benefits. The bush had socks, bras, tracksuit bottoms and even a sliotar attached to it. Not the most pleasant fruit that one could hope for on a tree, but the tradition seems to be strong in this area. In the back of my mind, I could hear John and the eco-friendly witches from *Féile Draíochta* objecting, but I still attached a bit of cloth to the tree and went down to the well for a paddle and a spot of light anointing. Sure what harm could it do, and I did have a light hangover, which strangely hadn't fully gone away since starting my festival quest. Weird!

Getting deeper into the mystic triangle, I eventually arrived at Leap Castle, the venue for that evening's festivities as part of the Slievebloom Storytelling Festival. It is reputedly Ireland's most haunted castle, and let me say that it has the feel of it, as eerie as a garden party at Fred West's old gaff.

I arrived early to try and nab a couple of people to have a chat with. It was dusk, and I was there on my own. As I was sitting in the van, it was beginning to get dark. I was toying with the idea of spending the night in the van on the grounds of the castle; sure it would be a bit of an adventure. A fuse popped in the van, and none of the internal lights worked; that was the end of my ghost-hunting aspirations. I had just seen the ad for the most recent *Paranormal Activity* film, with two kids saying 'Bloody Mary' three times into a mirror, and a strange presence appearing to them. The problem I have is that I'd be thinking, 'Whatever you do. Don't say "Bloody Mary" three times.' Then I'd think, 'Shit, I just thought the name "Bloody Mary" once, does that mean if I think it again something will happen? Shit, I just thought it again! Think happy thoughts, think happy thoughts...'. I'm not even superstitious, but I still wouldn't like to piss something off, even if I don't believe in it. I decided then and there that saying 'Large bottle of Bulmers' three times to a barman down the road in Kinnitty would be a much better way to spend the night. It turns out that there were plenty of spirits there too.

After what seemed like an age of being there on my own in the dark, people began to arrive for the storytelling. What a setting. A fireside in a haunted castle must be one of the best places for a night of stories, so long as you know that you don't have to sleep there. A huge crowd turned out for what was a wonderful night's entertainment. The storytellers came from the four corners of Ireland, as well as from all around the local areas. There were traditional stories, songs, poetry and yards of yarns.

I chatted to a few American tourists who happened to be in the area and had heard about the festival. How lucky were they? This event isn't that easy for an Irish person to hear about, my bloomin' satnav couldn't even find it. This wasn't the Bunratty vibe that the tourists usually get served up; the night at The Slievebloom Storytelling was the real deal. I was blown away by the experience on the night, so

I can only imagine how a tourist must take it, or maybe it's exactly what they expect. The woman beside me had travelled up from Carlow for the night, and she said to me: 'You would either be watching *The X Factor* or out in the pub, and God knows you wouldn't be in the pub long on €12.' She was right. The event lasted for over three hours, and people were left wanting more. It was a special night and great value.

I hadn't been long chatting with Christina, who is heavily involved with the festival committee, when she offered me a space outside her B&B for the van. She lived around the corner from the pub in Kinnitty, so this lifted my spirits no end. After the main event, a pleasant night was had in the pub, and the company was more than interesting. I found out that there is a difference between a harper and a harpist. It turns out that a harper is a person who travels around with their harp, whereas a harpist is more performer than traveller. Anya, who plays the harp with a group of poets under the name 'Catch The Moon' walked 2,500 kilometres the previous year with her harp on her back.

She had read the *Ryan Report*, published after an in-depth inquiry into child abuse in Ireland, and the contents of the report saddened and infuriated her. She struggled to find a way to react to it, until eventually she decided to set out from her home in west Cork and start walking across Ireland, across France and across Spain, playing her harp every day on her three month and three week journey. I'm glad to report that she felt much better after her stroll. Anya unfortunately had lost the run of herself, but in an altogether wonderfully different kind of way.

I was struck once again by the energy and effort that the people responsible for this festival invested in making their community a better place. The things they do happen regardless of recessions, and they will continue to enjoy themselves and help their neighbours enjoy themselves and bring storytelling to schools and punters, with or without deserved State support. Christina talked about how the midlands area is often neglected when it comes to festivals, tourism coverage and funding. She feels that the obvious areas get most of the attention, and she is told that this is because that's where the tourists go. 'Well why wouldn't all the tourists go there when that's all they know about?'

As I drove through the Slievebloom Mountains the next day, I couldn't help but appreciate Christina's love and passion for the area. When you take a turn off the main motorways, and stop to enjoy what the country has to offer, often for free, is when you see Ireland at its best. It's in the midlands that a lot of what we seek out in a traditional experience still remains unspoiled, be that music, walking, scenery or just the day to day. Of course, I could have been biased as this was only the second time ever that a festival official had bought me a pint. Two months into my quest, and it felt like I was definitely starting to get the hang of this thing.

The night before, one of the performers at the storytelling had told me that he had to go home early as himself and a Father Jack Hackett dummy were up on a High Nelly tandem bike the next day for a world record attempt to have the most High Nellies ever heading off for a spin. Needless to say, I was intrigued.

Durrow is the home of a High Nelly Club. Of course it is. This is the same town that brought you the 'Howya Festival' and hosts the All-Ireland Scarecrow Championships; they have a wonderful breed of head-a-ball in Durrow. No sooner are you within a couple of miles of Durrow on High Nelly day than the colour and characters start to wheel, wave and woo-hoo their way past you. This event is more fun than a Johnny Vegas and Lady Gaga Vegas wedding reception.

I was in Dublin days later telling a few of the Jacks what I was up to in Durrow. 'A high wha'?' they asked with scrunched-up, confused faces. For those of you who may be so far removed from your country cousins as to think that stew is an evil American cartoon baby, a High Nelly is traditionally an old, steel-frame bike, usually black with a leather sprung saddle. Some can have three gears, but usually just one with back-pedal and/or lever breaks. Mind you, there were some newer, more comfortable models available to rent and buy on the day in Durrow, but they were probably only there for any Dubs who were visiting.

The organisers were hoping for somewhere in the region of 300 bikes. I have a feeling that they got very close, if not beyond that, but I lost count as a particularly pretty girl on a High Nelly cycled past. It may be a kink deep down in our genetic coding, or it could just be me, but I found that there was something inherently sexy about a shapely calf and fine pair of legs powering the hefty frame of a High Nelly. Easy now.

The cycle went from Durrow to Abbeyleix and back (for those with the legs and lungs for it, and if the bikes didn't seize up or fall asunder). Given the age and condition of some of the bikes (and cyclists), this was no mean feat. I saw one man with a dog up on the handlebars, who looked like he was probably just making his way home and happened to end up in the middle of the jaunt by accident. As I stood by the side of the road with a grin on my face, it was obvious that here was yet another group of townsfolk having a great laugh. As the riders headed off into the sunset on their trusty and sometimes rusty black steeds, I heard a man beside me say: 'Jaysus, 'tis some sight all the same, isn't it?' It was.

The High Nelly cyclists were still creasing the laugh lines of my face when I reached Co. Leitrim for my next set of festival adventures. You couldn't get around a corner in Mohill without a member of the community out on the road shaking a bucket at you for their collection for cancer research. Every *bóthareen* and laneway was manned. The fire brigade lads were out washing cars and lending a hand. I stopped at the lights and rolled down the window to get directions, and threw a bit of change into a bucket. The auld lad on collection duty winked at me, stuck a flag on my lapel and said, 'Wear this, it will give you freedom.' WTF!? Some of the surrealism of what I was experiencing on the road was starting to get worrying. Being awarded the auld lad's talisman felt like being in some border-county version of *Alice in Wonderland*. Somebody, somewhere, was taking the piss. They were, and I found the whole lot of them, down at the local GAA club throwing eggs at each other.

It is safe to say that I'd been to one or two festivals at this stage, and I can tell you in all honesty that I hadn't laughed as much at any of them as I did at the Culchie Festival in Mohill, featuring, for the first time, the Irish Egg-Throwing Championships. Mixing together the Culchies and the Egg-Throwing produced an omelette of entertainment on a scale that had never been witnessed on any GAA club pitch in any parish previously.

When it comes to egg-throwing (and I can actually speak with a little bit of authority here, as my friend Ella took time out from her marathon training and we both actually practised for this event), it's not so much the throwing that's important, it's the catching of the fecking thing that requires skill. You have to take the momentum out of it, pulling your hands back from the flight of the thing as you catch it or you'll end up yolked. Competitors came in all ages, shapes, sizes and degrees of culchiness. Fair to say that everyone present enjoyed this immensely, and it only cost … FECK ALL, MISSUS! Yep, it was free. Donations from the event were going to a charity that trains dogs to become companions for autistic children, and you could buy a commemorative mug (and they were decent china mugs too) for €3, or two for a fiver.

When Ella and I were in the field, warming up for our egg-tossing heat, I was chatting to two of the culchie competitors about how there must be a clatter of pints torn into in the evening. 'I'm a pioneer, and he doesn't drink that much', says the lad with bailer twine holding up his pants to me. Here we go, back into Alice mode, I thought. 'No mushrooms either, only with the fry of a Sunday.' The lads were serious. They do it because they can have such a laugh at it without having to drink. One of them met his now wife at the event eleven years ago, and he was her escort at the *Macra* 'Queen of the Land' competition the following year. Two sound lads, but seriously deranged in the most wonderful way possible. Eoin actually won the title of Culchie King in 2003.

By far and away my favourite Culchie was Hughie. Hughie wasn't dressed up or play-acting, and definitely not hiding any mixed olive tapenade in the jute sack he had slung over his shoulder. Hughie was Hughie. He was pulling on a fag and drinking tea out of an old Lucozade bottle that he produced from his pocket when I asked him if I could take his photo. 'Fire away, lad, so long as I don't break the camera.' Hughie had earlier eaten six raw eggs, complete with shells; the evidence was in his beard. He didn't win the Culchie title during Sunday's final, but on Saturday he was certainly my man of the match.

There were egg-throwing competitions for kids, women, mixed pairs and men. All competitions were hilarious, with people busting eggs off each other like it was going out of fashion. There was even an official from the World Egg-Throwing Federation present on the day to help officiate and keep things above board.

It was just as well that the official English egg fella was there, because after the main men's event, there was a mixed pair of a lad from Mohill and a Dutch dude who had flown in especially (the two Dutch champions didn't even get a look in against the strong local contenders during the main event). The lad from Mohill, who was part of the winning men's duo, had an arm on him like a horse's leg. He's a road bow-ler (not bowler, that's a hat English fellas wear), and he used the bowls windmilling arm technique to fire an egg sixty-one metres across the width of the field, and in fairness to him, the Dutch lad caught it. Between them they set a new World Egg-Throwing Record. I felt humbled and privileged to have witnessed ... nah, I didn't, but I fairly enjoyed it. It was fitting for what was a great day's sport, in the widest possible meaning of the word.

When the fun in the field was over, that wasn't the end of the eggcitement (ah come on, I'm allowed one). We all adjourned to a hotel down the road for Egg Roulette. It's like that scene from *The Deer Hunter*, but instead of a gun loaded with just one bullet, you have six eggs, five boiled and one raw, that you must take turns in breaking against your head. I failed miserably. The first egg I busted off my bulb was far from boiled, 'twas raw. So with an eggy head and a pain in my face from laughing, it was back on the road. Phil and Eoin were right, you didn't have to drink in order to have a good time at this caper, but balance is good, so it was off to a Gypsy Jazz and Craft Beer Festival in north Tipperary.

Craft beer and gypsy jazz is pretty much a match made in heaven as far as I'm concerned, so Wanderly Wagon was in overdrive to get to Cloughjordan in time to settle in for the night. Upon arrival, the town was quieter than the Dáil bar in August. Was this the right place at all? It was the right place, but it was so quiet that I didn't think there were going to be many bodies at the gig that evening. I was wrong. Thirty-five minutes later, the hall was packed. The gypsy jazzers slunk out of the woodwork. The Lollo Meier Quartet was fantastic, banging out tunes that sounded like they were marinated in stored smoke from a 1930s Paris jazz club. If it was just the gypsy jazz, that would have been good enough, but this was also a craft beer festival, so it was off to the pub where all the gypsy jazzers, who had been playing and attending workshops all day, gathered for a session and a few bottles. The music was great, and the brew of the night for me was a lager called 'Brew Eyed', imported all the way from Co. Offaly, home of haunted castles and great-great-great-granddaddy Obama.

Chatting to Lilly who organised this shindig was another one of those positive stories of people going out of their way to do something in their town to bump up the feel-good factor. She had been unemployed since the previous year, and as a result she wanted to find something to do to keep her busy and to promote the area. She didn't receive any funding, so the cost of the event fell on her (an unemployed lone parent), with support from her partner, friends, family and the community.

This explained the lack of bunting, posters and hoopla around the village. It's difficult not to be impressed by some of the people who invest so much of their time, energy and money to promote and organise events in the hope that something good will come of them. Humbled yet again, I was getting well used to the feeling.

After the visit to Cloughjordan, some festivalling without intoxicants was called for; luckily, the selection of festivals on offer in Ireland is as eclectic as the range of glasses on offer in Elton John's local Specsavers. Over the course of one weekend, there were three children's festivals happening around the country, and luckily I knew a 12-year-old that I could borrow for the weekend; she's always great company, and she could give me some insight while we both had a laugh. Céilí's Mam and I had gone out for a few years and, since then, Céilí and I had been on a couple of camping trips. Just before starting the festival quest, we'd done a little tour around Scotland finishing up in Edinburgh for a couple of days at the Fringe Festival, where we saw the most amazing puppet show. We needed cheering up after a fruitless hunt for the Loch Ness Monster. Our experience in the area of puppets would stand to us; we were off to Bray for the International Puppet Festival, hitting Longford for Aisling Children's Arts Festival, but the first port of call was Galway for Ireland's largest children's festival: Baború.

The overlap in festivals for young folk wasn't accidental; it often happens that similar types of festivals in different parts of the country will run at the same time. It means that international acts can be brought in, and the cost shared between more than one organisation. It makes sense. Earagail Arts and Clonmel Junction Festivals have this symbiosis down to a tee.

In 1994, Baború International Children's Arts Festival kicked off, created and curated by the crew responsible for Galway Arts Festival. It's a great idea, and one that all three festivals we were attending had in common: bringing quality entertainment to young people, firing their imaginations and getting them interested in the arts. At the first show we saw, in Galway, there was a person onstage dancing in what looked like a huge inflatable plastic bag that resembled a cloud. Not only was it visually stunning, we were both delighted to finally find someone who could relate to the first line in Katy Perry's song, 'Firework'. Surely this was a person who must know exactly what it feels like to be a plastic bag? We both agreed that the shows we got to see in Galway were pretty cool, and we even got to play Bingo in Salthill. Who doesn't enjoy a card of Bingo?

Aisling in Longford was kicking off on the day we got there, so it was kind of like a launch party, with lemonade and buns instead of wine and cheese; I'd much prefer the latter any day of the week. There was a multitude of activities and distractions on which the younger folk could expend their lemonade-induced energy; the climbing wall caught Céilí's attention. It was raining, but she didn't care. Jacket on, hood up, and away she went. She loved the scramble, even though there was a little 7-year-old who flew past her. We both agreed that he was a little bit too monkeyish for his own good. The atmosphere was great, and all the activities were free, so we ended up staying much longer than expected. Why leave when you're having fun?

Geography was never one of my strong points, and I'm a bit ashamed to admit that I thought Bray was in Dublin. Céilí was pretty adamant that it was in Wicklow, so we consulted the roadmap. We were bound for Bray International Puppet Festival, definitely in Co. Wicklow. The 12-year-old had a better sense of direction than me. The show we caught there that night was a thought-provoking and poignant piece about a girl who heard stories from her grandfather about his time in the trenches during the First World War. It was great to experience a whole weekend of entertainment for kids that didn't patronise or dumb things down; on the contrary, it was challenging and stimulating. On the way home I asked Céilí if she was worried about missing *The X Factor* that weekend. 'Not at all', she said, 'I Sky-plussed it.' There's a Discover Ireland campaign in there somewhere.

We'd had a full and fantastic weekend, and even though the wind was howling and the rain bucketing down on the road home, Céilí was out for the count. It had been a pleasure sharing the weekend with her, and getting to hear her take on the festival experience. The weather was so bad driving home that I became acutely aware that I was responsible for the safety of that small sleeping girl beside me; throwing myself headlong into long nights on the road had never been a concern when alone. For a fella who doesn't have any kids, it was an odd feeling, and those occasional pangs of responsibility that popped up while out on the road with Céilí are probably as close as I'll ever get to fatherhood.

On that dark October night, with just the sound of the rain beating down on Wanderly Wagon and the pulse of the windscreen wipers, I was thinking about the nature of journeys. As you move towards somewhere new, you're bound to leave some places behind, thinking of them fondly, learning from them, letting them enhance your life. Hopefully, occasionally getting to revisit the really worthwhile ones makes the journey worthwhile. It was also possible that I was thinking too much, so I put the Katy Perry CD on really low, and wondered what it would feel like to be a plastic bag.

Childhood pursuits and family fun were to be continuing themes. I was setting sail for Freshford in Co. Kilkenny to try my hand at the All-Ireland Conker Championships. There are some people, God love them, who don't know what conkers are all about – probably the same types who were mystified by High Nellies. There follows 'Conkers for

Dummies': you get the fruit of the horse chestnut tree and take the brown round shiny bit (the nut) out of the spiky shell. Put a hole through the nut and thread a string, with one knotted end, through the hole. Find another conker fiend and proceed to lamp the bejangles out of each other's weapons. As they say in Monaghan, 'Chape, clane fun!' The square in Freshford, surrounded by horse chestnut trees, is an ideal setting for this type of pursuit, and on All-Ireland Conker Championship Sunday it has a carnival atmosphere. Brenda Cooper told me that they've been running the Conker Championships there for thirteen years, trying to keep the event as uncommercial as possible. Not a bad aspiration, and they are doing a good job. This is wholesome family fun, simple as that.

Well, fun to a point. The shin pads at registration were a warning of what was to come. I enquired about what they were for. 'Ah, don't be worrying about them, they're only for wimps', says the fella from the county where they feed babies hurleys instead of Farley's Rusks. I wasn't sure what he meant until I got into the practice ring for a few swings. Ow! Elbow, arm, knee and gongle-pouch are all areas prone to receiving the brunt of a poorly aimed swing. I don't remember conkers from childhood being an extreme sport. The fun gets toned down another notch when you enter the competition ring; this is a championship, and these Kilkenny folk take it seriously (if it were a league, you might have some hope).

You're not allowed to bring your own conker to the event, in case they've been knocking around with Lance Armstrong. All competitors choose their weapons blind from a cloth bag, and each match is assigned a referee. Three strokes each at a time, and, after a limit of five minutes, if there hasn't been a bust-up, whoever makes the most strokes out of the following nine strokes is the winner. If it's still a draw, then sudden death until someone misses and the other person doesn't. Are you still with me? See, I told you it starts to get serious.

Over the course of the day, I developed a technique of swinging in hard from the side rather than straight down. It seemed to work for me. Part of the trick of the thing is not to go full tilt at it or you run the risk of breaking your own conker.

After five knockout rounds, I was still surprised to be in with a shout. There's a lot of luck involved in this caper. In the heel of the hunt, I unbelievably got into the final, and was psyched up, ready to go the distance with John from Dublin. I was actually in the All-Ireland Conker Final!

Introductions were made, and the scene was set. I won the toss, and let John strike first. You could have cut the tension with a knife as hundreds of onlookers gathered around the finalists' platform. Bang! He busted his nut off mine first swing. That was it, I'd won! Crown, trophy and €500 all taken back across the bridge to the Deise. Bring on the World Championships in Honolulu in 2015. I'd love to tell you that I developed a knack and that I'm shit hot at conkers, but ... well, hang on ... actually ... I'd just won the All-Ireland Conker Championship, beat that, Tommy Walsh! Two months done, and one All-Ireland title, and 500 quid in the bag. This festival craic was definitely starting to suit me.

Later that week, I sat at home wearing my crown and polishing my trophy, mulling over the previous two months on the road, when I noticed something stuck to my jacket. It was the sticker from the auld lad collecting with the bucket in Co. Leitrim. Maybe the cryptic old dude was right; I hadn't managed to secure a mortgage six months earlier, but could his bit of sticky paper be helping to give me freedom? It could be that the Wiccans had cast some spell, or the scrap of J-cloth secured to a bush in the mystic triangle may have been having an influence, but whatever was going on, it felt like my journey was something I was meant to do. I was hungry for more road.

Festivals Attended in October

18. *Féile Draíochta* – Dublin City
19. Athlone Literature Festival – Athlone, Co. Westmeath
20. Ballinasloe Horse Fair – Ballinasloe, Co. Galway
21. Nire Valley Walking Festival – Dungarvan, Co. Waterford
22. Offline Film Festival – Birr, Co. Offaly
23. Slievebloom Storytelling Festival – Leap Castle, Co. Offaly
24. High Nelly Rally – Durrow, Co. Laois
25. Beck's Weekender – Dublin City
26. Baboró – Galway City
27. Aisling Children's Arts Festival – Longford, Co. Longford
28. International Puppet Festival – Bray, Co. Wicklow
29. Pumpkin Festival – Virginia, Co. Cavan
30. Culchie Festival and Egg-Throwing Championships – Mohill, Co. Leitrim
31. Gypsy Jazz Festival – Cloughjordan, Co. Tipperary
32. All-Ireland Conker Championships – Freshford, Co. Kilkenny
33. Imagine Arts Festival – Waterford City

Other Recommended Festivals in October

International Mushroom Festival – Killegar, Co. Leitrim
Guinness Jazz Festival – Cork City
Dublin Book Festival – Dublin City
Wexford Festival of Opera – Wexford, Co. Wexford

4 | *November – Laughter is preferable to tears*

*P*atient: 'Doctor, my brother thinks he's a chicken.'
Doctor: 'Here, give him one of these tablets three times a day and he'll be fine.'
Patient: 'I can't … we need the eggs!'

On the same day as Anglo Irish Bank's unsecured creditors were paid €200 million of Irish taxpayers' money, the retelling of this Woody Allen joke by Max Keiser at Kilkenomics on a Thursday night in November seemed to capture the essence of the barrel that the banks had us over. We still needed the eggs.

The audiences at Kilkenomics weren't really sure how to refer to the things they were attending. I heard people say they were going to 'a talk', 'a show', 'a gig', and even 'a Q&A session'. We'll stick with 'show' for now. The show on Thursday was 'What the Hell is Happening Now?' in the Set Theatre in Kilkenny. Things were changing so rapidly in the world of markets and finance around this time that it was difficult for anybody to say with authority what the hell was happening at any given point, but the consensus seemed to be that, whatever it was, it wasn't good, and that we'd be screwed altogether if we didn't have the Greeks to make fun of.

The show saw four economic luminaries and four well-known Irish comedians teaming up for the evening. To begin with, we had a sketch from the four comedians (Karl Spain, Des Bishop, Neil Delamere and Keith Farnan) using a horse racing analogy to explain our current economic position; the MC on the night (Colm O'Regan) commented that the sketch wouldn't have passed quality control for the John Player Tops. He was right.

One by one, we were introduced to each of the four scholarly economic guests for the evening (Max Keiser, Peter Antonioni, Martín Lousteau and the bold Davey McWilliams). They each spoke alone on the stage for a short period of time, before they were joined by one of the comedians to be asked some prepared questions. The addition of the comedians did lighten the whole affair, but it was difficult at times for the two worlds to blend smoothly, and some of the interviews were a bit strained. The highlight of the evening was when Max Keiser took to the stage, a bit more fire and brimstone and ballsy than some of the other speakers. Max used to be a broker type dude on Wall Street, and he told us that it has been proven that slightly brain-damaged people make the best investment bankers and brokers; if you lack empathy and have sociopathic tendencies, get yourself to Wall Street my son.

While all the other speakers shone light on what's happening around the world in terms of economic and social upheaval, it was Max who seemed to come closest to providing something practical that people can do to make a difference. He reckons that the war is on, and that we will never win it, but there are some battles that could be snatched if capitalism was fought with capitalism. I'd never be able to explain it with the same edge that he can. If you want to join the battle, check him out. He's been called a financial anarchist, and he's worth a look. Googletube him.

I'm still not sure what Kilkenomics is all about. It's not purely to engage in economic commentary, nor is it purely entertainment. If it is to inform and engage a diverse audience and interest them in the world of economics, I think it works. If it's a vehicle for David McWilliams to broaden a career beyond that of a cider-promoting economist, it works on that level too.

If I found myself in some Neo-Hiberno version of *Back to the Future* and ended up having a chat with a 21-year-old version of myself, if my head didn't explode from a disruption in the space-time continuum, I'd probably be willing to accept that Martin McGuinness would run for president someday, that down the line my prayers would be answered and Westlife would eventually break up (but not in the violent and lethal manner I had hoped for), and I'd even believe that Daniel O'Donnell got married (to a woman might be stretching it though). I wouldn't, however, be able to swallow that one day I'd end up at an economics festival in Kilkenny. 'An economics festival, are you mental?!' I can't say I enjoyed it in the same way I enjoy other festivals, but I was glad I went. I couldn't help but feel a little bit frustrated by the hopelessness and lack of control we seem to have over the world of high finance – a world that seems to exert absolute control over us. Best to stick to thinking about festivals, I decided; these were things I could relate to easily and control my relationship with ... mostly.

Although George Lee's analysis of the next budget would be made all the more engaging if he had his face painted like a member of Kiss and a flamethrower attached to a studded leather codpiece, it'd certainly make the fiscal farcical. Economics is not rock 'n'roll, it never will be. Maybe Kilkenomics and Max Keiser are as close as it will get.

Thankfully, the financial fug was banished by an odd tune playing over and over in my head as I trundled along the road in the van en route to my next destination on an unseasonably sunny Saturday morning in November. This particular dose of earworm wasn't that annoying: 'Ohhh I've got a brand new combine-harvester and I'll give you the key…'. It repeated on loop as I bounced northwards towards Donegal. Ardara Matchmaking Festival, here I come.

I drove into Ardara early on Saturday afternoon, and was met by a sign that read: 'Welcome to Ardara, Home of the Festivals'. There was every chance that I might like it here. It felt a little early to adjourn to the pub, so I decided to stroll around and take in some of the sights to keep myself out of mischief. Seven minutes later I was in a pub called The Corner House (well, at least I tried) talking to Stephen, the landlord, who was actually expecting me. He brought me down to meet one of several matchmakers who were on duty in the town over the weekend.

He asked me if I recognised Bernard, who was a bit of a celebrity around Donegal a few years back when he appeared on *Blind Date* with Cilla Black and stripped off on the telly. Good man, Bernard. I wonder what 'Our Graham' made of that? Bernard has experience in the field, and he told me that, although it's a bit of craic for most people, some do take it very seriously. It took one lady from Louth three consecutive visits before she found her fella, but find him she did, and now they're married with two kids. Bernard is single himself, and when I asked if he could chat up the women while he was taking down their particulars, so to speak, he was aghast. 'God, no.' I suppose that would be like insider trading and, as the lads at Kilkenomics would tell you, that never EVER happens.

After chatting with Bernard, Stephen asked me if I had met Martin McGuinness yet. 'Jaysus, Stephen, I didn't think this would be his scene?' I said, shocked. 'I suppose he needs to wind down after a tough day's first ministering.' 'No, not that one, the real Martin McGuinness.' A phone call later, and I was sharing a pint with the real Martin McGuinness – a fella who had spent twenty years working in London as a drag artist, and returned to his home of Ardara to work on the farm after his dad passed away in 2005.

By day, he wears overalls and wellies, tending to the livestock in the windswept fields of west Donegal, but by night he dons the six-inch heels and a sparkly dress to become 'Scarlett Rose'. This lad should be on the cover of the *Farmers Journal*. You'd think that life wouldn't be easy for a chap like Martin in a rural town anywhere in Ireland, and he admits that he was apprehensive about returning to his hometown, having hightailed it to London as fast as his shapely legs would carry him, but he loves being back, and the community have welcomed him and his alter ego with open arms. He's even a member of the Parish Council. He doesn't just perform in Ardara; he's all over the country. He does five gigs in different cities during Pride, and he runs a weekly club in Letterkenny. It should be no surprise that he has amazing legs; sure he spends his days looking after calves. He has an apprentice in the shape of Lucy Lashes, and they make up a duo known in the locality as the Donegal Divas. There are times when living in Ireland would drive you spare, but it's talking to people like Martin that reminds you of what makes us great: we're a little bit craic'd, but the cracks are what lets the light shine through.

After a delightful chat with Martin in Nancy's Bar, I had that awful quandary that can face festival-goers: do I break for something to eat, or do I throw caution to the wind and plough ahead making day, evening and night the one event? I consulted Twitter and Facebook, where, funnily enough, the depth of experience seemed to know no bounds. 'Bag of chips out of the paw' was the advice from Thurles. 'Drive it on' were the words of wisdom from the Deise. 'Have the grub, but not too much, you'll keep going longer and you'll be glad of it in the morning' came the wise words from Galway.

The economy might be shagged, but if the rest of the world could use some over-indulgence consultants, we could charge for this advice. I can see us heading off on private jets to advise Mardi Gras revellers on the best way to approach the arduous party: 'Porridge is yer only man, Britney, don't steep it too long though, so it'll have plenty of soakage.' We could hit the beaches of Thailand for their Full Moon Partys to offer sagacious tips to buzzers. 'Half a bucket of that stuff every twenty minutes is loads, 'tis a marathon we're running here, not a sprint.' So, back to Wanderly Wagon I went to scrape together some victuals, when the phone rang. 'Mark, what about ya, Stephen here in The Corner House. I have a couple of people here you'll want to meet.' That was the end of dinner.

A few minutes later, I was above in The Corner House again, and Stephen was right. He brought me out the back to meet two ladies who are steeped in the tradition of matchmaking. Marie and Gráinne Daly, daughters of the Lisdoon Legend, Willy Daly, who'd tried to set me up with the Ban Garda in September. The girls have gone into their father's line of work, and don't limit their matchmaking to Lisdoon in September; they travel around the country providing a service for the lovelorn from Limerick to Leitrim and beyond. Not only were the two girls in the house, Stephen brought in the Mayor of Ardara, Conal Haughey, to talk to us too. Stephen wouldn't rest till I had the hand shook off me.

After the chats and handshakes, it was off around the pubs for some festival research. Slowly but surely the place began to wind up a little, but it still wasn't the kind of night I was expecting. It just felt like a good Saturday night out in any town in Ireland. It wasn't until things kicked off in the Nesbitt Arms Hotel that I found the spark that lit up this festival. This shower could dance. Not big box, little box or shuffle slowly round in a circle kind of dancing: proper dancing. The place was hopping, and they were jiving up a storm. I was amazed at how good the dancers were, and they all seemed to be at it – every age, every shape, and all of them grinning like loons. I've been to the Rhu Glenn in Co. Kilkenny where the dancing is good, I took set-dancing lessons as a New Year's resolution a few years ago (don't ask), and I've cut a rug in the ballrooms of Lisdoon, but nowhere have I seen as large and as accomplished a community of dancers as I have in Ardara. This shower like to move it, move it.

I waltzed to 'The Homes of Donegal', how could you not? I sang along with three ladies at the counter to the strains of 'The Boys of the County Armagh'. Lisa McHugh and her Country and Irish band wouldn't usually be my cup of tea, but it was perfect for the night that was in it. The crowd was well mixed, and where Lisdoon is wild and reckless fun, Ardara is a bit more polished, and I'd go so far as to say that if you were a fella who was seriously in the market for a dance partner, I'd steer you to Donegal before Clare. Where Kilkenomics gave rise to a kind of educated humorous hopelessness, Ardara was about having fun. I was in the Home of Festivals; It was bound to go well.

This was a matchmaking festival, so the obvious question is how did I get on. I met a lovely girl, big lass by the name of Lucy, a friend of Scarlett Rose. She had a grip on her like a bear. She beat me in a couple of arm-wrestles, but we had a great time. For some reason, all the way back home the next day I had a new dose of earworm: 'Well, I'm not the world's most physical guy, but when she squeezed me tight she nearly broke my spine, oh my Lola, La-La-La-La-Lola...'.

I was being educated as I travelled around the leafy lanes and grass-centered *bothareens* of Ireland. I learned a lot of things that I should probably have known already. Things like the fact that one of the best sounds in the world is 'Lough Ramor', spoken in a thick Cavan accent, and that *Macra na Feirme* rocks. It's true, and I didn't think it would be. *Macra* is a club for young people who come from farming and rural backgrounds. Before my travels, if I had to play a word association game that involved someone shouting '*Macra*' at me, I would have shouted back 'Wellies'. Right now, I think I'd shout back 'Savage', and not in relation to muck either. The time spent in the company of farming transvestites in Donegal was to serve me well; my next dose of festival duty saw me spending a weekend at the most glamorous event on the *Macra* calendar. Similarly to Donegal, there was plenty of leg on show, but not one wellington scar was evident. Trust me, I was looking.

I was invited to Tullamore to take up duties as an escort for *Macra na Feirme*'s Queen of the Land Festival. I was so excited heading off to this shindig that I forgot my shoes. I ironed shirts (the first time since September), and even had a suit and a tux on hangers in Wanderly Wagon. As luck would have it, Ballinasloe, where I was parked up the night before, is possibly the best place in Ireland to go if you want to be shod. Not only do they have Ireland's biggest horse fair, I found a pair of boots in a skip. They were a little bit rough, but I think I just about managed to clean them up. When I say clean them up, I coloured in the scuffs with a black marker. What? It was a permanent marker.

Henry Healy, a recent celebrity on Irish shores by virtue of the fact that he's Barack Obama's eighth cousin, was one of the judges for the festivities at Queen of the Land. I can say in all honesty that he's such a gentleman it's understandable why the Obamas and their posse called down to him for a pint. Lovely fella. That actually became a refrain for me over the course of the weekend in Tullamore. They were all so bloody nice that the cynical bastard in me went off in a huff on Saturday night to watch the Munster rugby match. I met up with him again on Monday. He said it was a good game. I didn't know what to expect, heading to what I had envisaged as being a 'Lovely Girls' competition, similar to the one from Father Ted. Well, I can tell you now that even though I still don't have a fecking clue what 'Road Frontage' is, I enjoyed myself more than Shane McGowan visiting the Jameson Distillery in Middleton.

I hadn't a clue what *Macra* was all about before the weekend, but I do now. It's a social club first and foremost, and I mean social in the broadest sense possible of the word. The members are between the ages of 17 and 35, they come from all walks of life, and thankfully it isn't just for people who know what 'Road Frontage' is, although it wouldn't do any harm. The members of *Macra* are the barrister you dealt with that time you got off, the girl you chat with at the till in Dunnes, the fella who was playing in the pub last Thursday, and one or two of them might even be the farmer who supplies beef to your local butcher. Agri-experience is not a prerequisite, and I don't know if there are any prerequisites. There are city and country dwellers, and I imagine if you're not too far either side of the age limit you might be able to swing something, so long as you can bowl or look good in a pair of jeans.

Macra has been around for sixty years, and was set up to educate, train, develop, establish links and provide a social outlet for the youth in rural areas. It has about 9,000 members in 300 clubs around the country, and the sly feckers are having a great time without telling the rest of us about it. I couldn't help but admire the organization, the slick running of the event and the huge crowds of supporters that arrived in Tullamore with the banners they had made (it was like *Winning Streak* on steroids). I now understand why the IFA is such a strong body and lobby group: they're well trained as youngsters. This crowd of young, rural types has created a countrywide network that provides support and a strong community bond. The rest of us could learn a thing or two from them.

Our first real duty as escorts began at 2.00 p.m. on Saturday afternoon, when we got to find out who the (un)lucky ladies who would enjoy our company for the weekend were going to be. I was meeting up with twenty-six lads from *Macra*, most of whom were away from home for the weekend. We met in a pub that had a trad session laid on for us. Mick, one of the escorts, and his Dad played a few tunes, and the recently introduced Susan and I threw a foot at them to cut the rug. Pub at 2.00, dinner at 8.00, what do you think happened? Would you believe that we all actually made it to dinner without being carried? Well, nearly all – there is one Offaly escort who now answers to the name 'Sleeping Beauty': he'd had a late night the night before.

Having been introduced to the ladies, I was delighted to find that Susan was, unsurprisingly, a lovely girl. Then again, they were all lovely girls. The ladies went off to prepare for the night, and the lads stayed on for a drink or two, but nothing mental. A few friendly pints, and the banter among the escorts was good. One of my favourite quotes came from a Kilkenny farmer: 'That fella'd ride a cat gettin' out a sky-light!' He was describing one of our fellow escorts. I think it was meant as a compliment. There was an initial amount of discontent when the escorts found out how many of the girls had boyfriends, but sure didn't they also have sisters and friends travelling up for each of the nights? Sorted! The lad who was accused of sexually assaulting cats exiting windows even got a date, and if he'd do that to a cat, I shudder to think what he was going to do to a bird in a bowling alley.

Dinner went well, and we headed off to the ball. The fellas sat there like good little escorts, up in the front rows for a couple of hours, a few sneaking away occasionally to a bottle. You just knew that keeping animals like us penned up for that long would result in a backlash that would be extreme. It wouldn't be long before our fancy matching ties would be tied around our heads, like Rambo at a disco. As well as the ties, we were kitted out with white shirts and name badges. I was given out to by a woman for having a drink when I should have been in behind a busy bar. This was about the third time I was accosted as being a hotel manager. I couldn't blame them. At one stage I remember thinking, 'Would ya look at the cut of that fuc … oohhh!' as I walked past a full-length mirror. The band was rocking, and the place was hopping. There were about 1,000 people at this shindig, and they were all well trained in the art of enjoying themselves. *Macra* takes that particular branch of their training very seriously.

Sunday night was another ball, and the announcement of the 'Queen of the Land'. I have to say that, having spent three days sleeping in Wanderly Wagon at the side of the road, I felt an enjoyable mix of scummy and classy as I stepped out through the sliding door on Sunday night in a tux and skip boots.

The previous year's queen, Sherine, told me how the year went far too quickly, she was enjoying it so much. Sherine was part of the judging panel, and Henry reckoned that it was easier to get the Obamas to Moneygall than it would be picking just one of the girls to don the tiara. Henry reckoned that he'd be back as an escort the next year. You may as well start training now, buddy, 'tis no fecking walk in the park. Get the Milk Thistle into ya.

After another wonderful evening, the tension grew and we all paraded around the Bridge House Hotel with a bagpiper. The judges did have a tough job in fairness, but the girl who won it was really nice, and Mick and I were talking about it afterwards. Although it felt a little unfair to pick just one of them after the great weekend we'd all had, she seemed to be so humble, along with all her other qualities. It was just a shame that she had to be from Kilkenny. I suppose we all have to have one fatal flaw. Well done, Bernie Woods.

Learning was to be the theme on the road in November. I found out that you've never really walked in another man's shoes until you've gone skip-diving in Ballinasloe. I learned that I'd make a much better Cortina than an Escort. I discovered that the Bridge House Hotel has the only elevators in the world that defy physics: it's possible for someone to go down in them at the same time they go up, allegedly. I found out what Offaly girls do down on the farm for kicks, and that being a Stalwart of the Land is great fun, and it's possible to make it through a description of a weekend on the lash with *Macra* without using the expression 'craic' once. Not easy. My next lesson was to be an education in inappropriate online behaviour.

The following weekend, the festivals were close to home, so I spent a Friday night in my own bed for the first time in almost three months, and Saturday afternoon goofing around the house and doing some much-needed chores. There was a pair of socks at the end of the laundry basket that were shaping up to kick the shit out of me if they weren't washed. My next festival appointment was Saturday at 7.00 p.m. in Clonmel for their comedy festival. This festival was actually called the Bulmer's Pear Comedy Festival; no doubt an effort to redeem the sullied reputation of a drink that had some, how shall I put this, teething difficulties when it was initially launched. I'm not saying more than that; you can do your own research into the messy business. There's a new recipe now, and everyone at the gig that Saturday seemed to be happy in their nappies.

There was a clatter of comedians taking to the stage over the weekend, and I was surprised to find the main room in Hearn's Hotel full before 7.00 p.m. The punters were out in force, and they were ready to be entertained. You know that old *plámás* that you often get at gigs: 'It's really great to be here in [insert name of town the hack is appearing in here], you guys are beautiful.' Well, none of that from Geordie Chris Ramsey. 'Clonmel, what an armpit!' Now I don't know if you've ever been out in Clonmel before, but if you went around Danno's spouting the spiel that Chris was coming out with, they'd probably be fishing you out of the river in Carrick. But he delivered the abuse in such a way that the crowd were lapping it up. Maybe he was just telling the truth.

After Chris, I went to see Sanderson Jones, who has a unique approach to promoting his gigs. He endeavours to sell all the tickets for his gigs by hand, thus getting to meet everybody who's going to be there on the night. This creates an intimate atmosphere, with Sanderson welcoming everyone, by name, to the show. Where this aspect of Sanderson's approach comes into its own is when he delves into online investigations of the people who will be present in the audience. He knows who we all are, so he uses this information to trawl the web for embarrassing nuggets about the audience members. This is where the lesson began.

The projected presentation on-screen (or in the case of this gig, on-bedsheet) shows Facebook posts, pictures and inane tweets from audience members, but it's when the content gets a bit more cringe-inducing that things get much more interesting. My favourite moment was when Sanderson went to a tweet posted by the guy sitting across from me. This guy had wondered, in a tweet, how best to implement the domestic violence he had just witnessed in *Raging Bull* into his own home life. Judging by the looks and reaction from his other half on the night, mission accomplished.

I remember hearing someone say that you should never submit or do anything online that you wouldn't be willing to have posted on a billboard in your hometown. After this gig, it was a bit more immediate than that. Never do anything online that you wouldn't like Sanderson Jones to bring up in front of an audience in Clonmel. I was sitting there thinking, 'Hang on ... is there anything he might have found out about me?' Unfounded paranoia of course.

The highlight of the show was one of the funniest things I've seen at a comedy gig. Let me try to explain how it works. Sanderson has a webcam (his iPhone) attached to the stage wall. He clears out the front row of the gig and gets one attractive female to sit on her own in the front row, while the row behind her hold up a white sheet. From the camera it looks like a girl sitting on her own in front of a webcam. The audience can see all the on-screen content from the projector being used for the show. Sanderson is out of the shot on the laptop, and he opens a website that is populated by fellas who look for webcam links with women so they can 'interfere' with themselves whilst looking at someone who is also looking at them and interfering with themselves too. I think the idea is to set up a feedback loop of interference (Hey! Give me a break, I'm doing my best to describe this in as euphemistic a way as possible). Sanderson wasn't logged on for long when he got a bite. So he typed in some suggestive chat, and some poor eejit thinks he's linked up with some girl who's interested in watching him lamp the bejangles out of himself.

All the while, the audience is trying to keep quiet. The fella eventually starts tearing into it, and Sanderson counts down from three to one, and on cue the second row drop the sheet and the audience cheers, whoops, whistles, points and laughs; all of this audience activity now being transmitted to the masturbator via the webcam. The poor eejit now realises that he's being broadcast to an audience, and disappears faster than cocktail sausages at a twenty-first.

We did this three times, and it didn't get tired at all. This turn, without doubt, and in a subtle-as-a-brick-to-the-bulb kind of a way, shows that there are some who take their internet privacy as a given. Be careful what you type, what you post and at whom you pull your pants down. The really worrying thing is that Sanderson told me that sometimes the guys who are on-screen don't stop, relishing the opportunity to perform in front of an audience. Be careful out there.

After the depravity of the comedy gig it was time for some balance. Off to Kilkenny on a Sunday morning to attend the inaugural Kilkenny Die-Cast and Model Exhibition for some good, clean fun. Dinky, Matchbox, Corgi, tractors, trucks, trains, planes and whatever you're having yourself.

Why do you think a fella organises an event like this? In Brian's case, it's because he likes trucks. He drives them for work, and he collects them as a hobby. No other motivation. He wasn't selling anything, he wasn't advertising some service, in fact, he was worried that he wouldn't cover the €3,000 that it cost to put on the event. He spent days putting up posters, getting the hotel ready, making calls to publicise the event, to get people to exhibit and to pull the whole thing together. The man likes trucks, simple as that. I asked Brian's wife if he's mad, and she said that he's more obsessed than craic'd. That's okay then.

The highlight of my weekend was meeting Gavin and Grahame McLaughlin. These two young lads build and sell model farms. Some days they spend up to six hours making model farms for die-cast enthusiasts to populate with miniature machines, people and livestock. They reckon that one of their farms takes sixty hours to build. The night before the exhibition they had been up till 2.00 a.m. putting the finishing touches to their display. The young lads had sold five of these farms since September, and I'm not surprised they were getting customers. They had a laptop set up at their stand showing previous work, displayed on their Facebook page, and no sooner had I told them what I was doing than Grahame had the smartphone out and was on the blog. These boys are sharp, but so much better than that, they are genuine and enthusiastic. If you could bottle what these young fellas have, Joe Duffy would be juggling on Grafton Street. The future of the country might be rosy after all.

I'm delighted to report that, as I was leaving the Springhill Court Hotel in Kilkenny, the crowds were flooding in. You couldn't get parking, and the Waterford road was lined with cars. I think Brian was going to get the 500 bodies through the door that he needed to cover himself, and I've no doubt that the two McLaughlin boys got a few orders too. This event provided the perfect yin to the yang-a-lang-a-ding-dong from the night before. The potential and positivity being radiated by the McLaughlin boys put a spring in my step.

The next festival I hit kept those positivity levels brimming over. There was a DIY arts festival running in Cork under the title 'Trash Culture Revue'. The festival is run through the work, performances, skills and efforts of the members of the Mutantspace Arts Skills Exchange. Run by volunteers, programmed by volunteers, performances by volunteers. The entry fee to events? Voluntary contribution in the cardboard box by the door if you feel like it. As they say themselves, 'How good is that? It's fantastic! We are truly autonomous. Together, we can do anything.' The positivity of the crowd in Cork is almost sickening. It turns my inner cynic into Gollum, sent scurrying, cursing and hissing into the recesses of my psyche. At this early stage of my travels, he'd nearly been banished completely.

Mutantspace is a skills bank that was established in 2009 out of frustration with how things stood, both economically and socially. It's a proactive effort to deliver a real alternative to buying into a commercial existence that has spiraled out of control. There are over 1,500 Mutantspace members in eight different countries. They've all signed up to offer their skills to other members on a 'You scratch my back...' basis. The hurlers of Cork don't wear red for nothing. At its core, it's a skills bank into which you lodge your own skills and from which you can withdraw the skills of others. What does it cost to join? Nothing. What does it cost to draw upon the skills of other members? Nothing. What's stopping you from signing up as a member? I signed up a week before the festival.

It was great to find the beginnings of a solution to some of the doom and gloom scenarios that the economists were talking about at Kilkenomics at the beginning of the month. The Mutantspace Skills Bank is only a drop in the ocean, but it's proactive, and it certainly stemmed my feeling of complete helplessness. More importantly, it points towards a whole group of people who are hungry to find alternatives to broken banks. It felt as if nothing could go wrong with my festival quest, which is exactly when something usually does.

Festivals Attended in November

34. Kilkenomics – Kilkenny, Kilkenny
35. Waterford Film Festival – Waterford City
36. Ardara Matchmaking Festival – Ardara, Co. Donegal
37. AOIFE – Ballinasloe, Co. Galway
38. Queen of the Land – Tullamore, Co. Offaly
39. Waterford Golden Years Festival – Waterford City
40. Japanese Film Festival – Waterford City
41. Clonmel Comedy Festival – Clonmel, Co. Tipperary
42. Die-Cast and Model Exhibition – Kilkenny, Kilkenny
43. Cork: A Christmas Celebration – Cork City
44. Mutant Space DIY Arts Festival – Cork City
45. WexWorld Sci-Fi – Wexford, Co. Wexford

Other Recommended Festivals in November

National Circus Festival Ireland – Tralee, Co. Kerry
Ennis Trad Festival – Ennis, Co. Clare
Subtitle European Film Festival – Kilkenny, Co. Kilkenny
Cork Film Festival – Cork City

5 | *December – A Poxy Christmas*

On the first Wednesday in December, The Frames and Lisa Hannigan kicked off the Other Voices Festival in McCarthy's Bar in Dingle. At the centre of this affair is the filming of the *Other Voices* music programme for RTÉ television; it's not quite *Later … with Jools Holland*, but it's ours. The gig on Wednesday was the only event on the whole *Other Voices* programme for which you could actually buy a ticket, except you couldn't really; they'd sold out faster than Johnny Rotten with a butter ad contract. I had my sights set on getting a ticket for the filming of the TV show in St James' Church. Unfortunately, you can't book, steal or borrow tickets for this gig. It's by invitation, or you can enter a competition to win the few tickets that are issued to the public. The prospect of getting into the main event was about a likely as Van Morrison changing career to become a CBeebies presenter, but a dangle in Dingle is always fun, and there was music laid on around the town all weekend. It was worth a whirl.

During the week I shook a few trees to see if any tickets might fall out, but there was nothing doing. I didn't panic; I have a theory about tickets. I reckon that there are always ways to get into things. You may not actually find the way to get in, but that doesn't mean it doesn't exist.

Perseverance, and a neck like a jockey's undercarriage, is the key. It was about eightish on Friday night when Wanderly Wagon rolled into an extremely quiet Dingle, and I had a whole bag of bullshit ready to dip into, in an effort to get inside St James' church for Cold Specks and Lisa Hannigan's second stint. We sidled shadily up to the church gate, only to be met by the security cordon. 'Ah, go on in there, lads, and stand down the back, ye'll be grand', said the security man at the door. Is that it?! No *plámásing*, no ducking and diving, no hinting at vague assurances that weren't given by people I didn't know? I almost felt cheated. It was too easy. Hang on, there was a fella pointing at us, right, game face on. 'Lads, come down here, there's a couple of seats nearer the front.' Ah, this was too fecking easy. Once inside, it's plain to see why it's so hard to ticket this event. About 150, max, can squeeze inside the venue. When you consider performer guest lists, sponsors, politicians, press, industry types and hangers-on, it doesn't leave much room for you and me. The whole series of *Other Voices* is shot over this one weekend, so whether or not members of the public are able to win tickets to become part of the audience could be deemed irrelevant by the producers of a series that gets broadcast in twelve countries, but, in fairness to them, they make an effort to get members of the public in. To say the atmosphere inside the church on the night was special is an understatement: it was what Mass should be like.

I remember the first time I heard Lisa singing with Damien Rice, and how I was captivated by the quality and control of tone that she has. The slight variations and nuances that she's able to bring to a vocal are mesmerising, and I can't help but get sucked in by them every time. When I eventually got to listen to her solo work, the appreciation was even deeper. The feeling and emotion she can convey – not just through her lyrics, but through the melodic journey that she takes with each syllable, each phoneme – are the threads that weave the aural equivalent of that blanky you had as a small child. Have I mentioned that she resembles an elven princess? As you can probably tell, I can take her or leave her really. I ended up standing next to Lisa after she played at Electric Picnic one year, and held my breath when I realised that it was she. What the hell would you do? I turned around and said, 'Hi, Lisa, I think you're great.' Shit!

I have no idea what she said afterwards, because there was a ringing in my ears from the rush of blood that needed to get to my bulb in time to cater for the blushes and embarrassment to which I had just subjected myself. I'm sure that she smiled, thanked me and was very gracious about the whole thing, right before she walked away as quickly as possible. Do you know why I'm sure? Because I did it all again, and worse, in Dingle after the gig in the church. A word of advice: never talk to people upon whom you'd prefer to make a good impression at 3.00 a.m. in the residents' bar of a hotel in Co. Kerry. If you want the whole horrible, car-crash account, you're going to have to ask me in person, I'm not committing it to print. Saturday's hangover wasn't helped by a particularly spectacular dose of the 'Oh Nos'.

As a form of distraction from the memories of the night before, we took a spin out around the Ring of Kerry on Saturday before the *Other Voices* afternoon sessions started in the pubs. We stopped off in Páidí Ó Sé's for a game of pool and a cure; you'd be surprised at how unfriendly Kerry men can be when you express the opinion that football is a game for piano movers while hurling is more suited to piano tuners. Just as well the engine was still warm. The weather wasn't great, but the scenery was still spectacular. Fellow muso, and partner in crime for the weekend, Markie W. and I decided we'd risk a swim at Inch Strand to freshen up. I assured him that the water was only a couple of degrees off what it was in August, which is technically true, but it's that fecking breeze and the fact that the tide was out that was the killer. People were stopping to take photos of the freaks swimming in December. It certainly livened us up for the rest of the day's proceedings.

During Saturday night's socialising, we ended up in the company of a local fisherman, who has found that turning Fungi finder and tourist ferrier is more lucrative and regular than hauling nets and pots. Once Fungi the dolphin made Dingle his home, people began turning up in droves to go and swim with the friendly fella. The lone dolphin has done for Dingle what the Obamas did for Moneygall. I was telling the hardened seaman about my quest, and about how I hadn't managed to find anyone who had lost the run of themselves during the boom while I'd been on my travels. He went a little quiet for a moment, and started looking at his shoes. 'To be honest,' he said, 'I kinda lost the run of meself.' He went on explain that when the dolphin gawpers began to show up, he got a loan for another boat. Dolphin tourism was booming, and so, when some development was going on in the town, he went back to the bank for some refinancing to invest in property, and the bank obliged. He drew deeply on his pint, wiped the froth from his mouth with his sleeve and took on a serious expression as he looked off into the middle-distance. 'If that dolphin ever dies, I'm fucked!'

I admired his honesty; he could have been a poster boy for what went wrong with the banks: the hard-working fisherman who secured a couple of loans and a mortgage on the strength of the daily appearance of a socially dysfunctional dolphin in the bay. If Fungi ever heads for

Honolulu, don't be surprised if a replacement is shipped in, or if a resident of the town paints themselves grey and takes to eating live mackerel. I wouldn't be surprised if it's happening already.

As if to underline this insight into our financial woes, during our conversation a portrait of Charlie Haughey looked down on us from the wall. Charlie, our former Headcase of State, makes Berlusconi look like Tintin. C. J. is still venerated in *An Daingean* for having built the town one of the finest marinas this side of Monte Carlo. It is no coincidence that it was handy for him to sail from here to his private island off the Kerry coast. Maybe he even anted up for an animatronic dolphin too? Just as I was looking away to take another sup from my pint, I could have sworn Charlie's portrait winked at me.

In an effort to banish false idols, we took a spin down to Annascaul on Sunday morning to visit the pub that was once owned by the manliest of Irish men: Arctic explorer and sailor Tom Crean. I'd received a present of one of Michael Smith's books for Christmas many years ago, and was fascinated to read about the adventures that Crean had with Shackleton and Scott. There was a great story taken from one of Scott's diaries where he recounted how refreshing it was to have two Irish men on the expedition, as they brought much-needed humour to the tough conditions. Scott overheard Shackleton and Crean as they sat by the fire on watch duty one night, discussing which member of the party would be best to eat first if they ran out of food. Scott reckoned that they were joking, but I picked up some of the legendary Annascaul black pudding while we were in the village. If Crean had the local touch to fashion a companion into the tasty blood pudding, it'd make for some scran.

Clonakilty claims bragging rights when it comes to clotted blood pud. So ubiquitous is it in the picturesque Co. Cork town, you can get it in suppository form from the local chemists. As with other things, the Rebels are inclined to think themselves the best in many areas, but when it comes to black pudding, Annascaul is the dog's. I ought to know. I'm in a position to officiate on offal; I have lineage. In a small local shop, in front of the pudding plant, you can buy it by the block, suitable for putting between wafers, should the mood take you. Thankfully, there wasn't a jar of mixed olive tapenade in sight; it would have desecrated the memory of Crean. There is, however, a locally brewed beer named after the hero; it would have been rude not to raise a glass to him.

There were signs up all around Dingle for the Festival of Light, but I'd been quizzing a few people about what it was and where it was, but not a flicker. Then, lo and behold, didn't we end up in the middle of it as we left one of the watering holes after an evening gig on Sunday. There was a parade heading up the road the same way we were going, and they were carrying lanterns and implements of shininess. It was either the Festival of Light, or we'd got caught up in a Co. Kerry version of *The Wicker Man* (also possible).

There had been a market laid on for the festival earlier in the day, and in the build-up to the parade, the populace of Dingle had been making lanterns and torches at one of the stalls to bring with them on the jaunt through the town. They all marched up through Main Street as far as the hospital, where the large Christmas tree was then lit up. It had a lovely family vibe to it, and it was nice to see that it wasn't just the interlopers who were enjoying the weekend. I was told that something similar happens in the town on New Year's Eve. There are fireworks earlier in the evening, and then a parade down to the bridge, where the Dinglers ring in the New Year. The parade of lanterns seems like an apt way to signify the start of the festive season. The Wren festivities on Stephen's Day in Dingle are famous, and the town is the best place in Ireland for upholding this tradition. It's on my to-do list.

No sooner had the townsfolk of Dingle fired up their tree, than Christmas festivals of all descriptions started popping up all over the place. One of the hangovers from our period of prosperity is the insistence of some towns on trying to turn their local square into a Viennese wonderland, complete with ice-skating rink, mulled wine and overpriced geegaws once December rolls around.

On more than one occasion in my life, I've found myself saying, 'Okay, if I get through it this time, I promise never to do it again. JUST MAKE IT STOP!' You'd be surprised at the wide variety of experiences that can bring on these empty promises and declarations, and even more surprised by how soon they can be forgotten. As I took to the ice on a Friday night in Waterford City at Winterval, I remembered that I'd had this exact feeling of imbalance and foreboding before, and just as I was about to summon spiritual help and make far-ranging promises that were about as credible as Thierry Henry standing beside a broken vase with his hands in his pockets, whistling and trying to look nonchalant, a little voice in my head said, 'Not a chance, buddy! You've negated your last contract of protection by being stupid enough to go ice-skating AGAIN! Did you not read the terms and conditions? You're on your own.' Shit!

As soon as the skate hit the ice, all the reasons for not doing this made themselves known to me. There was that doctor from Cork who told of a 20 per cent rise in A&E admissions when their ice rink opened, and then there was the security guy who worked at one of these things who told me about the fella who landed, front teeth first, down onto the ice, ramming all his top teeth up into his gums ('We had to close for an hour to clean up the blood'). There were also the many falls that I'd suffered the last time I'd tried this malarkey. It seemed obvious now, as I floundered to find my feet, that if God had wanted Irish people to ice-skate, he would have made us Canadian. But here I was, nonetheless, flailing and skittering like Peter Crouch trying to tap dance whilst wearing roller skates. I had all the elegance, grace and poise of a baby giraffe in six-inch heels that has just discovered polished parquet flooring.

To add a soundtrack to my misadventure, it was a disco night at 'Waterford on Ice'. The irony here is that, even suitably anaesthetised at a club on a regular night out, I'd be reluctant enough to take to the floor, but sober me up, cover the floor with ice, throw in a bunch of teenagers wearing blades on their feet careering around the place at 40km/h and I'm all over it like Ryan Giggs on his sister-in-law. If the DJ decided to play Van Halen's 'Jump', it'd be carnage. It seems that the effect that ice can have on slowing down the rotting and withering of foodstuffs must be similar to the effect that it has on the natural processes of logic. After fifteen minutes, I was as happy as Wayne Rooney in an old folks' home on bath night.

It's when you start getting confident that things start to get more dangerous. You get faster and faster, then remember that you don't know how to stop, a bit like Kate Moss on a coke binge. Whilst overconfidently bombing along, a small child, no more than eight years old, cut across in front of me. I was about to plough through the child, full sure that both of us would not be any the better for the collision, when at the last second, I lifted the child up under the armpits, avoiding the crash and inevitable pileup. Sorted! Except that now I was flaking along at pace, holding a child in the air, unable to skate for fear I'd go over, and still unable to stop.

Eventually, I began to slow down, and placed the child back on the ice. He skated away happily. The next time this scenario presented itself, I smacked into the person and then hit the ice like a sack of spuds. The lesser of two evils, really. If I kept lifting up children, the gardaí probably would've been called. I fell once, took out one teenager (five points) and did a lap holding a child aloft, looking like I'd just been awarded the FA cup for ice-skating. Not really too bad, all things considered. I was never doing that again though ... well, at least not until the following Wednesday night. They had the biggest ice rink in Ireland in Mahon Point in Cork. I couldn't resist.

The Christmas festivals that started popping up were a little different to most other festivals I'd been attending. They were all about spending Christmas, if you catch the tinkle of my till. Not many flights to New York for shopping trips were being booked, and strudel at the seasonal markets of Vienna had been replaced by a Pot Noodle over the Argos catalogue. But there was still a few bob for socks and such to be stashed under the tree; we weren't totally down and out. At all these festive fairs, there were loads of lights, ice skating, merry-go-rounds, and lots of shops in which you could spend your money. It is pretty, seeing places lit up like Eamon Dunphy's rear-view mirror just before he gets pulled over, but if you can manage to go into a city centre near you during silly season and enjoy all its twinkly glory without it leaving too much of a dent in your pocket, fair play to you. Skating for an adult and two kids was €35 for an hour – about as much as going to the cinema, which ain't cheap either. It is more fun than Andy Reid at a post-match singsong though.

After the near-death experience on ice in Waterford, I headed for Co. Clare to check out a few of their festive offerings. You'd be surprised at how long it takes to drive through the Burren if you stop every time that there's something interesting to take a picture of. Even on a grey day in early December, I counted at least three coaches of tourists winding their way between the stony walls, which is actually quiet for this unique and picturesque part of the country. The previous week, down around the Ring of Kerry, it was nice to feel that we had some of the places of interest as much to ourselves as it's possible to have. The weather at this time of year obviously isn't going to be ideal, but if you wrap up well, it beats the shit out of queuing and driving up on ditches to pass coaches, which is par for the course in the summer. To see these places in the rain is to see them in their natural state.

I was heading for Ballyvaughan for the second time since my festival quest began. This time, there was a Christmas Festival underway in the scenic village. This was your proper country market type event, with a few fancy things thrown in for good measure. There was a small amount of livestock (chickens and turkeys), there was a clatter of baked goods, jam and some crafts and such. The atmosphere was homely and down to earth, with everyone on the stalls willing to chat and tell you about their wares.

There was a lady manning a fruit and veg stall outside the hall where most of the action was taking place. As a coach full of tourists drove past, she beckoned them towards the market. They probably would have loved the stuff that was on sale here. They would have been lucky enough to get a real taste of Ireland, but getting the Paddywagon to pull up was about as likely as Roy Keane asking Mick McCarthy to be godfather to his next Labrador pup. They were no doubt on a strict schedule, some overpriced soggy sandwiches at the café and interpretive centre on the Cliffs of Moher would have to do them. That particular tour boasts that it can cover all of Ireland's major sights in one day. It makes my three festivals a week seem leisurely.

No sooner was I through the door, than the monkey was on my back, and I started seeking out that olive-based foodstuff particular to Provençal, rather than some tasty morsels gleaned from the slaughterhouse floor. It's a hard cross to bear, but I am seeking help. I think that the trouble started years earlier at an All-Ireland Semi-Final in Croke Park. I'd travelled straight over from England, and didn't have the chance to prepare the usual tinfoil package of bacon ribs. A sandwich of brie, grapes and sun-dried tomatoes was forced on me at half-time, and it served as a gateway foodstuff. After that, I moved on to cured meats, and now I find that I've become a foreign fancy food fiend. I'd been doing well recently; nine bars of pure black pudding from Annascaul the previous weekend did me good, but I fell off the wagon in Co. Clare. A feta and chickpea samosa from the festive offerings in Ballyvaughan knocked me back, I couldn't help it. You know that the middle-class miasma is pulling at your sleeve when you're standing in the limestone wastes of the Burren, in the drizzle, on a grey December day, chomping into a feta and chickpea samosa. I've cleaned out my system since though, with a liberal application of Superkings and Karpackie.

Part of the reason for hitting Co. Clare was that there were two Christmas festivals on in relatively close proximity, and the link between the two was the coast road along by the Cliffs of Moher, through Lahinch, into Miltown Malbay, then down towards Kilkee to Doonbeg. A wonderful part of the country, and even on the damp day that was in it, it was a pleasure to be driving through this part of the world, with the 'Cliffs of Dooneen' as the earworm that was working through my head (better than 'Rocket' by Def Leppard, which had been clattering around in my bulb at the start of the day. What is that about? Somebody needs to do a PhD on earworm).

I wasn't far from Lahinch when I saw a sign on the side of a collection of ramshackle stone structures. 'New Home for Sale', it read. Above the sign, nailed to one of the collection of crumbling outhouses, were the plans for a house that hadn't been built yet. The auctioneer in charge of pimping this development must have worked for Brothers Grimm Agri-Sales before getting into the property game; they'd made their name flogging magic beans. I'd seen ghost estates, but this was the first of the ethereal bungalows. A sure sign that the economy must have been improving was that the bastards were trying to rip us off again, selling imaginary houses that hadn't yet been built.

The event at Doonbeg Lodge was a much more sophisticated affair than the gathering in Ballyvaughan. There were over fifty stalls, all named and numbered, and the organisers told me that 4,000 punters passed through the gates the previous year. Santa was in residence in a small thatched cottage with Mrs Claus and an Elf (I was informed I was on the good list. Yay!) There was mulled wine, fires lit in braziers around the grounds of the lodge, activities for kids, a Christmas train and some go-karts.

The festive fare on offer ranged from über-classy to incredibly kitsch. There were stalls selling imported shirts from Italy, luxury slippers, and one offering manicures for men (no I didn't, I'm not that bad). These were balanced by stalls selling pretty standard sweets, inflatable Dora the

Explorers and odd gizmos you'd expect to find on the shopping channel. As a place to go and browse for gifts for the family, it worked. As a place to go to spend an afternoon, I'm not sure if it was my bag.

If there is any doubt as to whether there was still a few bob left in the country, there was evidence here that there was. I stifled a guffaw as a lady exclaimed to her companion, 'Oh look, Marjorie, they have that delightful guinea fowl and wild mushroom pate', in an accent plummy enough to accompany turkey. Jaysus, this crowd were serious users; I was out of my depth! As if to underline the feeling that I had stepped over some socio-economic boundary, right on cue, a helicopter took off from the golf course. I couldn't help but feel that it lacked the homely character that was on offer up the road in Ballyvaughan, but, at about an hour apart, it was possible to get the best of both worlds.

If Doonebeg served no other purpose, it was clear that there was no escaping the madness now, the plump, jolly fella was all over the place. More ho's on the festival trail than Amsterdam's red-light district on the weekend of the Grass Cup. The whole aping of European Christmas markets was becoming a bit tedious, but I held out hopes for the festive version of Dublin's wonderful monthly Flea Market.

I headed up to Dublin on a Tuesday with an eye on trying to kill three birds with one stone. The Christmas Market was on down at the Docklands; an event called Dublin Castle at Christmas was also in full swing, and the Christmas Day *Sunday Miscellany* Concert was being recorded for Radio 1 in the National Concert Hall. The drive took longer than expected because it was snowing from Carlow to Dublin. How festive is that? Dublin Castle was *dúnta* when I rolled up, but I was swinging back in this direction on Sunday, so I stuck my tongue out at the gates, taking care not to get it stuck to the frozen metal, and headed down the quays towards the Docklands, where I hoped there was still something going on.

I lived up in Dublin for a spell, and it was down near the somewhat recently rejuvenated Docklands and IFSC area that I managed to shack up in student type accommodation; fairly salubrious surroundings for a skint scoundrel. I used to enjoy the fact that, behind the prosperous front that was projected towards the quays, lay Sheriff Street, part of the heart of auld jingle jangle Dublin where it's still possible for your bicycle to be robbed while you're riding it. One night, while I was probably watching a Champions League match instead of studying, with a flatmate who was a Liverpool supporter from Mauritius (he couldn't understand why two grumpy old men, aka Eamo and Gilsey, were on the telly, and why they talked such shite all the time), we heard a loud crack. Some lad with a gangland nickname that escapes me, but I think it was some kind of mammal, was shot in the head outside our building. Cops on horses were down in the IFSC for the next two weeks, putting the settlers on the investment bankers. Little did they know that it wasn't scumbags with shooters who were the biggest thieves operating down around the squeaky clean financial services district.

I'd been at the festive market at George's Dock a few times before, and was fairly familiar with it. It had all the expected stalls selling bits and pieces that might make a nice present for your auntie, it had a merry-go-round, trick-a-the-loopie stalls, but where this event came into its own was its surroundings and its food and drink offerings. They were expecting 150,000 punters to ramble around here over the two weeks it was open, and you can bet that a good proportion of those people would be folk from the surrounding office blocks and businesses down in the IFSC. There was a bar selling decent mulled wine, and shacks specialising in hot whiskies, bratwurst, fried spuds and more sweet things than Willy Wonka's larder.

It's a great place to wind down of an evening and have a drink or a small bite to eat. It stayed open until 8.00 p.m. most nights, and, with the lights and hurdy-gurdys reflecting onto the water at George's dock, it offered a nice, gentle break from the rabid madness of the shoppers foaming at the mouth around the city centre.

The gig on in the Concert Hall that evening was a good one, and set the tone nicely for the coming weeks. Julie Feeney sounded fabulous, and looked pretty good too; sparklier than the lights on Grafton Street. It was great to hear Paddy Maloney from the Chieftains playing pipes with the accompaniment of the orchestra. The short stories and readings on offer struck a real festive tone, and for €11 for the cheap seats it was wonderful bang for the buck, and a great way to finish off the evening. The orchestra sounded wonderful. Two programmes were recorded for RTÉ, to be aired on *Sunday Miscellany* (another guilty pleasure, similar to tapenade) on Christmas Day. We were bursting with festiveness as we left the Concert Hall.

Before getting back to Dublin for another shot at the festivities, I returned to Cork for a skate on what they were proclaiming as the biggest ice rink in the country. It's Cork – of course they'd have to have the biggest one in the country. Are you overcompensating for something there, lads? Having got away relatively unscathed from my last outing on ice, I might have been a bit cocky heading out, but it wasn't long before I got that knocked out of me. I got an awful slap, and gave my knee a good bang into the bargain. I think that I've filled my quota for ice skating for this decade. Not only was the rink bigger, but I also think that the ice in Cork is icier and the surface is slidier. That must have been it.

It was Sunday when I got the use of my legs back, so I headed back to the Big Smoke and secured Wanderly Wagon to a hitching post out at the Red Cow saloon at about noon. Waiting for the LUAS was great craic; you wouldn't see as much confusion trying to work the ticket machines on an All-Ireland Hurling Final Sunday if Longford were playing Leitrim. There must have been cows going unmilked all over the country with the shower of 'up for the day' shoppers that were champing at the bit to get into Henry Street for anything the Customs Officers didn't haul away the previous week. I felt almost cosmopolitan. Almost. It does no harm for the country cousins to head to town and make the Jackeens' lives a little cramped and difficult; God knows the favour is returned along the coast all summer.

I was really looking forward to getting to the festive version of the Dublin Flea Market. I thought it would offer some balance to the other Christmas Markets that had been popping up around the country, and thankfully it did. I loved it! I knew it was a good omen when the PA rigged up outside was playing 'Cay's Cray' by Fat Freddy's Drop. You can't beat a shot of decent reggae when you're out doing your Christmas shop. Sure, wasn't one of the Wise Men a Rasta?

There were clatters of stalls around Newmarket Square on the day. It's a Flea Market, so you kind of know what to expect, 'previously loved' goods, crafts, bits and pieces, and maybe some grub or a hot drink. I wasn't actually expecting it to be as good as it was. The weather was fresh, but things got a little cooler around Newmarket, literally and figuratively. The Flea Market crew describe what happens there as a 'Bizarre bazaar of vintage clothing, bric-a-brac and whatnots in Dublin's city centre' – that doesn't cover the half of it.

There were electric guitars, vintage toys, typewriters, cameras, clothes, a ZX Spectrum, and stuff so esoteric that I couldn't even hazard a guess as to what its original function had been. I love this kind of shit. There is something in me that craves a bargain; it's probably in a lot of us. Go into T. K. Maxx and stand in the corner and watch people start to glaze over and growl at each other – that's the bargain beast taking hold. The atmosphere here, though, was friendly and upbeat. I asked all and sundry if I could take their photograph, or photographs of their stalls, and all replied chirpily and positively and didn't seem to care what I wanted the pictures for. The chestnuts roasting on the open fire in the middle of the square were a nice touch. I would have been happy enough heading off after this, but that was only the outside of the place; there was much more going on inside the building of Dublin Food Co-op.

The inner market is based in the Dublin Food Co-op building. This organisation is a member-owned co-operative, run by volunteers, to sell organic, locally produced foods and the like, giving its members a chance to make a few bob, and its customers a chance to save a few bob, and get high quality produce too. IFSC or Food Co-op? Hmm.... The Co-op shop was also open on Sunday. I got talking to Catriona as I wandered around the market. She was offering an alterations service, for taking up your hem or letting out your waist. Jaysus, I'd say she'd even knock together an auld pelmet if you asked her nicely. Catriona tailors any clothes you might have bought around the place to fit you better, and she also takes jobs from people to mend stuff they bring from home. If you got to her early enough on Sunday, she could have your stuff ready for you by the close of business that afternoon. Mending, altering, tailoring second-hand clothes … have we gone back to the bad old days? Nice one! Can you tell that I liked it here? Just a little bit.

There was a lot of really good quality original crafts and artwork for sale, deadly posters and beady things and some top-notch scran. The falafels were truly rocking. I read a quote from Charlie Mingus one time, where he reckoned that if God had created anything better than heroin, he kept it for himself. Well, I don't know about the heroin, Charlie buddy, but I'd be including falafels (and rashers) in that sentiment. I reckon that Charlie would have agreed too if he'd dwelled on it a bit longer and had the munchies.

The falafels being served up at the Flea Market on Sunday were some of the best you are likely to get this side of Beirut, and slightly less addictive than heroin. Falafels count as one of your five-a-day festival foods, and are in no way related to tapenade. The Dublin Flea Market is on the last Sunday of every month, so you have no excuse.

After the Flea Market, it was down to Dublin Castle to experience some of their Castle at Christmas Festival: a series of plays, concerts and carols, all being offered to the public for free. As wonderful as a bargain is, free stuff is even better, especially when it's a festival to which parents can bring kids for a day out. The grounds were looking great in the December sunshine, much grander than the last time I'd been here for Iggy and The Stooges. There were a few tourists buzzing around, and a nice little gathering around the tree for the carol service. Fran Dempsey seemed to be in the choir or in charge or something. Who now? He's only the flipping fella who played Forty Coats on the telly, missus! Wanderly Wagon was delighted when I told him. I was pretty happy with the day myself.

I could have done with forty coats in the van the next night. It was the coldest night I'd spent on the road so far, and got down below freezing temperatures around the fields of Roscommon. I woke up looking at a bright sunrise making the frozen turloughs in the fields glisten and thought to myself, 'Shit! More ice skating, but this time on the road in a van.' The training I put in over the last two weeks stood me in good stead, though – there were a couple of slides and slips, but slow and steady got me home.

It was bound to happen sooner or later. I lapsed again, this time falling a week behind. I thought it would have happened as a result of a healthy mix of debauchery and late nights, but I had a proper excuse. I got Chicken Pox for Christmas. I have a doctor's cert and everything. Contrary to what the jolly dude told me in Doonbeg, I must have been on the 'bold boys' list. I can't imagine why that would be?

On the upside, I thought that if I played my cards right, I might find a fun-loving blind girl to whom I could offer a simultaneous romp and read, and although I found someone who I thought was going to be game, her heightened sense of smell worked against me and she did a legger. It was chamomile lotion and misery up to New Year's Eve. Ho, ho, ho my arse! After a week confined to barracks, I was one week behind. There was some catching up to do.

Festivals Attended in December

46. Other Voices – Dingle, Co. Kerry
47. Festival of Light – Dingle, Co. Kerry
48. Winterval – Waterford City
49. Ballyvaughan Christmas Festival – Ballyvaughan, Co. Clare
50. Doonbeg Lodge Christmas Festival – Doonbeg, Co. Clare
51. Dublin docklands Christmas Market – Dublin City
52. Dublin Christmas Flea Market – Dublin City
53. Dublin Castle at Christmas – Dublin City
54. NYE Festival – Dublin City
55. Winter Wonderland – Dublin City

Other Recommended Festivals in December

Winter Solstice – New Grange, Co. Meath
Richard Harris Film Festival – Limerick City
Éigse Dhiarmuid Uí Shúilleabháin – Coolea, Co. Cork

6 | *January – Spinning, Science and Sessions*

*B*arely recovered from the bok-bok pox, and still a bit scabby, such was my dedication to this festival quest that I headed off to Dublin to get the show back on the road. I was gutted to have missed the Christmas swim in the Guillamene, in my home town of Tramore; I'd been looking forward to it in a twisted, masochistic way. To make up for it, I headed for the legendary swimming spot in Dún Laoghaire, 'The Forty Foot'. This was the setting for 'The Big Dip', an annual New Year's Day swim that attracts a particular type of head-a-ball; loons like the lady coming out of the water who told me 'it's lovely!' You were fooling no one, you lying bitch! Even with the overexposed, sun-hardened skin on her like a Tunisian handbag, there is no way you could describe the water as being lovely, unless you're half penguin, half polar bear. It was fucking freezing.

There was a fair crowd of swimmers down at the Forty Foot, and a few obligatory gawpers too, but the majority were taking the plunge. Swimming in your togs in January in Ireland doesn't make any sense when you try to commit it to text. It's just wrong. But there's a feeling afterwards of rejuvenation and really being alive that makes having ingrown genitals almost worthwhile. Not a pretty sight in togs at the best of times, I was still a bit poxy and scabby, so it couldn't have been an aesthetically pleasing experience for anyone watching, but I thought the dip might do my complexion the world of good, and return me my natural Natalie Portman-type radiance. Well, it is the Irish Sea – at worst, it'd be like having a dose of chemo.

At all the best swimming spots in Ireland, you'll always get those people who take the craic out of it. More often than not they're male, and they have a thermometer on a rope. They're everywhere. They'll shout things like, 'half a degree up from yesterday!' or 'two degrees down from this time last year!' letting you know that they are sad enough to keep records of this kind of thing, and they will always, always tell you that 'it only changes by a few degrees from season to season.' The dope with the thermometer on a rope told me, 'it's eight today!' as I was shivering back to my towel. Eight what? I didn't need his assistance; I knew exactly what temperature it was... FUCKING COLD!!!

I made the rookie error of tying up my togs good and tight before taking the plunge, forgetting that I wouldn't have the luxury of feeling in my fingers when I got out of the water. Genitals, fingers and toes have the best union when it comes to body parts; when you subject them to stupid amounts of cold, they just plain refuse to work. Not easy to reef a pair of tightly tied togs off whilst standing on cold concrete, holding up a towel, without the use of your fingers for leverage or your toes for balance. I'm pretty sure someone got an eyeful of spotty arse. The Forty Foot is maybe the seventh best place to swim in Ireland, definitely in the top twenty, but that's another book altogether. With the James Joyce museum beside it, opening in the spring/summer months, it makes a very worthwhile place for a visit. During the opening passages of *Ulysses*, Joyce describes how Buck Mulligan and Stephen Dedalus head to the very same spot for a swim after a feed of rashers. 'The sea, the snotgreen sea, the scrotumtightening sea' is how Joyce colourfully rendered a dip at the spot … in June. I can only imagine how eloquently he would describe it in January. I'm sticking with fucking freezing.

In recent years they've done a sneaky job in Dublin of turning St Patrick's Day into a week-long festival that's now called … wait for it … St Patrick's Festival. Genius! But it has taken off, and where in years gone by New York was probably a better place to be on Paddy's Day than the Auld Sod, the people behind the festival in Dublin have done a great job in making it top nobber for the wearing of the green. For the full effect, they want you *in situ* for a week, to make sure that all of your pockets have been emptied fully before you waddle and stagger your way home. A similar approach has been taken for the New Year's Eve celebrations in Das Kapital. Say hello to New Year's Festival Dublin. Handy that New Year's fell on a Saturday for the first year of this shindig. The festival ran over Friday, Saturday and Sunday. Ideal!

The main event was a concert on College Green, smack bang in the city centre, featuring the current crop of Irish pop princes The Coronas, the elder lemon of trad/folk/middle of the road Paul Brady, and Dublin's own bruiser balladeer Damien Dempsey. The Bold Damo in the heart of Dublin on New Year's? The gig was sold out. Over 6,000 people attended the event, which, according to the girl I chatted with, who sported a clipboard and luminous vest, went swimmingly. I went down to the Electric Céilí in Meeting House Square on New Year's Day, walking through a Dublin that was eerily quiet; all the revellers must still have been in the cot. It turns out that Bono was right about New Year's Day, but don't tell him; he's just about bearable as it is.

The crowd down at the Céilí was an interesting mix of fresh-faced families and a spattering of tourists, but there seemed to be a majority of Irish people at the lunchtime hooley. More than a few actually looked like they knew what they were doing when the Caller announced that the Siege of Ennis was about to begin (poor auld Ennis is in a worse state than Fallujah; it's been under siege in the halls and parishes of Ireland for generations). My previous New Year's resolution of learning to bluff through a set-dance would stand to me here. I'd been around about at a few hops and gatherings where people had been shaking a leg, but I tell you what, lads: you know you're at a Céilí in Dublin when you end up swinging a transsexual to 'Gray's Knob Polka'. I couldn't help but wonder if she would have got past security on the crossroads to be one of Dev's comely maidens? 'Twould have steamed his glasses, I'll tell you that. I was awoken from my post-treaty reverie by the Caller instructing, 'Now take your partner home.' I looked at her Adam's apple, farmer's hands and huge feet, and thought to myself, 'eeeeehhhhh ... no!'

After stepping it out for a while, it was off to Ballsbridge for the annual hurdy-gurdy fest that is Funderland. An event that has achieved legendary status in the canon of Irish folklore, you're as likely to have your pocket picked as you are to puke your ring up. Doesn't that just sound like a wonderful day out? Luckily, neither happened on the day, but I'd say I wasn't far from either. Housed in the RDS in Dublin, the throngs of thrill-seekers that Europe's biggest travelling funfair attracts is not exactly an identical demographic to those who turn up in the RDS for the annual Dublin Horse Show. This bunch of carny folk have been coming to this spot, in this city, at this time of year, since 1975.

I come from a small seaside town where we have hurdy-gurdys spinning away all summer long, and we grew up loitering around them, so you would think that I'd be used to them. Wrong! I hate being spun around in different directions at the same time. I've parachuted, bungeed, and even risked going for pints at the Balinasloe Horse Fair, but spinny things that most 8-year-olds would hop onto at the drop of a hat fill me with dread. The ghost train was okay, but the other two things I managed weren't so hot. I went on the waltzers and got that feeling – you know when you're so locked that the room won't stop spinning, so you have to throw your leg out of the bed and put your foot on the floor just to make sure that the house isn't tumbling down a hill? That's what it felt like, and that, my friend, isn't a nice feeling. Having that nausea this early in the evening wasn't at all pleasant. In hindsight, even though a day out here is pretty expensive (seventy odd quid for a family of four), it works out a good deal cheaper to have that feeling induced by a spin on the waltzers rather than spending a fortune down the local. I got the biggest whitener since Tintin ended up on the Primal Scream tour bus with Bobby Gillespie. Pale and cold sweats are bad enough, but it brought up the still-lingering red spots and scabs wonderfully.

It might have been easier to laugh all this off if I wasn't in the company of a young lady I was trying to impress. The trip to Funderland wasn't just a festival jaunt, this was a date, and I was hoping it would be the first of a few. It wasn't. It's official: I am a wuss! It took the application of beer to my lips to restore the colour to my cheeks. Those hurdy-gurdys were much more fun as a kid, and a much better place to take girls.

For some reason, I imagined that January was going to be the most barren month on the festival trail, and although

I'd had to stretch my festival definition to its limits at times, during the last weekend of the month there were actually going to be six decent festivals happening simultaneously. Fate played another card to indicate that my festival quest was the right path for me to follow. RTÉ started their new reality/find a pop star show *The Voice* on Sunday nights; a night when I was nearly always on the road, and I didn't have Sky Plus to record it. I would miss all of it completely. Perfect! I knew that travelling around the country in a van was an inspired idea.

Most of my festivalling was still taking place at weekends, when Irish festival activity peaks during winter months, but I took a notion one Wednesday night, and headed up to Dublin in weather you wouldn't put Tom Crean out in. The wind was so strong that it would have blown a fella from Wexford off his sister. The initial draw was the Vibe for Philo. If you're a French pastry chef and the sound of this gig has got you all excited, sorry; this is an annual event that celebrates the life and music of Phil Lynott, arguably the coolest Irish man who ever lived (much better than a light pastry festival). Lads, Phil invented skinny jeans, and managed to pull them off (take that any way you want to) with flair and aplomb hitherto or subsequently unseen on this island nation. Phil is a proper legend, and a hero worthy of a black pudding feast with Tom Crean in Valhalla.

While on the rocky road to Dublin, I got a message from a friend asking if I was going to the launch of the First Fortnight Festival that was on in Dublin the very same evening. Squawk, squawk, thud. Two birds, one stone, happy days. It was well worth strapping myself to the ship's wheel, with the deck buckling and the masts heaving and groaning, braving the elements in order reach my festival destination.

I got down to the Button Factory in Temple Bar at about nine-ish, thinking I was a great fella for not ending up in a ditch in Kildare somewhere and delighted to be about to head in and get some shelter and a bit of decent auld Lizzy rock. Bad news, buddy, the fecking gig was sold out. Cool head now, breathe and let the bullshit flow. It was time to try the anti-Houdini blag routine and see if there was a way in. There was a fella called Justin who seemed to be the *buachaill* in charge of entry, and he told me to call back in about forty-five minutes to see what the craic was; better than a kick in the hole and your bus fare home I suppose.

Truth be known, it actually worked out perfectly. The Workman's, where First Fortnight was kicking off, was only down around the corner on the quays, and it turned out that the gig down there was just my cup of tea. I was enjoying more than my fair share of luck on the road, and was getting a bit worried that there was a karmic debt building up here that was going to be an awful bastard when it came time for payback. I wonder if there's a spiritual equivalent to NAMA?

First Fortnight is an arts festival that sets out to promote mental health awareness through gigs, exhibitions, discussions and whatever arts pursuit you're having yourself. I came across the festival when one of the guys involved tweeted to me about it a couple of months before the event. I think he thought that I actually planned my festival schedule well in advance, but the reality was still that it usually wasn't until the Wednesday before a particular weekend that I'd actually know where I'd be going.

I wasn't halfway through my quest yet, but already I'd reserved a special esteem for festivals that have a conscience and generous ethos behind them; festivals that are actually worth our while supporting; festivals where you're not being bamboozled or ripped off; festivals that stand for something and have a wholly positive impact

117

on communities and interest groups. I wasn't long on the road, but it was obvious to me that these should be the kind of festival that we hear more about, especially in a time when the Dark Lord of Negativity (aka Joe Duffy) and his ilk have us where they want us, applying the frighteners and sucking the positivity out of us like a Dyson caught on a curtain.

It was a gig in which I could have happily immersed myself all night, but I couldn't stay; I had a date to keep with a fella on the door up the road. It was oilskins and wellies back on, and out the gap. There were a couple of obstacles to getting in, but I played a blinder, and pulled some championship blagging out of the bag. 'Drove all the way from Waterford … year of festivals … covering another gig down the road…'. Justin came up trumps, and he got me in on the guest list. I have to admit, I was getting a kick out of blagging my way into some of these things; it was becoming a bit of a pastime for me. It was just as well: pushing my luck was the only exercise I was getting out on the road.

The rockers were stuffed into the Button Factory like socks down the front of Derek Small's pants, and there was more leather than a warehouse clearance sale in World of Sofas. It was loud, hot, sweaty and heaving; I think Phil would have approved.

There were rockers of every age, shape, size and state of excitement. Some of them had a gleam in their eye that belied their years, and lent them a youthful enthusiasm reminiscent of a time when they shook their heads to the thump of Phil's bass with such vigour that it would have given Mike Tyson whiplash. Somewhere in the region of 700 people in the Button Factory paid tribute to, and enjoyed the work of, Phil Lynott. I was on the dry, and had to run the gauntlet back home, so most of the wildness of the night was lost on me, but in the right company, in the right frame of mind, with Thursday off work, this would have been a rocking way to spend a school night.

One of the drawbacks of travelling around the country with your bed in the back of a van is that there's always the temptation to have a couple of pints and crash where you park, so to speak. I trundled down the road in Wanderly Wagon, patting myself on the back for such self-restraint, consoled by the fact that I'd be back in Das Kapital within two nights, and could have a pint or two then. Unfortunately, I may have promised myself more than two pints.

I arrived in Dublin that Friday, with a whole festival plan laid out for the evening. Nowhere in these plans did I allow for being beerjacked. I got into town in plenty of time to hit the festival hotspots, feeling at ease. I met up with a friend, and reckoned that I had some time to play with. Ones to Watch was a music festival in Whelan's that was running all night, and the Art O'Neill Challenge was kicking off from Dublin Castle at midnight. These may have been the root of the problem; I had too much fecking time. I had a great night altogether, but not a bit of it was festival related. I got to the places where there had been stuff happening all right, but not in the best of conditions. There was a Mother Hubbard's cupboardness to them by the time I arrived – not even a bone left to give a poor festival hound.

The Art O'Neill Challenge is an event that re-enacts the 1592 escape of Art O'Neill and Hugh Red O'Donnell from Dublin Castle. Participants head off from the city centre location just before midnight to cover the fifty-three kilometres that our two bold historical heroes hared across during their great escape. There were no Steve McQueen antics on motorbikes in those days, just

119

a mad scarper through the freezing Dublin and Wicklow hills. As the participants re-enacted the escape route and torturous trek through the mountains, I re-enacted the jailer arriving to find everyone gone. Shite! I wonder was the jailer having a few jars that night too? There was another batch heading off in two hours, I'd call back then … in an even worse condition.

In the meantime, I ambled merrily down the road to Whelan's, holding onto the hope that there might still be some bands playing into the small hours of the morning – it was a festival after all. Nah. There were drums, amps and the trappings of up-and-coming bands onstage, but these were pushed to the side to make room for the DJ, who was in fuller swing than a gibbon whose bananas have been dipped in ketamine. I was in time for the festival DJ at a live music event. Whoops.

I'd parked the van out at the Red Cow LUAS stop, and, after calling back to Dublin Castle and shouting abuse at fit lunatics, that is where I bedded down for the night. I don't think there were many disturbances; I certainly wasn't aware of anything anyway. Not the most ideal place to conduct my roadside ablutions the next morning, if you catch my drift, but there were a few hedges around the place, so I managed. The heavy frost did a great job of freshening me up. Life on the road wasn't getting any more glamorous, but I did have something uplifting to look forward to. Driving towards the RDS that morning was like being a crew member in Danny Boyle's film *Sunshine*, but in a camper van driving towards a blinding light of hope, intelligence, energy and youthfulness instead of hurtling towards becoming toast.

The Young Scientist and Technology Exhibition is a wonderful thing, and embodies everything I'd hoped to find when I set out on the festival trail. If you've never been lucky enough to get along to it, pencil it in for next year. I travelled up to it for the first time about five years ago with work. Waterford Institute of Technology had a stand, and I rigged up some pots and pans with amplitude triggers to work as a fully functional, realistic-sounding drum kit. It was whole school bags full of fun, and the young people who put together projects for the competition really seem to enjoy themselves over the few days spent mingling with other students amidst their wildly varying projects. But the science, fun and socialising aren't even the best bits. There's a positivity and enthusiasm on display here that will have the cynic inside the most stalwart of misanthropes cowering in the corner, rendered powerless by the kryptonite of honest endeavour, vivacity and keenness.

The Young Scientist and Technology Exhibition is a competition for secondary and primary school students, who submit science projects that are then judged in a number of categories, the main one being 'Young Scientists of the Year'. There are thousands of entries each year, and these get whittled down to the hundreds that end up in the final exhibition and adjudication process in the RDS in Dublin. The previous week, it had been in this exact same spot that I was turning white on the waltzers. I was pretty sure that I'd have a better time with the young scientists.

The exhibitions are amazing, informative, entertaining and bewildering. They ranged from how electricity affects plants to designs for stronger hurling helmets. There was a young drummer from Cork who had invented a single-pedal solution to the double bass drum pedal; surely he must also play another instrument (besides the bass) to display that kind of intelligence? One of my favourite projects on the day was entitled 'Do Redheads Feel More

Pain?' Conclusion: Every single day of our miserable existence, every day I tell you! It transpires that pain has a Mick Hucknall coefficient.

The winners of the 'Young Scientists of the Year' title had a project entitled 'Simulation Accuracy in the Gravitational Many-Body Problem'. It was very impressive, I'm led to believe. These two lads worked for a year, and discovered a new class of algorithm to work out projected orbits for multiple celestial bodies that come within gravitational proximity to each other – I think. I have the abstract in front of me as I write this. I am trying to make sense of it, and I'm still not sure about it. They won anyway, so it must be good. Did I tell you about the drummer with the pedal?

After the science, my head hurt even more, so it was high time for a trad session. Wanderly Wagon pottered all the way across Ireland from the east coast to the west coast, on something of a traditional Irish type Tupac vs. Biggie tip, only to screech to a halt behind a funeral parlour in Sixmilebridge, Co. Clare. It was the first time I had slept behind a funeral home, and was quite peaceful. I was just hoping that I didn't get caught in mid-mourning ablutions, if you catch the clasp of my coffin. It was mid-afternoon when I landed and, as you'd expect in Clare, there was a trad session being expertly thumped out in a comfortable and cosy local pub.

The Shannonside Winter Music Festival was in full swing, and I began an age-old and all-too-familiar argument with myself: 'Is it too early to start into a pint or two?' One of the great advantages of social media in your pocket is that as the good little festival monkey and the bad little festival monkey on either shoulder argue with each other around your head, you can pose the question to the

World Wide Wob (that's Mob with an upside down M). I was reliably informed that it was time for a nightcap in China. Sorted!

I thought that €25 for a ticket for the main Saturday night concert at the festival was a bit on the steep side, even though there were six different acts on the bill. Steep or not, the gig was sold out, and it's no wonder. I found out what this festival is all about, and it's a simple recipe: really good music.

I've loved the work of Ger Wolfe for a long time, and was delighted, driving back from a festival one night, to hear a documentary on the wireless about him. A down-to-earth and humble kind of fella who is something of an unsung hero, a kind of musician's musician; John Spillane immortalising him in 'Magic Nights in the Lobby Bar' is evidence of that. He was on the bill, and I was hoping that he might sing my favourite song of his, 'Curra Road', when, lo and behold, Zoe from a band called Trio Alatha requested it and Ger obliged, finishing his set with it. Happy days! There is a richness and depth to the songs of this Cork man that is enhanced by the seeming simplicity of the setting and lyrics, but peaceful waters run deep, and these waters can soothe, drown, buoy and quench.

The quality of the acts on the night was top shelf, with the Carrivick Sisters introducing me to a John Hartford song called 'Tall Buildings'; it has become something of an anthem for me. With a wonderful night wrapped up in The Courthouse, there was still more going on down the road in The Mill Bar, where Sarah Savoy and the Francadians were doing a brisk trade in two-step; the cajuns had come to Co. Clare. The back room of the bar was stuffed, and the crowd was ready for some serious buck-lepping. Can you do the 'Siege of Ennis' to a Bayou beat? No one fell over while trying anyway, well, not many fell over while dancing; standing still was proving difficult for some. It had been a long day; the Chinese nightcappers were getting up at this point.

In order to get through a whole year of three festivals every week, I needed to achieve some kind of balanced approach to the festival quest, and this visit to Clare and the night before in Dublin was tipping the scales in an enjoyable but draining direction. Striving to offset some of the madness with culture, I decided that the next batch of adventures would be an exercise in living out a BBC Radio 4 schedule. Classical Tunes, Astronomy and getting down with W. B. Yeats in the Valley of the Black Pig seemed to fit the bill nicely. These three festivals promised more culture than I'd seen since a PR crew were giving away free banana-flavoured Yop to beered-up hurling supporters at a Munster Final on a sunny Sunday in Thurles. Unfortunately, the culture on display that day was in the form of regurgitated curdled yoghurt in the gutter. Yop and cider get along about as well as Pat Spillane and Joe Brolly.

First on my classy festival hit list was Midwinter Festival: Intimate Voices in the Town Hall Theatre in Galway. Performing on that Friday night were the ensemble in residence, ConTempo Quartet, and their guests, Amstel Quartet, a visiting saxophone group from Holland. I was tempted to ask the Dutch lads if they were named after the beer, but thanks to my pocket-sized ignorance dispeller, some Facebookers were quick to tell me that Amstel is also a river. Blushes avoided (and yes, I am that thick), I was one piece of trivia closer to being invited onto a pub quiz team. I'll tell you what, though: I can't wait to visit Amsterdam again. A river of beer! I'm bringing my togs next time.

The Amstel Quartet filled the theatre with an eerie, enveloping sound that seemed impossible to make with the

SATB saxophones being used by the lads. It was exciting, engaging and wonderfully executed. The ConTempo Quartet wouldn't go out without a bang, though, and the Finnish folk-dance-inspired music of Sibelius was a rock 'n' roll way to finish off; fists in the air and headbanging into the night, figuratively speaking.

After the tunes, it was time for the tiles. It's hard to go to Galway and not do some light socializing; it'd be negligent, and I was worried about overcompensating this balance thing. The Crane was the first port of call for a quiet pint and a chat. The far side of the river isn't as busy as the centre of town, but it's well worth the extra bit of shoe leather. I always enjoy heading across the bridge and down Domnick Street; it makes me feel like a bold student again. The Crane is a proper pub, where you can sit downstairs and have a good auld natter or head upstairs for some of the best trad, not just in Galway, but possibly in Ireland if you hit it on the right night. Spookily, this was the second time in as many weeks that I'd sat down under a picture of tin whistler and general legend Sean Ryan. Sean is the fella who lives in the most haunted castle in Ireland, where I was lucky enough to meet him, hear him play and attend part of the Slievebloom Storytelling Festival. I ended up sitting under his picture at the festival in Clare too. I also had his CD playing in Wanderly Wagon, and there he was in a painting, playing his whistle, on the wall of The Crane. If it was some kind of omen, then its meaning, like the painting, was over my head.

Late one night at a festival in a field, I was chatting to a Rasta trapped in an Irishman's body. Martin spends half his year here in Ireland and the other half in Jamaica; he runs a Jamaican-themed festival sideshow called Trenchtown at a couple of our big summer rock 'n' roll circuses. We discussed that odd feeling you get that life is sometimes giving you certain signposts to show that you're on the right path. I took the painting of whistling Sean to be one of those signs that everything was as it should be. I ordered another pint without any concern about tipping scales or balance – the universe was telling me to do it.

After The Crane, we rambled back into town and ping-ponged around a bit until we ended up in An Púcán on Foster Street. Not the most obvious of watering holes on the trail in Galway, but there was a 'Come-all-Ye' band playing, and the waltzing was epic. The drinkers grabbed our hands and held them aloft for a rousing chorus or five of 'The Red Rose Café', and there was a reckless fecklessness in the air that made it the perfect place to be. The tin-whistle player gave me a knowing grin and sideways nod. Maybe all whistle players are part of some cosmic cult? I shrugged off the thought, and launched into another waltz.

The next morning was started red-eyed and bushy-headed, with enough time to spare between festival appointments to goof down by the Saturday morning market in Church Lane. Always colourful and worth a visit, it is one of few places in the country where you can have Samosas for your breakfast. Do you think that the Hare Krishnas spike their grub? If they do, they're some value for money. Tasty scran and drugs for a fist of last night's change. Whether or which, I had Kula Shaker's 'Govinda' in my head all day. The samosas were definitely riddled with earworm. After the odd but pleasing breakfast, and purchasing yet more of that fecking olive tapenade (heroin would be handier habit to kick), I rolled the van towards Astronomy Fest.

The Galway Astronomy Club has been running this festival for over ten years, and at this event they had about sixty-five people in attendance. There was a full day of lectures, observatory visits and sky-watching activities available for those in attendance. I went to a lecture by Brian Harvey on 'Future Missions to the Moon and Mars'. I do actually own a telescope, but it lives in a box in an attic. I had it set up when I lived down by the beach in Co. Waterford a few years ago. My experience of stargazing consisted wholly of drinking a couple of cans and looking at the moon while reciting the unchanging mantra of 'that's deadly!' In other words, I haven't a clue about any of it. Brian quoted Theo Pirard's assertion that if you want to follow space programs from now on, learn Mandarin. I'm not sure what small oranges had to do with Mars, but I was getting used to the universe working in mysterious ways. At least there weren't any tin-whistle players in attendance ... that I knew of.

When Brian talked about recent pictures of footprints on the surface of the moon left by previous missions, he quipped, 'If you believe that it actually happened', which got a good laugh from the assembled astronomers, who no doubt thumb their noses at conspiracy theorists who think that the moon landings were actually filmed in a caravan park near Spiddal. Little did Brian know that there was a sniper waiting on the grassy knoll for him when he went to the floor for questions. A brave and overwhelmingly outnumbered sceptic asked something along the lines of, 'how come, if the footprints on the moon were real, there was no scattering of dust from the take-off from the moon, and the flag didn't burn?' This question sucked the atmosphere out of the room quicker than opening the door of the International Space Station to let the cat out. Don't meddle with the catflapskis, comrade! Brian fielded it well, but your man was like a Sandworm of Dune with a bone; he just wouldn't let it go. It was riveting. If you managed to condense all the awkwardness Ricky Gervais has scripted in his career into one moment, you'd need to amplify it considerably to get close to the mood in the room. As a neutral, I was loving it, but eventually all the sceptics' questions crashed and burned. One of the events on the programme for later that night was 'Observing in Bearna Golf Club car park'. Observing, late at night, in a secluded car park? I passed on that one. Something like that could get you in trouble.

As the moon began to make its presence felt, I trundled up the road to a secluded spot on the cliffs of Sligo, having been told by the lads in Galway that there was a slight chance that the Northern Lights might be visible from there that night. I was standing out on a cliff at Rosses Point until 2.00 a.m., freezing my Brian Cox off, and all I got was a crick in my neck. Keeping sketch for the Dog Star passing through Uranus in a car park in Bearna may have been a better bet, but Rosses Point was a great spot to wake up in. Stunning scenery of the wild west coast with Ben Bulben as a backdrop. Sligo has a majesty to it that makes you understand why Yeats waxed lyrical about it.

I trotted along to the Yeats Winter School that morning to catch the tail end of an event that serves as a weekend taster for the fortnight-long summer school. Margaret Mills Harper was delivering the last lecture on the programme for the weekend. The room was packed, and Margaret began by taking us down through the 'Valley of the Black Pig'. I was expecting to be out of my depth here, and, let's face it, I'd be out of my depth chatting to Jedward in a paddling pool, but the material and delivery were pitched at a level that seemed to be all-inclusive, with the regulars nodding appreciatively and sagaciously and the newcomers sparking off revealed gems of insight and information.

I chatted to some of the attendees, and they couldn't have been more effusive in their praise for the event and for Stella G. Mew, the CEO of the Yeats Society, Sligo, and the lady who seemed to be pulling the strings for the weekend. I couldn't really blame them; she's a competent and charismatic lady who's on the ball when it comes to lining up punters for poetry, and a great character to boot.

Rita told me that she'd travelled over from London especially for this event, and she'd had an amazing time. She confessed to not knowing anything about Yeats other than the little she had learned in school (I'm with you there, Missus). A desire to learn a bit more is what brought her to Sligo, and although she was a bit worried about the winter school being pitched beyond her understanding, it was all well within her grasp, and she felt as if she'd been 'taken by the hand' through the works and countryside of Yeats. For €199 all in for the weekend, you get three nights in the hotel, all your grub, all the excursions and all the lectures. Rita felt she'd got a bargain, and left Sligo as a satisfied customer. It seems that there'd been a beast of a singsong the night before, and there I was freezing out on a cliff when I could have been down by the Sally Gardens.

After missing the singsong in Sligo I felt a bit hard done by. I needed another shot of trad; a belting tune or two would sort me out. It had been nearly two weeks since my last trad session. If I wasn't careful, I could break out in healthy skin and clear, sparkling eyes. I punched coordinates for Temple Bar Tradfest into Wanderly Wagon's onboard computer, and engaged hyperdrive.

I found myself in Das Kapital yet again, heading along to catch a young fella from Cavan, whose name is Kavan. He's lucky he's not from Bastardstown, Boyle, Twomileborris or Horesbridge. He can play the harp, though, and wail a bit on those uillean pipes too. Kavan, a 19-year-old UCD student, can also add proficiency on low whistle and guitar to his armoury of skills. Sure, God love him, he has nothing going for him. He played the harp with a dexterity and edge that gave the instrument a youthful exuberance that I've never heard it voice before. It was an enjoyable gig, which was made only slightly drab by a *bodhrán* player (2010 Irish champion, Niall Preston) who played really well, but had a head on him like he was in the waiting room of a doctor's surgery with an unknown, but awfully embarrassing, venereal disease.

Back out on the mean streets of Temple Bar there were two stages set up along the drag of Dublin's prime drinking district, offering free entertainment to the punters who turned up in big numbers for the high-quality trad gigs that were on offer. The highlight of the weekend had to be the lads who were driving livestock along the streets of the capital, an honour I thought extended only to Bono and Stephen Cluxton. The misplaced drovers were part of the Tradfest, bringing a slice of rural Ireland to the city slickers. The taxi drivers were firing out abuse thicker than shite from a slurry spreader in spring, but the culchies could give better than they got, with the added advantage that the taxi drivers couldn't understand a word that they said, infuriating them all the more. The lad with the cow was stopping cars and asking the drivers to blow into a pipe. He put the other end of the pipe into the cow's mouth, and informed the drivers that it was a garda cow − if its eyes didn't light up when they blew into it, they needed to go and have a pint immediately, if not sooner. These were fecking funny farmers.

The *piss de résistance* (they were farmyard animals after all) was when the lads with the donkey arrived too, and they were all outside The Mezz bar, the animals placid, but the handlers seeming a bit edgy. The lads stopped a couple of foreign tourists and asked if they'd mind holding the bridles of the animals for a second. The flustered tourists accepted, whereupon the lads all headed into the pub and started lowering pints. I wouldn't be surprised if the bemused tourists were there, bewilderedly holding the bridles still, while the farmers were at the bar pissing themselves laughing. Beware of crafty culchies with cows cruising the streets of Das Kapital.

After five months on the road, I was getting used to seeing Irish people do odd things for a laugh, and I was feeling blessed to witness them and sometimes join in. My delight in the confused look on the Brazilian tourists' faces as they wondered how long they were meant to stay holding the cattle and donkey underlined how much I was enjoying this. When I started out, I was hungry for more road, but wasn't sure if I still would be enthusiastic by this stage. Now there I was, a bit shaken, poor Wanderly Wagon booked in for some treatment, but knowing that spring was on the horizon, the evenings were getting brighter, and the festival diary was getting fuller. People often asked me why in the name of all that's reasonable was I doing this, and I'd come up with lots of reasons. There were lots of really good ones to choose from, but I got asked in an very interesting way at the end of January, and it got me thinking deeply about what I was doing and why.

During one of those quiet times of contemplation in the van, one of those meditative moments on the road that were becoming as enjoyable as the festivals themselves, I realised that one of the reasons for doing this was that it just felt right. Everything that had been happening just seemed to fit, and occasionally a tin-whistle player would nod at me to let me know I was following the right path – either that, or tin-whistle playing leads to violent, involuntary ticks. Whatever the links between synchronicity and tin-whistles, spring was on the horizon, and Wanderly Wagon had new tyres and an oil change. There was no stopping us.

Festivals Attended in January

56. The Big Dip – Dún Laoghaire, Co. Dublin
57. Vibe for Philo – Dublin City
58. First Fortnight – Dublin City
59. Funderland – Dublin City
60. Ones to Watch – Dublin City
61. Art O'Neill Challenge – Dublin City
62. Young Scientist and Technology Exhibition – Dublin City
63. Winter Music Festival – Sixmilebridge, Co. Clare
64. Mid-Winter Festival – Galway City
65. Astronomy Fest – Galway City
66. Yeats Winter School – Sligo, Co. Sligo
67. Temple Bar TradFest – Dublin City
68. One-Act Festival – Bray, Co. Wicklow

Other Recommended Festivals in January

Out to Lunch Arts Festival – Belfast City
Mozart's Master Works – Dublin City

7 | February – Thy Kingdom Come and Priestly Fun

S ooner or later there were bound to be a couple more grains of sand in the Vaseline. I'd been swanning around the country having a blast for months, with only Tuam Trad Festival proving a minor blip in the merriment. Enter the Bray One-Act Drama Festival, an event that runs from the end of January into February. This wasn't just a festival for viewing one-act plays; it was also a competition for amateur dramatic groups to pit the best of their thespian skills against one other in an event that has been banging the boards for over thirty-five years. On paper, this festival fit perfectly into my template of positive Ireland, with lots of volunteers coming together on a not-for-profit basis to form their own community and entertain the masses. The problem is that, unfortunately, amateur drama can trigger my gag reflex. It wasn't them, it was me.

Performing on the night when I was kicking back on a well-upholstered seat in the Mermaid Arts Centre were Delgany ICA (Irish Countrywomen's Association, or *Macra*'s Mammies), Square One Theatre Group and Dalkey Players. There were moments when the possibility of a glimmer of entertainment almost revealed itself to me. The highlight of the first offering was when one of the actresses ate a bit of a carrot, which then began to repeat on her to such an extent that both talking and controlling her false teeth became a gargantuan struggle. I don't think it was scripted, but it proved to be the most dramatic moment of the night. I was left more than a little cold by the whole thing, but putting me and amateur drama together is like getting the Pope to go and visit Ian Paisley in hospital. Lacerated ulcer says no. I'd made my own bed here.

There is no doubt there are many folk for whom this kind of thing is a wonderful night out; proof of this was the theatre being sold out. Chock-a-block! I would have been more content eating dry rice-cakes in the back of a camper van in a deserted Lidl car park in Greystones on a stormy night. In fact, when I eventually escaped the theatre, I was more content eating dry rice cakes in the back of a camper van in a deserted Lidl car park in Greystones on a stormy night.

It may point to me being a bad person that the evening took a turn for the better when a lady returning to her seat after the second interval (two intervals and three plays, it was a fecking long night) stumbled on her scarf and managed to simultaneously trip and choke herself. Genius! Definitely my pick for the Fred Lee Festival Award, but they gave that to Lord and Lady where-d'you-get-the-accents for services to something or other that people of a lowly socio-economic standing would never remember or appreciate. Can you tell that I was having some craic?

Soiling myself became a possibility during the longest raffle in the history of humanity, not from excitement, but due to the seemingly never-ending nature of the thing. What made this raffle even more thrilling was that the Master of Ceremonies had the most wonderfully plummy diction, meaning that each of the seventy-two tickets

Bog Snorkelling Championships

Chief Culchie - Hughie Duignan

Durrow Scarecrow Championships

A fine specimen at the Moynalty Steam Threshing Festival

Enjoying the buzz at Harvest Food Festival, Waterford

National Hen Racing Championships

Forbidden Fruit

Clonakilty Random Acts of Kindness Festival

Prize-winning performance at Bucket Singing Championship

Road signs in Co. Cork

Heading into town for Ballinasloe Horse Fair

In the van

Festival heads

called out took five times longer to process than it should have. I hadn't experienced that much excitement since the combination play in rubbers during the great bridge symposium of ninety-three.

There was no escape from the raffle: I was hemmed in on all sides by auld ones rifling through their wads of tickets in the hopes of bagging the Yardley Pink Lace gift set. They would have savaged me if I distracted them. Interrupting an auld one during a raffle or bingo is the equivalent of dipping your genitals into the feeding bowl of a pit-fighting Rottweiler who's been given his first taste of Chum after an enforced two-week lentil diet.

Eventually it came to an end, and I escaped to the safety of the van and just sat there for a while to readjust. I hadn't been eating badly while traipsing around the country. The fridge and two-burner stove were well used. Soup, steak, falafels and pitta bread filled with all manner of items were the staple. The reason for the dry rice cakes in Greystones wasn't that I was getting a taste for torturing myself: my larder was bare. Nabbing a packet of Meanies while piping diesel into Wanderly Wagon the next day was feeling like an option as I trucked down the M9. While busily keeping sketch for a service station, I spotted a sign offering directions for a national event called 'Food and Bev'. I had no idea who Bev was, but I knew I was hungry, and I had a feeling there was going to be some top scran at a shindig like that, so I made the appropriate hand signals and put the foot down.

There were bound to be times when I pushed my festival definition to its limit, testing its elasticity to the max. This was one of them. At its core, this was a trade show for professionals in the food and beverage sector, but it was an annual event that celebrated Irish produce, and such a celebration had to be offering up high-quality food and drink, and that was good enough for me. Technically, I shouldn't have been allowed in at all, but I told a couple of tall tales, had a camera slung across my back, bandied the word 'blog' around the place a lot, and eventually swung myself an access-all-areas pass. I was more than a bit dubious about finding kicks at a catering trade show, but the sign on the M9 seemed like fate was sending me a dinner invitation – it would have been impolite to ignore it. There weren't any winking tin-whistle players at this gig, but the Bartenders' Association of Ireland was having the final National Cocktail Championship, and the competitors were shaking up a storm and the cocktails were flying out. Oh happy day!

Wandering around with cocktail in hand, delighted with myself, I heard a lady with a clipboard say to her colleague, 'You'd think it would be easier to find volunteers to sit for a three-course dinner cooked by contestants in the All-Ireland Chef of the Year competition.' I nearly pulled the arm out of her socket with the tug I gave her sleeve. The poor woman was still shaking with shock as she tucked the napkin into my T-shirt collar. There is no such thing as a free lunch, but I can testify that there is such a thing as a free three-course dinner cooked by the best chefs in Ireland. 'Waiter, any chance you'd nip up there and get me another prize-winning cocktail to go with this starter? Good man.'

Iron beef brisket à *la niçoise* served with truffle vinaigrette dressing. Fillet of halibut with braised vegetables served with red caviar and passion fruit sauce, and creole mousse with strawberry and chocolate, served with a cocoa meringue. Tough gig. As a friend of mine said afterwards, 'If ya fell out a window, you'd go up the way, you jammy bastard!' I reckon I'd earned this twist of karma after the raffle from hell at the am-dram marathon. Jammy bastard?

Maybe, but I would have to say it's more of a fortuitous summer berry coulis than jam.

One of the most surprising things about the competitors in this cook-off was where they puffed their pastry and plied their trade. You'd expect the fancy restaurants to have their chefs in the running, and they were, but one of the top dudes on the day for me was the chef from Dublin Zoo, who did a pretty neat thing with purple mashed potato and wasabi. I imagine he has occasion to get access to some pretty interesting offal offcuts too. Where do you think the All-Ireland Chef of the Year whisks his yolks? An upmarket eatery in Dublin? A country manor getaway? A five-star castle spa? Nope. This dude works in the canteen at Google. Now that's a sign of the times. Alin Garvil is the Executive Chef at Google Ireland. I've had a few jobs at this stage in my life, but I've never had one where I was sitting in the canteen thinking to myself, 'Whoever managed to instil this lasagna with the personality of a comatose ferret and the consistency of a tyre should be entered for Chef of the Year.' I hear they have iFood in the canteen at Apple that gets beamed straight onto your taste buds; it makes grown men cry, women faint and can cure oigher. It was going to be difficult to munch diesel-tainted Meanies after this.

With a full belly and my taste buds tingling, I set a course for Co. Tipperary. Fethard Ballroom is the site for the annual Tipperariana Book Festival, one of Ireland's largest and most atmospheric book fairs. Putting my feet up with a book would be ideal after the feed I'd had. My discomfort at amateur drama evenings can be traced back to overexposure as a child, not to imagined notions about it not being rock 'n' roll enough. The truth is that I'm about as hip as Pat Kenny at a Dubstep night. There's a nerd in me that enjoys nearly all of these festivals, and this was not the first time I'd been at the book bonanza in Fethard. I still had unread books from the previous year's visit, to which I could now add the books from the most recent visit – this sort of stockpiling is not uncommon. As unbelievable as it might sound from reading this, I bought a copy of *Eats, Shoots & Leaves* in an effort to improve my delinquent punctuation. I haven't had a chance to read it yet. Still in the pile. One of the things that I'd been enjoying most about my festival adventures was the people I had been meeting along the way, and in Fethard Mr John Ryan was added to the ever-growing list.

> Irish Festival Rule No.17: *Always make time to chat to a cat in a flamboyant hat.*

It was inevitable that I would have a chinwag with the dapper dude in the fedora. John Ryan wasn't just selling books; he had vintage cinema posters, showband memorabilia, copies of the Clonmel periodical that he publishes and stacks of vinyl LPs. It was while rooting around in one of the crates under his table that I happened across a relic of Irish childhood: a squeaky-voiced freak in the stripy pyjamas. Bosco! The album is called *This is Where I Live*, and features Bosco's unmistakable voice, which, when it wasn't being used to scar the memories of Irish children, could also be used to cut glass. Before Bosco got his break in television he actually worked as a master cutter in the Dungarvan plant of Waterford Crystal. The album was bound to be *ufásach*, but I desperately wanted to add it to my ever-growing collection of useless shite.

After chatting with JR (to his friends) for a while, the subject of the Bosco LP was eventually broached. Anyone who has ever struck a deal outside the cities of

Ireland knows that you never discuss the matter directly; it's a delicate dance, and I learned some hard lessons whilst hawking some of the debris of life at Ireland's finest car-boot in the very same town as this book fair. John Ryan did one of those things that makes me love being Irish: he enjoyed the chat, and was such a nice fella he said, 'Ah, g'wan, sure, you can have it for nuthin'.' Either that or he was just happy to be rid of it. It's possible that the album is the audio equivalent of the videotape in *The Ring*.

It's often at the rural festivals where you get to have deeper and less hurried chats with strangers. A ballroom in Co. Tipperary was a perfect spot for this, and especially suited to chats when you think that all the people here were into books and they were selling, browsing, collecting or just in on a goof. The Tipperary Historical Society started the festival in 1996, exactly when the economy started necking financial steroids, but, unlike our banking system, the Fethard Book Fair has managed to keep itself in check, and people are still enjoying it. There's everything here from ancient tomes to *Beano* annuals, all of them attracting their own brand of enthusiast. For anyone who fears that e-readers will wipe out books completely, head down to Fethard for the book fair and just stand in the hall and breathe in the musty wonderfulness of the gathered goods.

It had been almost two weeks since my last dose of trad. Driven by fear of gum disease and rickets brought on by a diddly-eye deficiency, Ballyferriter was the next destination in my sights for *Scoil Cheoil an Earraigh*. Well, at least I thought that Ballyferriter was my next destination. When I got to the small village on the Dingle Peninsula later than I'd hoped, there was a trickle of traffic still arriving, so I thought I'd timed my journey just right. I joined the people heading towards the lit-up building, went inside and found an empty seat. It was only when the old lady who shuffled in beside me kneeled before she sat down that I started to get the feeling that I was in the wrong place. 'Excuse me, is there a concert on here tonight?' 'Not at all, love, this is eight o'clock Mass.' Shit! I barely made it out before the priest took to the stage for his headlining performance.

I crossed the road to the local shop to enquire about the concert, and that didn't go well either. Technically this was not my first festival in a Gaeltacht, but it was the first one in a full-on proper *Na-bi-ag-caint-Béarla* Gaeltacht. I decided that I'd try to conduct my business through Irish, which is fine when you have time to compose the questions into what seems like a coherent arrangement in your mind's mouth. You're never quite prepared for the quick-fire response though. After asking the lady to repeat herself for the fifth time, I felt it was time to skedaddle down the road to Feohanagh before she started lobbing stale *rolla ispíní* at me. Thankfully, I only had to ask her how to spell Feohanagh four times. Any of our American brethren who might be reading this, please phone me to relay your pronunciation of this village name; it's an even better one for a laugh than Youghal. Take heart though, I can't say it properly either.

Scoil Cheoil an Earraigh is primarily about teaching musicians and dancers the style of trad and steps particularly associated with the *Corca Dhuibhne* peninsula of Co. Kerry, but all styles are catered for. *Sean-nós* dance workshops and remedial Irish classes for poor dopes like me are also on the agenda. It doesn't come much more Irish than this, *mo daoine*. I was aiming to hit a concert that featured some of the musicians who were in the area for the weekend. The hall was packed, and the tunes were stomping. Even

Stephen Hawking would have been tapping his feet, with his voice box tuned *Seán Bán* mode.

About halfway through the proceedings, the *Bean an tí* for the night told us that there was a surprise special guest in the house who was going to give us a *cúpla amhrán*. She was fairly bigging him up before she told us who it was. I wasn't expecting to be familiar with the performer at all, but, lo and behold, Christy Moore was in the gaff. Christy sang a few appropriately placed songs to suit the environs, singing first of the fuchsia in the hedgerow, and then moving on to St Brendan's trials and tribulations in the locality. Christy welcomed *Fear an tí* Brendan Begley to the stage, and together they sang a song that remembered the lives of two fishermen brothers from the Aran Islands lost at sea, a song of Christy's that Brendan had recorded.

I have a special place in my heart reserved for Christy Moore, not only a gifted interpreter of songs and a songwriter of depth and compassion, he's a man who doesn't court controversy, but certainly doesn't shy away from it when he feels it appropriate. There's been an integrity and consistency to him over the years that is a rare commodity. I can't help but feel that, a little like Johnny Cash, Christy won't be fully appreciated until he's gone. The next time you hear of a factory closing or bondholders being bailed out again, go listen to Christy sing 'Ordinary Man'. In the meantime, though, search out Christy's take on Richard Thompson's 'Beeswing'. It's a fine thing.

There was a time when I wouldn't have crossed the road to see Christy, until, one summer's evening in my seventeenth year at the racecourse in Tramore, I heard him playing to a festival crowd that he managed to hold in the palm of his hand all through the raucous singalong sections and, even more impressively, through the quiet, lovelorn and melancholy tunes that garnered a reverential silence, impressing and converting me. I've seen him many times since, on his own, with Declan Sinnott and with Planxty (the reformed version). That night in a hall in Co. Kerry was special. Christy was here out of friendship and for the love of the place and its music; he wasn't getting paid for this one, it was from the heart. There wasn't the thumping feet and overeagerness to sing and clap along that there usually is at some of Christy's shows. There was no shouting suggestions at him from the floor either; there was a respectful reverence. He eventually cajoled the crowd into joining in with him on a song, and when they did, Christy murmured under his breath, 'Oh baby'. I couldn't help but crack a smile and feel like a proper jammy bastard for being in that place at that time. It was a rare thing. It struck me that, no matter what happens with banks and bonds, we'll always be able to enjoy people and music. The Dingle Peninsula might be one of the finest places in the world to enjoy both.

I was pretty sure the weekend had peaked with the night's music in the hall at Feohanagh, but the best was yet to come. The next morning started dull and drizzly, with the prospect of a walking festival and five-hour A-rated trek in the mountains seeming like not such a hot idea for a fella who'd been chewing caffeine-laced Lemsip tablets all weekend. But that familiar little bastard nagging voice in the back of my head started whining again: 'If you let the weather stop you doing stuff, you might as well just stay at home, ya wuss ya!' So I pulled on the wet gear and traipsed down to sign up for the early morning edition of the Dingle Walking Festival. A sincere thank you, bastard nagging voice.

The weather cleared, and the full majesty of the Dingle Peninsula and surrounding countryside revealed itself dramatically, like a diva arriving late to a party for dramatic effect. 'God's own country' said the fella from Conor's Pass who was on the walk. A resident in the area all his life, this was the first time he'd taken this walk through the hills overlooking Mount Brandon, and he was loving every minute of it. They know how to do two things in Kerry really well: scenery and football. Thankfully, the Dubs haven't stolen the scenery from them yet. 'The Kingdom' is how Kerry is known, and on a day when its full regality was on show, I found myself swept away and thinking for the second time in as many days that this was indeed a rare thing.

This was only the second year of the Dingle Walking Festival, but the numbers were well up on the previous year. Over 300 people headed out on the three different graded walks on each day of the festival. I heard a statistic that Bord Fáilte released from market surveys they carry out on tourists as they leave Ireland: close to 90 per cent of people surveyed said that the thing they enjoyed most about Ireland was the people they encountered. I can tell you first-hand that there are people walking around the hills of Dingle who would are a living testament to those statistics. The other 10 per cent could probably be accounted for by the fact I didn't get to talk to everyone.

I spent a while chatting to a fisherman from Donegal who had travelled down especially from Killybegs for the weekend; that's a fair trek in and of itself. All walks of life, ages, interests and creeds had pulled their boots on for this stroll. Conor, a landscaper from Limerick, provided a good deal of the day's distraction, and was willing and able to discuss hurling all day long if needs be. I also met two wonderful Kerry girls who, although living away from The Kingdom, made a point of returning for the Dingle Walking Festival.

I find it difficult to do justice to how deeply enjoyable a weekend this was. There was none of that manic wildness that I'd immersed myself in at other festivals; it was more a deeply satisfying experience that had me worried that I might have been finding religion or something. But possibly better than finding religion was discovering a deeper appreciation and sense of the country, and probably even of myself. People had begun asking me if there weren't some weekends when I'd rather stay at home by the fire with my feet up. After a weekend like this in Kerry, I was able to answer them without hesitation. When you get a chance to spend time drinking in all the things that makes Ireland and its people special and unique, a night by the fire isn't that attractive.

I was halfway through my quest, and I was well and truly hooked. I'd been chatting to a truck driver from home around this time, and he quizzed me about my adventures on the road. As I was banging on about some of the things that had been happening, barely pausing for breath, I saw him crack a wry smile. I stopped and gave him a quizzical look. 'The road can become addictive, you know?' I was beginning to appreciate exactly what he meant.

After the almost spiritual experience in Kerry, some grounding was needed, so I pencilled in two festivals with a bit more built-in hedonism for the next leg of the adventure. I was heading for the legendary Tedfest on Inis Mór, and for Ireland's first Sex Festival. Hold on to your habit, sister, this could be a bumpy ride.

10.30 a.m. On Friday morning, the ferry pulls out from Rossaveal, Co. Galway, heading for Inis Mór, referred to henceforth as Craggy Island. This ferry was carrying a cargo of crazed clerics to Tedfest – a celebration of all things *Father Ted*.

10.45 a.m. A young fella dressed as a priest arrived on the top deck of the boat and announced, at the top of his voice, 'We're all going to Heaven!' to which he got the appropriate response, 'Wayyy-Heyyyy!' Evidently, for some, we were.

10:50 a.m. The first chorus of 'My Lovely Horse' broke out.

11.00 a.m. The weekend was pretty much in full swing as the sun shone down on the top deck of the ferry where Nuns, Brothers, Bishops, Priests, Pat Mustards and Mrs Doyles were downing cans and smoking fags in a frenzy that suggested Father Jack was on his way.

Overheard on the deck of the ferry: 'It's our anniversary this weekend. Some fellas would take their Missus to Paris. I take mine to Inis Mór and dress her as a priest.' Sounds like a pretty healthy relationship to me.

It's probably worth mentioning here, for any poor unfortunates who have never experienced this facet of Irish culture, that *Father Ted* is the holiest man ever to have lived in Ireland in the recent past. So holy and amazing was Ted that he doesn't just get a feast day, he gets a whole weekend in February. Soon he will be made Saint Ted (based on the 'That money was only resting in my account' miracle, among others), and will then be the new patron saint of Ireland, and Saint Patrick's Day will be celebrated only within the confines of the Guinness Storehouse by tourists wearing appropriately branded clothing. *Capisce*? Sound.

My plan was to head to Craggy Island for the day and catch the last ferry off the island that evening, and strike out for the Micho Russell festival in Doolin that night. That was about as good a plan as the night Bono turned around to the Edge and said, 'I know, why don't we make Spider-Man into a musical?' Lemon! I was actually making my way towards the pier for the last ferry when it dawned on me that leaving Craggy Island was a ridiculous thing to do; there was far too much fun to be had on the island. The fact that the walk to the pier had been the longest I'd been away from the bar all day might have had something to do with my train of thought. I enquired about digs for the night, and managed to find a room (which was surprising given the size of the religious rabble that had arrived for the festivities). Joel sorted me out with a boudoir in the hostel, and I went back to the pub to join in the fun again. Tally-ho!

There were events laid on throughout the day for the happy holy hordes to enjoy. Speed dating with Nelly, Craggy Island's Got Talent, Dancing for Peace in Shebangos, and the ever-popular Lovely Girls Competition. The real attraction of Tedfest, though, is the head-a-balls who attend it. This crowd is up for a laugh, and its members take their vocation very seriously. It's all 'Howya, Father?' 'Feck, Drink, Girls' and 'G'wan, g'wan, g'wan…'. One of my favourite comments of the day was from a terse nun, aimed at an over-amorous priest: 'That would be my arse, Father!' She got the narrowing of the mouth and delivery spot on.

The spirit entered into by the crowd in attendance was impressive. Lots of people came with three different costumes: one for each day they were on the island. I was praying that there were foreign tourists on the island for the day who didn't have a clue about *Father Ted* or what was happening. Somewhere in the world there may be a family who think that this is how clergy behave on the Aran Islands all the time.

I got chatting to Peter, one of the lads responsible for organising the madness, and he was telling me about a year when four lads arrived in full Nazi regalia (à la the 'Are You Right There, Father Ted' episode). The four boys decided that it would be a bit of sport to march, full jackboots swinging in the air, down to the ferry when they were leaving on the Sunday. They had a little crowd of nuns and priests join in the procession. As they made their way towards the pier, the ferry was docking with a clatter of foreign tourists aboard for a visit to the scenic island for the day. They froze and stared open-mouthed at the procession of clergy led by four Nazis that came to greet them. The only reason that many of them got off the boat at all was because the Nazis and Nuns were getting on. Many of the tourists stayed huddled together and didn't stray far from the pier until an empty boat showed up to ferry them back to safety. Peter told me that they were expecting about 300 lunatics on the island for the weekend – a crowd that was more pro-session than procession, if you catch my Corpus Christi.

So there I was, on the island for the night with not so much as spare underpants or a toothbrush to my name. What was I going to do for a costume? There is not much choice when it comes to drapers, gentleman's outfitters and haberdasheries on Craggy Island of a Friday evening. I rambled into the Spar, and came out ten minutes later with five pairs of black tights, a baby's dummy, a rattle and some old newspapers, and miraculously transformed myself into a creature with the body of a spider and the mind of a baby. Spider-Baby!

'That is really disturbing', said Lily. 'Holy Fuck!' said Trish. 'A bit more *Mighty Boosh* than Ted', commented Jennifer. Strangely, I blended in perfectly. I was standing outside the American Bar on Inis Mór at one point in the night, chatting away with a fisherman from the island about The Butcher's Bar down in Dunmore east, and comparing notes about this and that. It was only afterwards, when one of the crowd I was with ended up laughing about it, that I twigged the getup of me chatting away to the auld boy, blissfully unaware of how ridiculous I looked. In fairness, though, I didn't have the stocking over my face at the time, just the ones over my underpants and the two pairs stuffed with newspaper hanging from my torso. Not so bad so.

As if I wasn't looking freaky enough in my rigout, it turns out that I don't know how to pull tights up properly. What with all the dancing (we were dancing for peace after all), the crotch of the tights needed regular adjustment to stop them from sagging, which just wouldn't have looked right. The constant incorrect technique of just grabbing the sides and pulling them up resulted in a ladder in the under-arse of them, and this spread as the night went on. I barely got away with not creating a Rift Valley on the Aran Islands. I must have made some picture when strolling the roads of Inis Mór heading back to the hostel that night/morning. Thinking about it since, it'd probably be worth staying on the dry one night, getting up at sunrise, and sitting on a stone wall at a crossroads with an 'I Shot JR' T-shirt on you, just to witness the most colourful and surreal walks of shame known to man. I'd say Attenborough would get a series out of it.

I was meant to get the ferry off the island at 8.15 a.m. If I had made it, it would have been a miracle of which St Tibulus would have been proud. I missed another ferry. The difficulty with this one was that I was due in Dublin, about 1.30ish, for a radio interview about my festival quest. The next ferry off the island was at 5.00 p.m. I got a flight off the island, hitched a lift to Wanderly Wagon from the airport, and made it in time for the interview, and even managed to sound somewhat coherent. That afternoon in Dublin, I felt like Padre Pio after a particularly tough night wrestling demons, but there I was in Das Kapital, and just in time for Bliss Festival.

Bliss promised sexual health, freedom and pleasure in mind, body and spirit. The organisers were at pains to tell me that this wasn't a festival *of* riding, it was a festival *about* riding. I'm paraphrasing there.

A few weeks earlier, a friend sent me a link to an article about Ireland's first 'Sex Festival', and I obviously got very excited. After a bit of rooting, a lovely lady called Beth got in touch with me and asked if I was interested in attending. Er ... like ... YEAH!! It wasn't a sex festival though, it was a festival about sexuality, which is a different thing altogether, as she told me a few times. I wasn't sure what to expect, but in the spirit of adventure, and of putting myself through all kinds of experiences to seek out the Ireland that was still managing to happily exist despite the broken banks, I signed up for a 'playshop' entitled 'Awakening Your Senses'. I'm a martyr for the cause.

A blindfold was applied by a nice lady in the corridor of the Gresham Hotel, and I was led to a room that had atmospheric music playing, where I was invited to sit on a cushion to await whatever might happen. About twelve people were taking this playshop, and we were all instructed not to speak and not to remove our blindfolds unless we found we needed to leave the room in a hurry for some reason.

One of the first sensual experiences I noticed was the different types of smells that were changing regularly, and wafting quite close to my nose; thankfully, they were all pleasant. After a while, things were brushing against my arms and face, some of them feeling like feathers and very soft material. I'm not going to lie to you, this felt very pleasant indeed. Did I neglect to mention that everyone entered the room fully clothed? Well, at least they all were when the very pleasant ladies applied the blindfolds in the corridor. In addition to the sound, smell and touch sensations, we were then fed things, which is an odd thing to have a stranger do to you when blindfolded and tickled by feathers. A strawberry was placed into my mouth at one stage, and it felt weird (are you sure that was a strawberry, buddy?). The hairs on it made it feel all rough, but when I bit into it, there was a scream! Only joking. When I bit into it, it was obviously a strawberry; I had just never noticed how rough the surface of them actually is before.

This whole blindfolded-awakening-senses buzz was an interesting experience, unsettling but enjoyable. Among the unexpected aspects were the noises that other people were making in the room. While I was sitting there blindfolded on my cushion like Terry Waite in an erotic fantasy, I was getting increasingly curious about the noises being made by some of those around me. There was someone next to me groaning away like a bull seal in the throes of fellatio. It was getting so intense at one stage that I was wondering if other people were having things done to them that I wasn't. On the other side of me there was some Olympic-standard lip-smacking that sounded like an auld fella who had lost his false teeth trying to eat sour gooseberries. It was fecking unsettling, to say the least. I wasn't sure whether or not I was sitting blindfolded in the middle of an orgy, fully dressed with everyone else getting it on around me. It turns out that I wasn't; some people react differently to being stroked with feathers than others – simple as that. After a whole day of this type of carry-on, it's easy to understand why some people were a bit more sensitive. You try being tickled by feathers and fed chocolate cake all day. You wouldn't be right after it.

The first weekend after my near spiritual experience of music and mountains in Kerry, and I'd laughed my head off all night whilst dressed in tights, and the next day I was erotically tickled and fed chocolate cake by lovely ladies. Six months on the road, and I couldn't wait to give the next person who asked me 'Are you not tired of it yet?' a very full and detailed answer, or just a short monosyllabic one. More please!

Festivals Attended in February

69. Shore Angling Festival – Curracloe, Co. Wexford
70. Chinese New Year Festival – Dublin City
71. Haitifest – Dublin City
72. Food & Bev – City West, Co. Dublin
73. UCC Tradfest – Cork City
74. Tipperariana Book Festival – Fethard, Co. Tipperary
75. Dublin International Film Festival – Dublin City
76. Cork Spring Poetry Festival – Cork City
77. *Scoil Cheoil an Earraigh* – Ballyferriter, Co. Kerry
78. Dingle Walking Festival – Dingle, Co. Kerry
79. Tedfest – Inis Mór, Co. Galway
80. Bliss Sexual Health and Freedom – Dublin City
81. Festival of Russian Culture – Dublin City

Other Recommended Festivals in February

Glen of Aherlow Walking Festival – Aherlow, Co. Tipperary
Russell Memorial Weekend – Doolin, Co. Clare
Corofin Traditional Festival – Corofin, Co. Clare

8 | *March – Half a Pig's Head for the Ramblon Mon*

*I*t's hard to believe that the picturesque and unspoiled village of Carlingford is so close to one of the country's main motorways, and less than an hour away from two of Ireland's biggest cities. The village was a hive of activity first thing on Saturday morning for their annual walking get-together. The clients buzzing around looked fairly serious about their trekking, and I overheard snippets of conversations that mentioned Gobi Desert this and Kilimanjaro that. Uh oh!

Like the eejit that I am, I'd been signing up for the grade A/1 walks when I'd been arriving at these strolling sprees, and I may have had overestimated my ability as a result. It had been working out okay, but, even on paper, the walk here was a tough-looking jaunt. Fourteen kilometres across the mountains, hitting four peaks (I counted five while on the bloody walk!) I definitely got the impression that, from a difficulty perspective, this was up a notch from the traipsing tours I'd been on so far.

Once we were underway, one of the first things that struck me as we walked through the Cooley Mountains was that, for a small island, we have a huge contrast of countryside, scenery and people. The hills and views in this neck of the woods were totally different to the surroundings that I'd experienced at the other walking festivals. The difference in scenery was underscored by an assortment of strong border accents that also highlighted the diversity. Throw into this mix the fact that for much of the day we were looking across Carlingford Lough at the towns of Rostrevor, Warren Point and further up to Newry, all across the border in Co. Down, and that feeling of variety and localised uniqueness was underlined further still.

When we stopped for lunch looking down over Carlingford Lough, a member of the Mourne Walking Club from across the border quipped, 'That's Rostrevor over there, where yer last president came from. Ye always came across the border to get the best of politicians.' There came a quick and good-humoured response, ''Tis a pity ye didn't hang on to a few of them, ye might have sorted yerselves out years ago.' Ouch!

The historical and cultural significance of this part of the country is something that has been subliminally planted in lots of us Irish folk from a young age. We were reared on the stories of *Cú Chulainn* and his band of hurley-wielding warriors, a crew who used these hills as the backdrop to their greatest escapades. Supposedly, after Queen Maebh and her crowd stole a load of cattle, the *Fianna* lads were up here in the hills, picking off her bravest and best with slingshots from a distance of about five miles. They don't make slingshots or men like that any more.

You can blame these stories for the batch of weird and wonderful names that some poor little creatures have been landed with in the recent past. Mícheál Ó Muircheartaigh won't complain about the spurt of folklore names; I think he used to orgasm during commentary every time Setanta Ó hAilpín was on the ball in a match, using the hurler's name as an opportunity to launch into tales of the Hound of Ulster, or comparing an oncoming opposing player to

Balor of the Evil Eye (Tipperary's John Leahy springs to mind for some reason).

This was a tough walk, worthy of the Fianna's playground, but it was also an enjoyable one. There was retina-blowing scenery and, yet again, some great people out on the walk. Two recently graduated students from DKIT were telling me about their Erasmus year in China. Kevin from Dublin was hoping to set up his own business, taking people for walks in the mountains in the east of the country. The leader of the walk lent a bit of colour to the proceedings with some local knowledge and folklore as we ambled along. I was particularly impressed when he suggested that we all put on our rain gear while we stopped for a *sos beag*; five minutes later it started milling down. I had a chat with Frances, one of the organisers, after the walk, and she shed some light on the leprechaun hunt that takes place in Carlingford every year. Only a spotting hunt, mind you; Carlingford has been deemed an EU area of special protection for little people.

Not having a creamy pint after a hard walk in the mountains would be like going on tour with the English Rugby team and abstaining from adultery and midget-throwing (if they tried throwing little people around in Carlingford they might end up with the evil eye on them). I held off on the reward pint until I got to the trad festival I was heading for later in Co. Cavan, thinking that I'd also need to quench the thirst I'd work up on the dance floor after a few sets.

My ability to blag my way through a set or two was being tested to the full, but so long as I was sides and could get a good look at what was expected as the top couples stepped it out, I was just about able to get away with it. My dance partner would need to be wearing steel toecaps for safety reasons though. The New Year's resolution that led to my meagre set-dancing skills seemed like a perfectly reserved and normal goal in comparison to trying to get to three festivals in Ireland every week for a year.

When I got to the wonderfully named Swanlinbar, Co. Cavan, for the inaugural John Joe Maguire weekend, the village was swinging, stepping, circling, advancing and spinning round the house. There's something wholesome and earthy about the enjoyment that people who are into this craic get from a night's exertion. Thankfully, there was no beer in the hall to further muddle my moves, but plenty of tea, brack and ham sandwiches at the halfway point.

No matter where you are in Ireland, I'd be willing to wager that there is a Comhaltas group near you that organises set-dances and classes on weeknights during the winter. I'm not in a position to say whether or not it's more fun than Zumbaba Hot Yogic Tango classes, but it's ours, and that's why I thought it was worth a whack. The Copperplate Céilí Band in Swanlinbar did a great job keeping the crowd spinning, and the caller was the most glamourous set-caller this side of the Ramor. I have a hankering to be a set-caller myself when I grow up – you might say it's a calling. After a little skip around the hall, and an egg salad sandwich, I hopped out the door to sample the sessions around the town and to lubricate my knees.

It's not uncommon to find a traditional music and dance festival in a small town that's been established in memory of a local legend. In this instance, that legend was flautist John Joe Maguire from Co. Fermanagh who passed away in 2010. This was the first year the weekend had been run, and they were expecting over 2,000 bodies to pass through the village. It's a wonderful way for the life of a musician to be celebrated, teaching future musicians and dancers new skills and keeping tradition alive, while also bringing some vibrancy and a few bob into a village at the same time.

I gave Martin Donohoe a shout before I hit Swanlinbar. Martin is a musician, Comhaltas operative and trad festival fiend. Martin's a bit of a legend in these parts. The session he was playing at was rocking and, just in case I missed him, he sent through a text description: 'Big hairy boy with accordion'. He was right; you couldn't miss him.

Martin can take a good deal of credit for the success that the *Fleadh Cheoil* in Cavan had been in recent years. He was first to establish a theme that would be repeated for the night, offering me a bed and extending hospitality above and beyond the call of duty. In the middle of the session, between calling on singers and musicians, Martin gave details of the *Sean-Nós* Pole Dancing workshop he said was happening the next day, and later informed the crowd that the girls selling the raffle tickets would give you two strips for a fiver – wink, wink. At the end of the night, when I was chatting to Martin, he gave me a CD that his young fella had just released – Kavan from Cavan! The very fella that I was complimenting at the Temple Bar Trad Festival. It's a small country, but some of this symmetry was getting spooky. If the harpists were going to start carrying on like the tin-whistle players, there was a good chance that I'd start to get really freaked out.

The previous week on Inis Mór, PJ, the boss man in *Tí* Joe Watty's, offered me the couch in his house if I found myself stuck for a bed after I'd missed the ferry. I thanked PJ, and said that I reckoned I'd find something. ''Tis Ireland', said PJ, 'you won't be stuck.' This was a simple, throwaway comment as he put a pint in front of me, but the statement and sentiment has stayed with me ever since. The wonderful thing about it was that he was right on so many levels, and thankfully he continues to be right. On at least six different occasions during the night in Swanlinbar I was offered a bed for the night, well above the average in my rambling experience, and proving that, contrary to popular opinion, Cavan people are extremely generous.

One of the oddest accommodation offers came as I was at the urinal, doing some recycling. The big fella beside me grumbled at me, 'Orhughdaramblon mon hoy?' What now? 'Or-hugh-da-ramblon mon hoy?' A little bit of panic was setting in now, because there's only so many times you can ask a fella to repeat himself while you both stand beside each other holding your lads in your hands before things spiral out of control. He thinned out the Cavan accent somewhat, and it turned out that he wanted to know if I was 'The Rambling Man'. It turns out that I am, and that he'd heard me on the radio, and he also wanted to offer me a bed for the night. Odd circumstances in which to do so, but odder still was how deeply I appreciated it.

The banjo player up at the session in the Welcome Inn was one Darren Maloney, a fella I hadn't seen since we played a few gigs together in Norway all of ten years ago. He was straight in with the whiskey and the beer. Any notions of temperance were tempered, and I ended up over-medicating my knees to such an extent that they felt no pain and became anaesthetized to the point of uselessness.

I love the Cavan accent, and the earthiness and sense of fun on offer in Swanlinbar on that Saturday night just added to that *grá*. Driving through the county the following sunny Sunday morning, with Kavan Donohoe playing his harp on Wanderly Wagon's stereo, It felt like I had the scenic north-west section of the county to myself. I drove past lakes and signs that echoed place names from songs I heard sung while growing up in my parents' pub – Killeshandra, Ballybay, Ballyjamesduff, Ardee.... Although my most recently acquired favourite Cavan town name isn't a song, it should be. I'm still not sure of the best way of working Killywilly into a come-all-ye though. It felt like there was some neglected ancestral memory getting tapped into as I enjoyed the lakes and Kavan's touch on the harp. Once more, I found myself content and satiated. If a part of our country was broken, I was thankfully looking in all the wrong places. It was on mornings like that, spinning through the glorious countryside in Wanderly Wagon, I found time to reflect on some of the things I'd been getting up to. An interesting thought occurred to me: I'd heard it said that Cavan has a lake for every day of the year. I wondered if anyone had ever visited or swam in each of these lakes, every day, for a whole year? I've filed it away as something to do if I ever find myself at a loose end.

There was a good deal more Irish culture and mayhem being dealt out in the days that followed the trip to Cavan. I could have been living on tins of cold beans in a cave in Connemara and have still managed to find myself at three festivals in the days that followed. It was Paddy's weekend – a time when it's almost impossible to avoid festivities. I probably drove through more festivals than I attended while heading for west Cork.

I was bound for the *Fadó* festival in Bantry, Co. Cork. The set-up of this event had captured my imagination. *Fadó* translates into English as 'long ago', and many storytellers would have traditionally started their tales with a plaintive '*Fadó, fadó…*', which is where George Lucas got the idea for the *Star Wars* intro. Really! Sure wasn't Yoda a tailor in Caherciveen before he made it big in Hollywood; got his big break as an extra in *Darby O'Gill and the Little People*. The idea behind the *Fadó* festival in Bantry is to shun modern-day distractions, turn off the electricity and rip it up in an old-school style.

One of the first things I stumbled across in Bantry was a horse and trap ferrying classically clothed characters from pub to pub. More pub trawl than crawl. After I moored Wanderly Wagon and strolled through the town, I noticed that many of the businesses arranged vintage window displays for the festival (some of them inadvertently). The atmosphere in the alehouses was homely and engaging: candles flickering, locals dressed appropriately (not inadvertently in most cases), tunes being belted out, and a welcome at every counter I leaned on. This *Fadó* craic was creating a chilled and comfortable atmosphere. I liked it.

A recurring theme as I spun around the sprees of Ireland was how some Irish men seem to have a penchant for dressing up as old women. At the drop of a headscarf, it's on with a pinny, surgical stockings and haphazardly applied lippy. The amount of burly, bestubbled Mrs Doyles on Inis Mór for Tedfest was staggering. No doubt our predilection for cross-dressing has something to do with British oppression and the Famine. Deep-Freud potatoes. There was a gaggle of good-humoured old-lady-boys who I swear were winking at me over one Bantry bar; it may have been the flickering of the candles though.

The prize for the most hospitable hostelry has to go to the Bantry Inn, where I was offered a share in the soda bread and half a pig's head that were sitting on the counter. As strange as this might sound, the offer made me feel right at home. Cork and Waterford people may have many differences, but we are united in our mutual appreciation of offal. Tripe, drisheen, crubeens, pigs' heads and pudding are what many of us were reared on. Welcome to the deep south, y'all. I passed on the head, but tucked into a crubeen, hoping that the pig's foot might curb the craving for mixed olive tapenade.

The electricity was off, but the town was buzzing with music, drama, stories and chat, all building towards a pageant of fire on Saturday evening. Most of the activity and life could be found in any one of the many pubs in the town. It was in one of these pubs, while chatting to one of the friendly locals about the weekend's proceedings, that I was reminded of:

Irish Festival Rule No. 14: *Some of the best information you receive on the festival trail will smell of beer. Make sure to follow it well.*

It was such beer-soaked advice that took me to the small village of Kealkil the next day for what could be a contender for the best St Patrick's Day Parade in the country.

I landed in the village, and it was all of about five minutes before I met the lads responsible for the parade. They were working since 7.00 a.m. to get the village ready for the party that would ensue. The lads explained that this was a small village, and everyone involved in the day's festivities was a local, all working voluntarily. One of the first clients I met was an old boy with two large teeth poking out of his head. Just the two, mind you, but they were at jaunty angles, so he got good value from them. It was the dental equivalent of a comb-over. Have you ever noticed that talking to an auld lad with just two teeth is a lot like talking to a fine-looking lady with an over-obvious bosom; it's hard work not to stare.

The crowds began to gather early at the main intersection of the village, where the only two pubs in the place face each other. It was a grand spot for the main proceedings. It seemed as if everybody from the village (and beyond) had taken to the streets. One of the reasons that the parade in Kealkil is totally community-based is because there are so many large-scale parades on around the country and county that the main marching bands and street entertainment groups are always going to be lured to the larger parades. Bigger audiences and the possibility of earning a few bob can't be ignored. What these groups gain, in exposure and monetary benefit, they lose in bonding with their community and gaining a deeper, more meaningful appreciation of what a festival can often be about. Even though this was a really small-scale community parade, it still cost €3,000 to put the thing on. This was raised through sponsorship and fundraising. There was a raffle on the day – I'm not sure what the prize was, but I reckon it was either a tractor or some livestock; these were the most common elements of the day.

The sun was shining, and there was music, song and dance to be enjoyed before the parade itself began. Not surprisingly, the two pubs were doing a brisk trade. There were a couple of food vendors on hand to supply soakage; the double-dentured dude was sucking a bag of chips to death. There was a bouncy castle and a dangerous-looking bucking bronco machine, that threatened to be far too much fun, flinging festive fools around the place later that evening. There were a few different trad groups on the trailer over the course of the morning/afternoon, some singers, set-dancers, a brush dancer and a young girl who sang Amy Winehouse's 'Rehab', which seemed awfully appropriate for the day that was in it.

I went down and found a spot by the roadside for the parade as it was about to begin, but there was no hurry; we weren't just working on Irish time, we were working on Irish rural time. I was standing next to an elderly lady with flashing shamrock earrings who had travelled in from Bantry for the parade, as she had done for the past few years. She explained that she'd been up late the night before playing cards and drinking whiskey, but it was well worth the effort of getting organised to catch the parade in Kealkil.

Bantry used to have a St Patrick's Day Parade, but like many other mid-sized Irish towns, it wasn't actually held on St Patrick's Day any more – a victim of the demands made by the parades of county capitals on anything in a uniform that can walk or make noise. In terms of budget and resources, some towns just can't run parades on the seventeenth, so they wait until the day after, when the groups become available and cheaper. This lady felt that a parade not actually on the day itself makes the whole affair a little less special. She made a good point, and one that was reinforced by the fact that that nothing had been imported to enhance this parade, which made it all the more special. This was a matter of local people and community groups that were out to celebrate our national day, and to celebrate their place with their neighbours. Well, they were nearly all local. Seán Óg Ó hAilpín was leading out the parade. Not surprisingly, the lady beside me (and many others around the village) were very happy to see the tall, dark, handsome former county hurler in the flesh. She was not overly impressed, though, that he wasn't togged out in his legendary tight-fitting knicks.

The anticipation was building, and before the parade revealed itself by turning the corner onto the main thoroughfare, you could hear the plaintive refrain of the lone piper setting a traditional and appropriate mood for paraders and gawpers alike.

When the procession did start, it was a colourful, fun and irreverent affair. There was lots of laughter, and something that surprised me: there were at least six elements of the parade that had messages of protest, all delivered in a good-humoured way. There were two floats that had toilets on them, lampooning the recently introduced septic tank charges. There were at least three messages that referred to energy charges and the restrictions introduced on turf-cutting. There was also a group of schoolkids carrying a banner that read: 'Save Our Small Schools'. I'm not sure if this was something that was echoed in other towns around the country, but it was an interesting and often comical way for people to vent frustrations with what was happening politically and economically. Maybe it could be interpreted as a sociopolitical barometer, pointing towards the beginnings of revolution, or maybe it was just a bit of fun born of frustration and an all-too-familiar feeling of helplessness.

Besides a donkey of protest, there were some sheep, horses and a calf or two. But the most common element of the parade was tractors. If you're fond of tractors, Kealkil on Paddy's Day is the spot for you. All shapes, makes, flavours and colours were on display; Janey but there was even a fella from west Waterford in full *Déise* hurling kit driving out a John Deere lawnmower. Kealkil might just be the tractor-porn capital of Ireland.

For the first time since I started my journey, I felt like I was missing home a bit. It could have been the lad in the Waterford gear, it could have been lack of sleep, but I've a feeling that it was the sense of community, fun, belonging and pride of place that was on display by everyone who was out on the streets here. It was great to witness it, but I wasn't really part of it; I was just an onlooker. The parade and day that I would have really been a part of was taking place much farther down the coast in Co. Waterford; a parade that I walked in myself as a young fella with the scouts, and later as a teenager with the Sea and Cliff Rescue. I've worked on a few St Patrick's day parades for the week-long festival in Dublin and, while the pomp, ceremony and spectacle of a city parade is great entertainment, ideal for bringing in tourism revenue and a prime marketing opportunity for the country, take me out to the countryside and give me a fella on a lawnmower any day of the week, especially if he's wearing a Waterford jersey.

It wasn't until reflecting on the festival activities from March that I realised that everything I got up to during the month could have been done 100 years ago; probably not as comfortably, mind you. Mountain-walking, trad music, set-dancing, candlelit chats and old-school Paddy's day parades were all awfully enjoyable distractions. I was beginning to suspect that it was the simplest pleasures that were giving me the deepest satisfaction of all. It was also interesting that much of this stuff didn't cost a fortune to enjoy, if you cut out the excessive pints and diesel. I'd suspected that the country wasn't in the awful shape we were being led to believe, but I had underestimated how rich we were in character, imagination, generosity, curiosity, creativity, hunger for arousal, fun and divilment. You'll often run into German tourists who are in Ireland seeking to draw down on those very reserves of which we cultivate a studied embarrassment. The way I was feeling about what was happening around the country, twelve months of it probably wasn't going to be nearly enough.

Festivals Attended in March

82. Carlingford Walking Festival – Carlingford, Co. Louth
83. John Joe Maguire Festival – Swanlinbar, Co. Cavan
84. Barrow River Arts Festival – Borris, Co. Carlow
85. *Comórtas Peile na Gaeltachta* – Belmullet, Co. Mayo
86. *Seachtain na Gaeilge* – Belmullet, Co. Mayo
87. Windsurfing Inter-Varsities – Belmullet, Co. Mayo
88. Fadó Festival – Bantry, Co. Cork
89. St Patrick's Day – Kealkil, Co. Cork
90. *Moby Dick* Festival – Youghal, Co. Cork
91. Waterford Writers' Week – Waterford City
92. Waterford Festival of Learning – Waterford City
93. Festival of French Culture – Waterford City
94. Winnie Fennell Festival – Cappoquin, Co. Waterford

Other Recommended Festivals in March

Ennis Book Club Festival – Ennis, Co. Clare
Cork French Film Festival – Cork City
Connemara's Four Seasons Walking Festival – Connemara, Co. Galway

9 | *April – City of the Dead, Town of the Deranged*

*I*t can't have been a coincidence that in the same year Dublin was designated the UNESCO City of Literature, the One City, One Book Festival chose James Joyce's *Dubliners* as the target of its approbation. This choice was made more poignant by the passing away of the last original member of The Dubliners: Barney 'Banjo' McKenna, just before the festival kicked off. Not only was the name of that most influential of trad groups relevant, but the current incarnation group was actually scheduled to play at the National Concert Hall as part of the festival. The festival celebrated Joyce's text, but underneath was the theme of a send-off for Barney. If you're not overly familiar with The Dubliners, Barney was the one with the beard.

One of the more accessible of James Joyce's books, *Dubliners* is a collection of fifteen short stories about ordinary people going about their lives in Das Kapital. One of the chapters is entitled 'The Dead', and as part of the programme of events for the festival, there was a Joycean tour of Glasnevin Cemetery. I'd been threatening a visit to this most interesting and historically rich graveyard for years, and so, somewhat happier than most of the people who usually visit the place, it was off to Dublin's City of The Dead.

You wouldn't guess it from all the crosses and saintly figures, but Glasnevin was established as a multi-denominational graveyard, and it still is. Daniel 'The Liberator' O'Connell set up the boneyard to give people of all religions a place to find their final rest. Once the graveyard opened its gates for business, he even built a new road to it, bypassing the other two toll roads, so poor people wouldn't have pay to get to the graveyard. O'Connell was responsible for the emancipation of Catholics in Ireland, and helped to inspire the abolitionist movement in America. His political approach and methods were studied by many human rights activists, most notably Gandhi and Martin Luther King. O'Connell was one serious dude, and, from the little I know about him, I'd have to say that I count myself among his fans. I don't have a tattoo or a T-shirt or anything, but I have a well of respect for D. O'C.

Possibly one of the most powerful orators the country has ever known, thousands of people would gather at his mass meetings that were held all over the country, the Bruce Springsteen of his day. He represented Ireland in the House of Commons, and four-time Prime Minister of Britain, William Gladstone, described him as: 'The greatest popular leader the world has ever seen.' Gladstone was a fan too. Legend has it that he was a bit of a boyo, and a scurrilous rumour of yesteryear suggested that it would be difficult to lob a rock over a wall anywhere in the country without hitting a child that looked remarkably like dear old Danny. No one's perfect, I suppose.

One of the first stop-off points on the tour of the graveyard is O'Connell's tomb, under the huge round tower that was built in his honour. I'm reluctant to lash out the superlatives to describe the experience of being in O'Connell's final resting place, so instead I'll tell you a little story. While visiting Ireland, a former President of

Brazil paid a visit to O'Connell's tomb. So moved was he by the experience that he sent out his entourage to gather wild flowers as a mark of respect to a man, who he felt transcended royalty. The Brazilian minions scoured the shops, parks and gardens of Glasnevin, and returned with floral tributes that were then laid around the tomb. The Brazilian *buachaill* became a fan too.

You can still enter the tomb on tours of the graveyard, and reach inside the sarcophagus through the latticework panels to touch O'Connell's aged wooden casket; legend has it that this will bring you luck. Not for the first time since starting my travels, I had what could only be described as 'a moment'. I found it overwhelming. For a slice of Irish history, and a chance to feel the presence of a lingering legend, a visit to the tomb is just not recommended; I'll give you a slap if you don't go!

It felt like an eerie privilege, being allowed such intimate access to this sanctum; not just of O'Connell, but also of his family and relatives. This is a family-sized tomb, and he's not on his own down there.

We also visited the graves of Joyce's family, whose story of hardship and poverty is echoed all around the graveyard. Two of Joyce's siblings died from typhoid, which was rampant in the tenements of Dublin. As you pass through the graveyard, you are told of paupers' graves where there are thousands buried in one small area, stacked on top of each other. There is also the cholera pit, where tens of thousands are buried having died from disease, poverty and famine. I was never a great one for history in school (actually, I was just never a great one for school), and I wonder if a trip here would have been wasted on a teenage me (probably), but I'd like to think that it wouldn't have been – some seeds would have been planted.

A visit to the graveyard gives an immediacy and relevance to events, names, literature and Irish society in general that I certainly didn't appreciate before. Even something as simple as comparing the amount of flowers (placed by members of the public) on de Valera's grave to those on Michael Collins' grave suggests that historical events that shaped our nation are not just academic; they still have a strong meaning and relevance to many citizens of the Free State.

It didn't feel right visiting a graveyard and not going to a pub afterwards (ethnic programming); even some of the graves in Glasnevin get pints. The tour guide told us that you can usually identify Brendan Behan's grave by the pint of Guinness sitting on top of it. No doubt Benny would appreciate the sentiment more than a bunch of pansies. The Gravediggers pub is situated right beside what used to be the main gate for the graveyard. The inn was opened in the same year as the graveyard by a savvy publican. There are over 1.5 million people buried in Glasnevin. I'll let that sit for a moment. There are only 1.3 million living in Dublin. Just imagine how much porter has been peddled to almost 200 years worth of mourners that have passed through the gates of the cemetery. The Gravediggers has been in the same family for six generations, and when you step inside, you feel it. None of the fake rustic codology you get down Temple Bar. That's not paint on the walls and ceilings – it's nicotine. The Gravediggers: straight in at number seven in my top ten pubs in the world. I savoured the creamy pint, relishing every drop. The following day was going to be a dry Good Friday in Galway.

I was impressed by how seriously the populace of Galway was taking the whole Easter devotion thing when I landed there the next day. There were processions of solemn people with downcast expressions, made all the more dramatic by some weeping and cries of anguish. The Passion play in Oberammergau couldn't have created such a sense of compassion and loss. As I heard an American girl console her male companion, I twigged what was going on here: 'Don't sweat it, Steve, Dignity will be open again tomorrow.' Steve was going cold turkey for both alcohol and Galway's liveliest gay bar. The sullen pedestrians were suffering one of only two days that pubs close in Ireland. Whatever the Catholic Church might think of selling drink on a Good Friday, selling drink to homosexuals on a Good Friday? A little more hip than your usual original sins. That bar has closed since, but I don't think there's any truth in the rumour that it was due to a plague of locusts. Mind you, Galway always did have a touch of Sodom and Gomorrah about it.

There were many bewildered tourists wandering aimlessly around the streets of Galway, trying to get to grips with the fact that there are actually some days when the pubs don't open in Ireland. Help was on hand, though, in the shape of the distractions being offered by Galway Food Festival.

There was free coffee and hot cross buns in Vina Mara wine bar. No alcohol, but free stuff is good. Over sixty people turned up to the restaurant and wine bar on Middle Street, and they ran out of buns within thirty minutes. Sure the crowds were only wandering the streets crying out for something to do, poor creatures.

After a bun and some scald, I enjoyed the sight of another few forlorn tourists shaking the locked doors of pubs, before heading towards Co. Clare for a full moon walk on the Burren. The trouble with my navigation skills is that Letterfrack is in Connemara, not the Burren, which I didn't twig until I had started out towards Clare. I'm five-eighths dope, and it's amazing that I'd managed to clock up over seven months of festivals without the whole quest falling asunder. U-turn. Letterfrack, ho!

The event I was headed for was Diamond Moon, a midnight walk up one of the Twelve Bens Mountains to coincide with the full moon. The idea is that the moonlight adds some atmosphere to the experience – the slight hitch was that it was misty and raining on the night. Thank God for that Lidl head-torch, which worked perfectly all night, for a change.

Seven months on the road and it was becoming clear that I may have misplaced a couple of ball bearings. I walked up (and down) a mountain in the rain, wind, mist and pitch dark at an hour when most people were in bed, and I thoroughly enjoyed it. This was not normal behaviour for me, or for most reasonable people. Even in the dark, there was the usual good-humoured banter that you get on these walks from the other folk who were taking part. Yep, there were actually other people taking part too. Paul Phelan, who was leading the walk, was in control all the time, filling in details about the area as we went along, and sometimes telling us what we would see at certain points, had we decided to do the walk in the daylight. Paul knew his way around these hills, even in the dark. I was impressed; I can't usually make it out of the bed for a piss without clattering into something.

The work that has gone into making paths and walkways through Connemara National Park made this night-time ramble possible. Without the stone slabs and gritted paths, it would have been a much trickier and more hazardous affair. Even though the moon and stars didn't reveal themselves on the night, I really enjoyed the darkness and the somewhat isolated experience of not knowing what was beyond the limited pool of light that was spilling out from my head-torch. At one point, the wind died down completely, and it became very eerie indeed. Getting emotional rubbing coffins, communing with psychic tin-whistlers and wandering around mountains in the pitch dark – I was starting to build up a CV that would get me a job as an Igor.

After the highs of the midnight walk, there were bound to be some lows – I just didn't realize how low festivals could go. I had some clue what I was getting myself into when I rambled in to the Ideal Home and Motor Show in Tralee two days later. The event was surprisingly listed as part of the *Tir na nÓg* Family Festival. There were people selling solar panels, back massagers, gates, solid fuel stoves and curtains. Not much for kids to do though. It might have worked as an event for a family festival, if you were a family doing up your house and the kids were off on a school tour. Dull as Jedward after a frontal lobotomy.

I decided to hightail it to Ballybunion, quick smart, for the Easter Music Festival. As I was leaving the Ideal Homes Expo, the very friendly doorman asked if I'd like a stamp to get back in later on. I declined, and he pleaded, 'Ahhhh, go ooooon'. Poor dude was desperate for distraction. Time to leg it! I was delighted to be on the road, heading for another festival, given the disappointment felt after the pelmet party in Tralee, but when I arrived in Ballybunion, things weren't exactly moving and shaking either. Actually, that's not entirely true: there was a girl in leopard-print high heels vomiting outside one of the pubs.

When you need to find out what's going on in a small town in Ireland, it's a good bet that somebody at the counter of a pub will know. I went to about eight pubs (all in the name of research), and asked repeatedly about the Easter Music Festival. 'Never heard of it' was the consensus. I'm still not sure what exactly you could call what was happening in Badger Kelly's: it resembled music, but you definitely wouldn't call it a festival. I just about managed to finish my bottle before a deep need to leave finally moved me.

In the next bar they knew nothing about a festival either, but they had a fella playing and singing The Eagles' greatest hits, while a pissed dude stood beside him with a toy guitar and occasionally shouted 'Wayhey!' at something that was only happening in his head. Maureen fell on top of me at one stage, before she told me her name and added that she was very drunk because her pet lamb, Paul, had died that day. Next!

I'm no shrinking violet when it comes to pulling a stool up to a strange counter, but there were a couple of bars in Ballybunion that evening where I was watching my P's and Q's. I only saw one fight, but I wasn't staying in many of these places long enough to qualify for a ringside seat. It was Easter Sunday night in a small town in Ireland. I wasn't expecting cravats and Pimm's, but kids ducking in and out of pubs in pyjamas after 11.00 p.m. into very drunk adults isn't what you expect either. In fairness, though, in this case I think the kids were wearing those all-day pyjamas, which isn't as bad, I think?

By about pub five, things were starting to get better, and not just because I was throwing myself headlong into the hunt. The Exchange re-established relative normality. There was a decent band, and none of the clientele was wearing pyjamas. Undeterred by previous experience, I asked the barman about the phantom festival. He drew a blank, but he asked where I'd heard about it. I told him my source, and could even whip out the phone and look the thing up online. He gave a wry smile, and told me that there is a fella in Ballybunion who is 'a law unto himself' when it comes to tourism and promotion of the town. He didn't seem at all surprised that the individual he suspected of being behind this elusive festival would promote it without actually doing anything or telling anyone else. Discover Ireland even had it up as part of their Easter weekend festival listings. It seemed that there may have been a festival in Ballybunion that only two people knew about: me, and west Kerry's answer to Walter Mitty.

I definitely didn't make it up, but it was proving to be a difficult festival to nail down. Nevertheless, I was getting into the swing of my research now, and by the time I got to Merry's Bar, I was in the humour to have a little festival all of my own. Luckily, I arrived just in time for the singsong. At the counter was the finest country and western yodeller you're likely to hear this side of the Rio Grande. The man had skills. Cahersiveen's answer to Conrad Twitty he was. The owner of this pub echoed earlier investigations, and named the same suspect as before as the likely festival fabricator. A few songs were sung, chats were had, and by the end of it all I felt that the festival mystery was solved: Walter McMitty was a prick, and I could conclude my research for the night. Just as well – festival fatigue was setting in.

Ballybunion was an odd experience to say the least, but there were lessons to be learned from it. Beware of false festival promises, and vomit away from your new leopard-print high heels, lest you should add extra bleached spots. The town boasts that Bill Clinton came to play golf there once. This was such a notable event in the history of the place that they stuck up a statue of Billy swinging a club right outside the garda station – probably the best place for him.

After the events in Kerry, pulling up Wanderly Wagon's handbrake in the grounds of Carlow Mental Hospital seemed like a step up. The Pan Celtic Festival was underway, and the grounds of the local sanitarium provided a leafy sanctuary for a drop of tea and slab of steak in the van before another bout of festival investigations began.

The Pan Celtic Festival is nothing to do with Gaelic kitchenware or Scottish skillets. This is a festival where Celtic Soul Brothers and Sisters get to sing, dance and be merry in each other's company for a week or so. It turns out that the Irish aren't the only ones who know how to hooley. Who exactly are our Celtic cousins? Alba (Scotland), Breizh (Brittany), Cymru (Wales), Mannin (the Isle of Man) and Kernow (Cornwall). Remember that really good wedding you were at, where all the in-laws and outlaws got on great? Well, that's what getting all the Celts together is like, but with better music, less embarrassing dancing, fewer fights and no cousins trying to get off with each other (does that just happen in Waterford?). Nope, scratch that, there actually were cousins throwing shapes at each other, but only very distant cousins. If it's good enough for royalty, it's good enough for Carlowthians. There was even an embarrassing uncle there on the night – Dáithí O'Sé was on MC duty.

Delightful Dáithí was *Fear an Tí* for the night, and he kept things moving along with a string of jokes and quips that suggested he wasn't quite match-fit for the Rose of Tralee this early in the season. Cue a *Rocky* montage, with Marty Whelan as coach Mickey getting Dáithí in shape by lifting weights with his eyelids for prime winking and practising his puns in a disused cheese factory.

Whatever about Dáithí, I had my work cut out talking to an auld lad from Wales – he must have got the Connemara Linguaphone box set from Santi for Christmas. The Welsh boy was well able for the *cúpla focail*, but the accent made things a little more confusing. My lack of *blas* wasn't the problem at all; it was definitely his accent. That's my excuse, anyway. Here, though, was a Welsh man who took Irish classes in his spare time simply because he wanted to learn another Celtic language. You have to admire that. He was also fond of putting turnips in his shoes, smothered with mountain jam; at least, that's what I think he said to me. That fecking accent threw me off.

The solitude of the Mental Hospital grounds proved perfect for a peaceful night's sleep. Thankfully, the guy standing outside staring in the window all night was very quiet. On my next stop, in Dungarvan, Co. Waterford, I made the rookie mistake of parking on a migratory path between a popular local watering hole, The Anchor, and the late-night bolthole disco, Minnies. This was about as clever as building a salmon-canning factory on a polar bear migratory path. Interaction with the wildlife could be expected. I was lying in the van late on Friday night/ Saturday morning, when there was a tap on the window. The reveller wanted to know what festivals were on the next weekend. The odd thing was that the drunk dude sounded exactly like me after a few bottles. It was nice to be back in the home county.

It was early afternoon in west Waterford, and, although I had the makings of a late lunch in the van, I decided that it would be criminal to be at a food festival and not sample some of the local victuals. The first port of call was an obvious one. The Tannery in Dungarvan is an institution that owner and TV chef Paul Flynn has made it a requirement to visit on any culinary tour of the country. I've eaten there before, and enjoyed what was probably one of the nicest desserts I've ever had tingle my taste buds. The Tannery had finished serving grub when I ducked in, and I'm kind of glad they had. As an alternative, I went into the heart of town and ended up in Nude Food – the name was obviously the draw for me.

A very late lunch on a Friday afternoon consisted of O'Flynn's cumberland sausages with caramelised onion and beetroot relish, herb potato cakes, spicy chickpea and tomato thingy, olive tapenade toastinis (yep, olive tapenade. What? They didn't have any offal on the menu!), artichoke and pepper yolk-a-me-bob, large-cap mushrooms with halloumi cheese, all washed down by bottles of Helvick Gold from the Dungarvan Brewing Company. To say that this was a decent feed is an understatement akin to saying that the blue furry googly eyed fella who shared the same street with Bob and Susan was fond of cookies. I wasn't working on a food baby, I was working on twins! Afternoons like this made me give thanks and praise to the officials who'd refused my mortgage applications. As I sipped on the craft beer and tucked into top tucker, I toasted the tapped-out tellers.

Thankfully, The Swinging Bluecats offered up some infectious tunes later that night to help burn off a few calories. Let's be honest, though: I would have had to do a month on *Strictly* with a speed-freak lindy-hopper to make a dent in the levels of gluttony I had reached.

I took a stroll through the town to get a flavour of what was happening in some of the other smaller pubs. I had begun taking my research very seriously since Kerry. Up at the counter in Downey's, lo and behold, were two of the big names from the epicurean elite, Paul Flynn and Angela Hartnett – the glitterati of gourmet! The guys had finished a busy night in the kitchen, and were out for a well-deserved tipple and nibble. I was heartened to see them tucking into pints and, would you believe, bags of crisps! I salute the pair of them. Fine food is all well and good, but snobs in any walk of life are boring. It was nice to see that they can lock horns with the best of global gourmands, but can also let their hair down with the rest of us. Keep up the good work, lads. Now if I can get Jamie Oliver on the Buckfast and bacon fries, Gordon Ramsey on the Karpackie and KP nuts and Ainsley Harriet on the Hooch, we'll have a right night on our hands.

Before beginning my festival quest, I never really saw the point of food festivals, and thought them an excuse to buoy up an industry that was bloated and overpriced. There's still probably an element of that in the more elitist end of the foodie spectrum, but the craic in Dungarvan strived to be inclusive and cater for all tastes and ages, and even arranged fringe events for people who might not be fired up by food. It was one of the better food festivals I'd been at.

When not shoving food into it, you may not be surprised to hear that sometimes my mouth works faster than my mind and I end up making promises and declarations that will cause me untold problems down the line. On New Year's Eve, two years ago, after one or two sarsaparillas, I came up with not one, not two, but three resolutions. One of them was to go bog-snorkelling (check!). Another involved mountains and many early morning treks (check!). I've referred to the final resolution in passing already: I vowed to take set-dancing lessons. I went to a few classes and céilís, picking up a few steps, but it kind of fell by the wayside after that. It was great craic though. Skipping around a hotel ballroom on a Monday night at a *céilí* beats the shit out of watching Vincent Browne chewing the head off some poor dope or other. It also revealed to me yet another thing I want to be when I grow up. The auld boy playing drums with the *Céilí* band was about ten years older than God, happy out, tip-tapping away on the drums, tucking into his bag of cans of Dutch Gold. He cracked open a fresh can for each new set, and that kind of activity is a darn sight more enjoyable than *Murder, She Wrote* and Complan in my book. I always had a buzz at the set-dancing nights, and it was in this frame of mind that I was bouncing towards the Glen of Aherlow for *Fonn Rince* – a *Sean-Nós* dancing festival – where I was going to take a workshop in the ancient Irish art of buck-lepping. Hup, ya boy, ya!

I arrived at the community centre in Galbally, and there was already a good crowd in there ahead of me, limbering up their ankles, but thankfully there was a chance to have a chat with Roy, the man whose brainchild this festival is. Roy is one interesting dude. A retired dancer from the Irish National Ballet, he also plays trad flute, and has always had an interest and exposure to trad sessions and such. When he retired from ballet he didn't think there would be any more dancing for him – that was until he gave the *Sean-Nós* dancing a whirl. Hooked! He talked about the freedom, fun, expressiveness and inclusiveness of it. Anyone can do it, no matter what his or her ability or agility. That's part of the charm of the thing for Roy. I asked if he thought that ballet dancers would look down their noses at *Sean-Nós* dancing. Roy asked me not to quote him, so I'll paraphrase: ballet dancers look down their noses at everything.

So, what is *Sean-Nós* dancing? Well, forget about Riverdance, ringlets and keeping your hands rigidly down by your side. Roy was at pains to point out that this is the only form of traditional Irish dance that has elements of improvisation in it; *Sean-Nós* dancing is the jazz of the trad world. At its core, it's that freedom and room for full-on kicking and hopping that makes this craic such fun. Flailing your arms and throwing a couple of shapes to get a yelp of encouragement from onlookers is actively encouraged. I once saw an auld fella use his flat cap for slapping his knees exuberantly as he lepped and skipped around the place; he would have put a Wexican with strawberry-rimmed sombrero to shame.

There were people of every age, every level of ability and experience, from every hop, skip, shuffle and walk of life. I was surprised with the distances people had covered in order to get to this shindig. It felt like an underground movement. I met a wonderful lady there by the name of Bridget. She's 82 years old, and she shuffled, stepped, skipped and spun all day long. She was even waltzing during the tea break. I hear people talk about being 'festival fit' or 'up for it' – this lady would put us all to shame. This Tipperary minx can mash it up big style, and Bridget instantly became one of my festival heroes. If this lady can get out and enjoy herself this much, there's absolutely nothing stopping the rest of us. Bridget, you rock!

After the workshop, it was up the road to Moroney's Pub in Lisvernane to see the beast unleashed in its natural habitat. There was a clatter of musicians in the corner and a sheet of ply on the floor, and the dancers took turns in battering it into submission. This was my first *Sean-Nós* dancing session; I popped my cherry that Saturday in Co. Tipperary. I want to be a Dutch Gold-sponsored *Céilí* band drummer, a set-dance caller AND a Sean-Nós dancer when I grow up, doing all of the above with the *joie de vivre* of Bridget. Surely that's not too much to ask for?

I shuff-heeled and left-righted my way out the door, and tapped away on the clutch and accelerator of Wanderly Wagon all the way to the leafy, sunny suburbs of well-to-do south Co. Dublin. Hoards had descended upon Howth to celebrate, of all things, the prawn. Not just any prawn, though: the Dublin Bay Prawn. The difference between this prawn and other prawns is quite simple. When you see the Dublin Bay Prawn on a restaurant menu, it will cost you a few bob more than similar shellfish of unspecified origins. This is understandable when you consider that Dublin Bay Prawns do come from some pretty highfalutin neighbourhoods, and that they're caught in Louis Vuitton nets, Jean Paul Gaultier pots and well-heeled creels.

One prawn peddler at this festival, however, was offering his wares to passers-by for free. If you wanted, you could make a donation to the RNLI lifeboats. You didn't have to, but you'd have to be an awful hungry bastard and super-confident swimmer not to.

The variety of smells was mouth-watering, and attracted clatters of salivating punters to sample the sizzling seafood. You have to read the next part imagining me doing a poor and possibly politically incorrect impression of Bubba from *Forrest Gump*. Anyways, dey wuz lots a different type a prawn dere. Dey wuz barbecue prawns, prawn cocktail, prawn salad, deep-fry prawn, prawn skewers, prawn curry, chilli prawn, prawn bake, baked potato with prawn, brown bread with prawn, crab and prawn mix, plain prawn, breaded prawn, prawn vol-au-vents ... dat ... dat's about it.

If you weren't fond of prawns, there was some ... nope. If you weren't fond of prawns, you were in the wrong place. As I was walking into the main marquee of food stalls, I heard a young American tourist on his phone: 'There's a helluva lot of people and we're all eating prawns. That's pretty much it, dude.' The young yank hit the nail on the head. The focus was fishy food, and we were all getting down at a prawn party.

There was a light-hearted and good-humoured atmosphere on the seafront at Howth, and I heard many locals greeting each other and with an element of surprise, commenting on how well the festival was going. One guy said, in shock, to a stallholder, 'Hey, this is really working, isn't it?!' It wasn't just the locals and nearby Dubs that turned out in force for this event; there were lots of tourists who got the DART in from town. They seemed to be enjoying themselves too, although it took them a while to grapple with the concept of changing their euro into Prawn Punts, the currency used for the festival. Thankfully, the euro and Prawn Punt were on parity all weekend.

Howth is a pretty fancy-pants place, and I have to admit that bedding down in my camper in one of the most expensive neighbourhoods in Ireland gave me a little buzz of satisfaction. I may have been refused funding for a house of my own, but for a little while I enjoyed the same view as the some of those who may actually have been the architects of our economic woes. I even pissed on their hedges. Even after such a classy caper, it was still onwards and upwards: I was heading for Hollywood, baby!

Hollywood, Co. Wicklow, was the setting for a Vintage Rally and Tractor Run. This Hollywood is situated up in the Wicklow Mountains, and a more scenic spot you'd be hard pressed to find. It might not have the glamour and glitz of its Californian namesake, but it makes up for this with a wealth of tractors and sheep. Lots of sheep.

The idea here is that you get as many tractors and vintage cars together as possible, the drivers pay twenty quid for the privilege of spinning around en masse, we get to indulge in some serious tractor-porn, and all the proceeds go to a designated charity – a pretty sweet deal for all involved.

As with many of these festivals, it's not the events or attractions that make the thing interesting and fun, it's the people who are buzzing about that create the atmosphere. The crowd in Hollywood were having a field day. Literally! This was the same 'chape, clane fun' that the Leitrim lads like to indulge in. People out to have a laugh for the afternoon in the fresh air. No airs or graces, no politics, no getting fleeced, no agro, just wellies, tractors, smiles and goodwill. Welcome to Ireland. I'm tempted to bang on about how there was a spell where we seemed to be throwing out and turning our back on lots of things that were important in helping us retain a deep sense of who we are, but I think my time on the road was mellowing me out. I no longer think that Brown Thomas represents many of the things that turned our heads and led us astray. That particular corner shop has its place, and without it and its ilk, maybe I wouldn't appreciate a field in Wicklow full of tractors as much. There's a lot to be said for balance. I'll never be in danger of turning Rural Zen Master, but seeing so many different facets of Ireland was definitely having an effect. If there were ever any danger of turning monk, it was about to be blown out of the water. Summer was just around the corner, and the hedonist factor was about to get cranked up a notch or twelve.

Festivals Attended in April

95. Ballydehob Trad Fest – Ballydehob, Co. Cork
96. Telling Small and Tall Tales – Dublin City
97. One City, One Book – Dublin City
98. Galway Food Festival – Galway City
99. Hot-Air Balloon Fiesta – Trim, Co. Meath
100. *Tír na nÓg* Family Festival – Tralee, Co. Kerry
101. Ballybunion Easter Music Festival – Ballybunion, Co. Kerry
102. Racing Home for Easter – Mallow, Co. Cork
103. Fairyhouse Racing Festival – Fairyhouse, Co. Meath
104. Titanic Festival and Experience – Belfast City
105. Pan Celtic Festival – Carlow, Co. Carlow
106. Titanic 100 – Cobh, Co. Cork
107. *Cruiniú na bhFliúit* – Ballyvourney, Co. Cork
108. Tramore Racing Festival – Tramore, Co. Waterford
109. Latin Film Festival – Dublin City
110. Waterford Festival of Food – Dungarvan, Co. Waterford
111. Five Lamps Festival – Dublin City
112. Punchestown Race Festival – Punchestown, Co. Kildare
113. Waterford New Music Week – Waterford City
114. Cork World Book Fest – Cork City
115. *Fonn Rince* – Aherlow, Co. Tipperary
116. Record Store Day – Cork City
117. Dublin Bay Prawn Festival – Howth, Co. Dublin
118. Carlingford Set-Dancing Festival – Carlingford, Co. Louth
119. Hollywood Tractor Rally – Hollywood, Co. Wicklow
120. Guitar Festival of Ireland – Dublin City
121. Waterford Festival of Architecture – Waterford City

Other Recommended Festivals in April

Phase One Electronic Music and Arts Festival –
Carrick-on-Shannon, Co. Leitrim
Cúirt Literature Festival – Galway City
Tramore Skafest – Tramore, Co. Waterford
Clifden Traditional Music Festival – Clifden, Co.
Galway
The National Leprechaun Hunt – Carlingford, Co.
Louth

10 | *May – Cheoil in the Bucket*

*T*here was a time when I used to look forward to bank holiday weekends, but since starting my festival quest, they were driving me demented. The first weekend in May was manic. There were well over thirty festivals happening around the country in the space of three days. Picking which to attend was a nightmare, giving rise to crippling doses of FOMO (Fear Of Missing Out).

Planning out my trips well in advance is something I've never got a handle on. It was usually the Wednesday before a particular weekend when I decided on my plan of attack, and even then, the plans were always fluid. One thing that I purposely planned in advance was starting my quest in September, allowing me to build some festival fitness before the last section of the adventures hit peak festivalling season in the summer. May bank holiday weekend is the starting pistol for full-on festival mayhem in fields, and with the crack of the starter's shot ringing in my ears, I was out of the blocks and powering towards two big ones.

It never does any harm to have some history and a good backstory to lend a festival some depth and gravitas. Festival of the Fires on the mystical hill of Úisneach has skills when it comes to tall tales and historical significance. The guys in Co. Westmeath sell this shindig as being the oldest festival in Ireland, and it's possible that they're on to something. For thousands of years there were fires lit on this hill to celebrate the festival of *Bealtaine* (May) and the arrival of summer. Liam Ó Maonlaí and Kila, who were lined up to play this gig, were buzzing on the whole Celtic mysticism thing, right up their ley line. The tradition of the place is at the core of the new incarnation of this festival, which is still running as a one-day gig, but hopefully will stretch out to a weekend affair in the future.

The festival is run by the same crew who're involved with Grouse Lodge Recording Studio, a very high-end recording facility that attracts some pretty big names. Michael Jackson shacked up there years ago to get some tracks done. When I gave the lads a shout to quiz them about the festival, Paolo Nutini was squawking away in the studio. The recording industry has been changing quite significantly over the past decade, and not just in the retail sector. Advanced recording technology has become much more affordable, and capable of giving good results. Seth Lakeman recorded a whole album in his kitchen that ended up being nominated for a Mercury Music Prize. Studios with reps like Grouse Lodge will always be guaranteed some business, but in changing times it does no harm to diversify. It was a love for rock 'n' roll, and an appreciation of the history of the spot, that led the lads to put the festival together.

Being on-site in Westmeath felt like a good way to welcome summer; the vibe was as laid-back and as friendly as a stoned Californian beach bum. It was child-friendly, hippy-friendly, Viking-friendly, dog-friendly and horse-friendly. I arrived at the field well-prepared, a case of my favourite brew under my arm. I was tucking into the first of the day, nice and early, when a security guard stopped me. 'Sorry there, you can't bring glass bottles into the gig.' Shit! 'Hide them in your bag there like a good man', said the bouncer as he winked at me. This was a good start, and a breath of fresh air, since most large festivals in fields are pretty tyrannical when it comes to protecting their valuable rights to a monopoly on beer.

At this point in my travels, I was starting to bump into some familiar faces at many of the festivals. There are lots of folks who make festivals their weekend out, and will hit several over the course of the year, so the more reasonable the ticket, the more likely it is that the gig will attract a cohort of seasoned festival freaks. Festival of the Fires ticked the money box. It was nice to feel that you weren't being ripped off, and that you might even be getting a bargain for a change. Forty quid for the day was very decent for what was happening in the field. €4.50 for a can of beer was a bit much, but you could bring your own tinnies. Does anyone ever bring enough?! I've yet to see anyone carrying a slab back to the car after a weekend's festivalling.

There are lots of class festivals in Europe that attract a few Irish punters every year: Roskilde, Sziget, Sonar, Benicassim etc., but Glastonbury has to be the daddy when it comes to days out jumping around in fields. There are a number of significant parallels with Michael Eavis' bash and this do in David Clarke's pastures.

Both shindigs are based on a cattle farm – Eavis even used to include a weekend's supply of milk in the price of his tickets. The historical and mystical significance of both places share a lot of similarities, with ley lines, druids and all that malarkey being part and parcel of both events; one taking *Bealtaine* as its focus, and the other the summer solstice. Most importantly, when you leave both festivals, you don't feel like the sole purpose for its existence is to empty your pockets. Festival of the Fires has one up on the

Somerset spree though: the stone circle in Glastonbury is not ancient or mystical; it was built for the festival, and most of the freaky earth energy stuff is centred around the tor in the nearby the town of Glastonbury, not at the site of the gig itself. On the Hill of Úisneach you're in the middle of all that druidic craic, so it's perfectly positioned to tap into any mystical mainlines that might be running through the place. When they lit the bonfire late on Saturday night and started getting their freak on, it had an air of authenticity about it. Even before the first band struck a chord, I knew that Festival of the Fires was going to be a good one, for it was a great example of:

Irish Festival Rule No. 7: *The quality of a festival can be judged by the ratio of barefoot crusties and free-range dogs to corporate branding and fake tan.*

The great thing about that rule is that it works in two different ways, providing a satisfactory indicator to both Rastafarians and Tallafornians.

On the Sunday morning, after an epic night on the Hill of Úisneach, a little rough around the edges, I made my way to Bellurgan Park in Co. Louth for Vantastival, and a second dose of serious al fresco sessioning. The sun surprisingly decided to shine, which didn't actually help my condition at all. Thank God for sunglasses. Typical! You wait eight months for summer, and when it arrives for an hour or two you squint and groan like a dehydrated Victor Meldrew. I needed a cure.

The first noticeable thing about Vanastival was how happy and friendly everyone was. The atmosphere was almost Disneylike as you walked around the field. I parked up Wanderly Wagon, and, wait for this, camping was in the same field as the stages for the gig. You could go down and park your van beside the main stage if you wanted. I met a crowd from Waterford, and they were parked right beside one of the smaller stages – it was the perfect place for them; they don't sleep much. No lugging your gear around with you for miles when you pack up your troubles on Blue Monday. As the young fella of the Buckleys once said, Hallelujah!

Arriving with your bed and baggage laid out in the van is a wonderful way to festival, and one of its many advantages was brought home at the Helium Festival in Co. Longford. Having stayed up far too late/early the previous night/morning, I was extremely dismayed to be woken by somebody who had filled their boot with a subwoofer, parked nearby and decided it would be a great idea to treat the neighbouring campers to 'Boom Boom Boom' by the Outthere Brothers at the ungodly hour of 11.00 a.m. In normal circumstances this would lead to confrontation and friction, but I simply checked the lie of the land, left down the handbrake, rolled twenty yards down the field to a new neighbourhood, pulled up the handbrake again and went back to sleep with a smile on my face. Returning to tent life has become difficult.

Vantastival seemed to have a more family-orientated vibe to it than Festival of the Fires. I imagine that a lot of families who own campers find this festival ideal, with the mix of room, friendliness and activities organised for the kids. The crowd here wasn't huge, but that isn't a bad thing. There was atmosphere, but there was space too. Kids under 14 were free, under 18 it was €30 for the weekend. Adults were €40 for the day, or €89 for the weekend – pretty much the same price as Festival of the Fires down the road. I stocked up Wanderly Wagon with what I thought would be enough beer for the weekend on Thursday before hitting the road. I was all out by Saturday night; I reckon

I must have spilled some. So I wandered up to get a can; it would be criminal to walk around a festival with my arms swinging. It was only €2.50 for a beer here; it would have been rude not to support them, with them being so considerate and all.

There was plenty going on besides the music. One of the main fringe events on Sunday was the camper cook off. The idea is that you get a crew of cooking campers to circle their wagons, give them all the same ingredients, and get them to compete à la *Ready Steady Cook*. The bonus was that these folk of the road were a bit more competitive than the lads on the telly, and you don't have to keep checking your pockets to make sure that Antony Worrall Thompson isn't picking them.

I'd love to tell you who won, but I don't have a clue. I still wasn't totally together, so I went off to Wanderly Wagon for a disco-nap before the serious shenanigans began that night.

I was working on a theory that was starting to become more concrete the longer I was out in the road: the line-up attracts the crowd to a festival, but it ends up being the crowd that actually makes the thing swing. The shower at Vantastival were über-friendly. I had people coming over, chewing the fat about Wanderly Wagon and about camper-van life in general. We swapped tips, tricks and horror stories. Tanya called around out of curiosity, since she has the female equivalent of Wanderly Wagon. I lent her my fold-up table and she invited me to her place for Irish Coffee. Her van smelled much nicer than mine, and she had a *Winnie the Pooh* kettle. It was obvious that her van was female, while mine would always smell slightly of socks.

I'd been quizzing the people I'd been meeting all weekend about how they cover the costs of their festivalling, with times being tight and all. Most of them hit a couple of festivals every month of the summer, which seemed pretty costly on the surface. The hardened festivallers explained that, instead of going out every weekend, which they can't afford to do, they save up and hit a festival once or twice a month instead, knowing that they're guaranteed something different, and usually getting much better bang for their buck than if they went out in their local venue or nightclub. It made sense. If you give people something special that they can't get every other week, and you give them good value, they'll pencil the festival into their diaries and put away a few bob to get there. It's one of the things that make festivals special, especially when times are tough. People have been really looking forward to whatever event they have their sights on, and have made a real effort to be there, so they are primed for good times.

I enjoyed the field day in Belurgan Park just as much as I'd enjoyed Úisneach, but it was a different vibe. Part of the enjoyment was just getting out for a jump around in a field for a weekend for the first time since taking to the road. It felt like summer was arriving, and, as I'd been building up to this for the last eight months, I may have overdone welcoming its arrival somewhat. But I still had some juice left in the tank, literally and metaphorically. It was a bank holiday weekend, and I had an appointment in the deep south – an appointment to sing with a metal bucket on my head.

Dungarvan, in the west of Co. Waterford, is home to a unique branch of the traditional Irish arts: bucket-singing. Singers place a metal galvanised bucket over their heads, and sing their little hearts out. Once a year the town hosts a competition to find the best bucket-singer in Ireland and the world. The history of this branch of the traditional arts is shrouded in mystery. Stories tell of our auld buddy

Daniel O'Connell encouraging singers in Co. Waterford to use the bucket to sing outlawed songs for him when he was being entertained as he passed through the area for one of his legendary Catholic Emancipation rallies. O'Connell, being well-versed in the law of the land, maintained that you could not be prosecuted for singing outlawed songs in public if you were inside a bucket on your own.

Other stories tell of how the bucket was an integral part of rural life in years gone by. Under the bed for night-time relief, it was then cleaned out in the morning and used for gathering eggs, milk, fetching water, carrying feed and many other essential tasks of the day. It makes sense that the bucket would be close to hand when friends and neighbours called around to the rambling house for songs, dancing and music in the evening. Did the bucket end up on a singer's head to enhance the acoustics, to fight bashfulness or just for a laugh? However it happened, the tradition is alive and well in west Waterford.

Sean Murphy told the crowd assembled in Downey's Pub for the All-Ireland Championship of how the Kellys of Kilgobnet were particularly fine exponents of the art. A relation of theirs ended up in Australia many years ago, and this former west Waterford resident gave birth to a son whom they christened Ned. Ned Kelly would have been exposed to bucket-singing from an early age, as his father Tom was particularly gifted when it came to lilting in a pail. Sean suggested that outlaw Ned Kelly's sense of fashion and self-preservation would have been influenced heavily by his early exposure to the art form. Look up a picture of the infamous outback outlaw, and see for yourself how bucket-singing shaped the story of one of Australia's most legendary characters. Tales and myths abound, but whatever its origin, the bucket is still placed with pride over the heads of singers in Dungarvan every year when their trad festival rolls around.

The competitors vying for the crown (or bucket) this year had flown in from America, Austria, the UK, and even from Carrick-on-Suir. The competition was fierce. The tinny ringing of the bucket suited the style of some singers more than others. The adjudicators took a long time to deliberate after all the performers had rattled the rusty receptacle, and who would have envied them, given the line-up of talent on display in Downey's that bank holiday Monday afternoon.

Eventually, they decided to award the crown/bucket to a man who actually had some Dungarvan blood in him, after his somewhat nasal performance seemed particularly suited to the acoustics of the metal bucket. That man was me. No shit! Not only had I won the All-Ireland Conker Championship, I was now crowned/bucketed the All-Ireland Bucket-Singing Champion. You could not make this stuff up. I was starting to feel pretty confident about the All-Ireland Turnip-Tossing Championships that were coming up in Ballydehob in August.

Mystical tin-whistle players aside, I was starting to freak myself out. It still hadn't sunk in by the time I was being interviewed on RTÉ Radio 1 the next morning. I got some slagging for singing on the national airwaves with a bucket on my head, but fuck it, I was an All-Ireland Champion ... AGAIN!

After the amazing win, I was worried that my head might get a bit too big for my bucket, so I thought that the earthy Dunderry Country Fair would be a perfect way to keep my feet on the ground. No chance of a champagne and cocaine lifestyle there, much more tea and colcannon. I'd been to a clatter of village fairs at this stage, so I thought I knew what to expect at this one. Wrong!

The first thing that was obvious about this gathering in Co. Meath was that it was pulling a huge crowd, a much bigger crowd than you'd expect for the usual farmers' market and bouncy castles that often get passed off as a country fair day. This was a big deal, and it was attracting punters from far and wide.

There was every kind of stall and sideshow in the main traders' field. If you were in the market for power tools, super-strength adhesive, inflatable dinosaurs, tractor DVDs, a unicycle, a stuffed badger, Country and Irish CDs, apple tarts, horse-drawn carts, overalls, beach balls or bales of hay, this was the spot for you. That was only the market field. The whole village and its surrounding pastures were given over to the fair. Would you like to see someone reassemble a tractor engine lickity-split, or the best chainsaw-slingers this side of the Rio Grande, maybe a bonnie baby competition or even some fancy dogs? No matter what your taste or rural pursuit, there was a field for you.

This wasn't the village fête that I was expecting; this thing was massive. As well as three stages of music, there were huge fields of stalls and traders, the GAA pitch was a fairground, dancing, competitions, grub, demonstrations and a bit of livestock thrown in for good measure – all delivered with a tilt of the head, a wink and a bit of country charm.

The common denominator all around Dunderry was old-school, simple pleasures. This fair day had many elements that would have been the exact same at a fair fifty years ago, and they were still as enjoyable on this particular Sunday. Dara Ó Briain once commented that nostalgia is heroin for old people. If that's true, there were a few junkies knocking around Dunderry. I'd spent the wee small hours of a previous night in the busiest club in Dublin, wondering why people were using plastic to pay for pints and getting cashback, making the twenty-five-minute wait at the bar even more excruciating. Dunderry was the tonic I needed. There were no pin numbers needed here. When I bought a plate of colcannon, the only question I was asked was 'Would you like a fried egg on top of that?' (the Dunderry equivalent of the supersize question). There isn't much in life that can't be improved by putting a fried egg on top of it, for instance Simon Cowell's hair.

I was gobsmacked while walking around the fair at how the seemingly ancient, traditional country market vibe seemed perfectly at home today in this little village. There were tinkers hammering designs into tin cups and brass coal scuttles, the squeak of a pedal on spinning wheels, spuds being boiled up on open fires in skillet pots, extremely unhealthy and wholly delicious butter being churned by hand and set-dancing on the streets. Forget about Bunratty Folk Park; the living tradition was right here. It might just be for this one day every year, but it's an enjoyable day, and I can't recommend it highly enough. If you should ever find yourself in Dunderry on fair day, for the love of God try the colcannon ... with a fried egg on top.

As I was leaving Dunderry, the Country and Irish band on the main stage had invited up a guest vocalist who gave a wonderful rendition of 'I'm Going Home to Nobber'. Perfect!

Dunderry was rich in unique Irish character, something that I was finding increasingly appealing as I drove around the country. The activities and buzz all around the village of Dunderry were a universe away from bank bonds, and the only foreign market influence here was the French lad selling crêpes. The nature of the fair harked back to bygone days of blacksmiths and drovers; I couldn't help but wonder if there was something similar that could capture that creative do-it-yourself community spirit, but in a more modern context. It was with this in mind that I hopped on the ferry at Doolin to take the short spin over to the smallest of the Aran Islands: *Inis Oírr*.

I've spent more time on *Inis Oírr* than any of the other Aran Islands; I'm not sure why, but it has a place in my heart. Peaceful evenings spent enjoying the changing light while sitting on the wonderful white sandy beach by the pier might have something to do with it. On a sunny day, the fresh Atlantic waters turn emerald green, and you'd be hard pressed to find a better place in the world to be. It is an idyllic setting for a contemporary arts gathering. Drop Everything was the name given to this series of events, and it promised dynamic talks, installations, screenings, concerts, DJ sets and impromptu pop-up happenings from a restaurant to an acting workshop. I landed smack bang in the middle of the acting workshop.

The exercises and activities at this workshop not only broke the ice for people attending, making sure that people got to know each other very well, but it also got the creative juices flowing. It was a laugh and, more importantly, it kept some of us out of the pub for a while. I only popped in to take some pictures, but I didn't even manage to whip the camera out before Lara and Vicki had me making a tit out of myself too. This was childlike fun, and we laughed a lot.

At one point, I was lying on the ground with my head on a girl's stomach, and another girl was lying on the ground with her head on my stomach, when I got an awful paranoid feeling that maybe this whole thing wasn't actually part of the festival, and I was mistakenly lying with strangers, getting a flashback to accidentally ending up in Mass at *Scoil Cheoil an Earraigh*. I relayed my paranoia to the girls, and they thought that waiting until being in such a compromising position to ask was both odd and hilarious. It was part of the festival, thank God. It was safe to continue lying with strangers, so.

This event was conceived when a couple of visionary young ladies (Mary Nally and Síomha Nee) decided over a few pints that it would be a great idea to have an arts gathering where they could showcase some of the best of contemporary Irish creativity, and also include some artists, musicians and creative heads from Iceland too (the girls have some links going on with the icy place and the arty folk there). A get-together like this costs money, and usually this is made back by punters paying for tickets. Not in the heads of these girls. They launched a campaign on fundit.ie, and managed to raise the twelve grand needed to just about cover the costs of all the events. With that done, it was then free to attend all events. No tickets, no credit card booking lines and no corporate sponsors. You dig? The community spirit was fostered even before anyone set foot on *Inis Oírr*. The people who funded this festival made sure it happened, and then they attended. The girls and their friends, families and anyone they could rope in were working on this gig, and the people attending were the sponsors. Not only did the girls build a communal arts event from scratch, they picked the perfect place to hold it. Here it was, that same do-it-yourself spirit from the village fair, in a modern context; fostering an online community to fund and populate a new breed of event. I was into this.

One of the events that summed up the spirit of the whole thing for me was the pop-up restaurant. The organisers have some mates who are pretty handy when it comes to banging together some wholesome and scrumptious scran. A café on the island was commandeered, and the food elves began to work their magic. That evening, we were invited to eat the results. It was gorgeous. Chickpea and chorizo stew, home-made tortillas, wood-smoked baked potatoes, a cornucopia of varieties of humus, and some of the best flatbread since the night Jesus offered his body up as a fresh living loaf. Some of the ingredients were even foraged from around the island. How much for a plate at this feast? There was a jar on the table, and you could make a donation if the mood took you. It was that kind of gig.

Inis Oírr is the only Aran Island that has its own arts centre and theatre: *Áras Éanna*. This was the hub for some of the bigger gigs and exhibitions, but the whole island was being used. You didn't have to buy tickets, but you did need to pre-book in order to ensure entry into the events (if you didn't pre-book, I have a Ronnie Whelan that you might have got in if you hung around, pouted and batted your peep-lids). When a captivating gig from Icelandic singer Sóley was finished in the theatre, it was outside for live video mapping and a light show projected onto the walls of *Áras Éanna*. This added nicely to the vibe of the whole night, and put a spring in our step as we skipped carefully through the dark country lanes, down to the *Óstan*, where Don Williams was spinning out a DJ set to keep the party splendidly swinging on the small island. The fun and games continued into the wee small hours of the morning and, if I'm not very much mistaken, for the first time since I began the festival quest, I saw the sunrise on my way to the cot; a combination of staying up quite late and the sun beginning to rise earlier now that summer had arrived. Waiting until I was on *Inis Oírr* to catch my first sunrise on the road seemed fitting, and a stupid grin spread across my face as the first light shone red over the distant mainland.

The fun and games at Drop Everything were continuing through Sunday, but my festival quest was taking me back to Co. Clare to visit a town that was having three festivals in one day. It broke my heart to leave *Inis Oírr* on what was easily the most summery day since my travels had begun; not having my togs with me made it just a little easier.

The main street of Ennistymon was taken over with horses, ponies, donkeys, traders and trailers. The small town in the west of Ireland took on the guise of a wild west watering hole with bareback riders and bucking broncos replacing the usual Sunday traffic. There was a horse fair on the hoof. Being in the town had the feeling of travelling back in time. The sights, smells and sounds on the streets felt like stepping back to fair days of old, but without the romanticism of the black-and-white photographs you often see on the walls of pubs. There was a lot of shite around the place that added a certain unexpected colour to proceedings. But it was horse shite, which for some reason is more acceptable than the canine variety. Cow shite, and strangely elephant shite, aren't that offensive either. This is a phenomenon that I may need to look into in the future – there could be a thesis in it.

The livestock on show was interesting enough, but the heads and characters holding the reins were priceless. There are few clients cagier than a well-seasoned horse trader. Throw a few canny Travellers, some shrewd country folk and a gallery of gawpers into the mix, and you had a wholly enjoyable show that needs to be seen, smelled and heard to be experienced properly. People-watching par excellence!

The horse fair was not the only show in town. In different units and shops dotted around the place, booksellers had set up stalls and were dealing out the literature just behind where other traders were hawking horses. A book fair, a horse fair and a Dylan Thomas festival made for an interesting combination, and, although some might think it better to spread out these festivals over different days, having the three events happening simultaneously gave the town a real shot of vibrancy and an eclectic mix of punters.

These events converging meant that you got people with an interest in one area experiencing something that they might never have considered sticking their nose in before. It was certainly the first time I'd strolled from a festival of ponies to a party of publications in fewer than five steps. The book fair featured a few pop-up shops. The pop-up phenomenon was becoming increasingly common: using empty premises as venues for festival events, adding some energy and creativity to thoroughfares and giving the streetscapes a facelift – a sign of the times.

The third shindig that I rambled along to was celebrating the life and work of Welsh poet Dylan Thomas. Why Dylan Thomas in the Co. Clare town? Thomas' wife was from the Ennistymon, and her auld fella (Francis MacNamara) was also a poet. Frankie opened the Falls Hotel in the town, having converted Ennistymon House to provide accommodation for visitors to the health-enhancing spas in the locality. I wonder what the auld fella would make of the hot-stone massages on offer in the hotel these days?

The link with the hotel in Ennistymon is something that the management of the gaff is obviously trying to cash in on. When you walk into the joint, the first thing to catch your eye is the Dylan Thomas Bar. The festival was based mostly in the hotel, with readings, lectures and a documentary screening all happening on-site. On Sunday there was a walk around the town hitting hotspots that have a Dylan Thomas connection. It would seem that this Co. Clare town is the best place in Ireland for a dose of the DTs. That was a stroke of luck.

It's not often you get three festivals in one place in one day. I was in my element, even if the Welsh poetry offerings seemed more than a little drab compared to the colour of the horse fair out on the streets. Meeting my festival targets in one day in one town meant that I had some wriggle room going into the next weekend, which I knew would be sorely needed. For the first time since beginning my festival quest, I'd be playing at one of the festivals that I was attending. (Singing in a bucket doesn't really count.)

The Life Festival in Westmeath was the event, and knowing what I, and the rest of the lads in our band, am capable of, I knew I'd be working at reduced capacity once I got out the other side of the post-gig gluttony.

I began the Life Festival in the same way as I began many festivals: by sitting on the stoop of Wanderly Wagon and supping on a beer. The difference here was the shorts, sandals and sunglasses were out. If you'd put out a whole terracotta army of children of Prague and whipped the heads off the lot of them, you would not have been blessed with better weather than the shiny, sparkly day in which Life Festival was basking. It was one of those days that Irish travel agents hate. Driving through the greenery of the countryside on the way to Westmeath, the lustrous hedgerows were bursting with life, and by the time we arrived at the grounds of Belvedere House, the theme from *Grizzly Adams* was on a playback loop in my head. I was on an at-one-with-nature buzz.

Belvedere House in Westmeath was the setting for this AGM of hardcore hedonists. Many of the people who manage and work on this gig also work on Sonar in Spain, and you could see the T-shirts and tans to prove it. A good deal of the crew were Spanish, and, while trying to make our way backstage in Wanderly Wagon, there was more than a little bit of a *Fawlty Towers* banter going on. At each barrier I was asked if I had equipment in Wanderly Wagon that couldn't be carried to the main stage from the car park. I insisted that I had. There was no way I could have carried that fridge as full as it was.

This was the sixth Life Festival, and it is touted as being the best electronic music festival in the country. Not knowing anyone on the bill is more a sign of me being old than it is a commentary on the line-up. Jamie Jones came pretty highly recommended, and he had the place heaving when he was banging out the tunes. The whispers around the pastures were that the festival had scaled down somewhat this year, and the headliners had taken a bit of a hit too. Jaysus, they had King Kong Company on the bill for feck's sake. Talk about dropping their standards.

At ten o'clock, we took to the stage, and let's just say that I'm glad I had spare underpants in Wanderly Wagon. I was planking it! We had played our first gig in ten years the previous February. The last time we'd played at something like this was in 1999 at the Homelands Festival. After a break of a decade we were back, actually sounding better than we ever did, but maybe not cutting as fine a figure (personally speaking of course). Two of the lads spearheaded getting the band back together in a turn of events that I like to refer to as Midlife Crisis: The Musical. They're not the sports-car type. Having spent the last nine months attending festivals, this was a real buzz. We got a decent crowd up at the main stage, and they even danced. Not only that, the feckers clapped and cheered too. There weren't too many mistakes, and by the time we got to the second last tune we were rocking and actually enjoying ourselves. We were delighted to leave the stage to chants of 'One more tune!'. Obviously, we'd brought some friends and family along.

With all the playing out of the way, it was time to get stuck into some serious *après-gig*, and it seems that we were in the right place to do it. There were three large stages lashing out electro beats and bass. The dubstep was pulling a big crowd, and if you needed something a bit rootsier, there was some dancehall and dub available closer to the lake. The crowd was a friendly bunch, and not half as rough as I'd expected at a gig that appealed mainly to clubbers. There were a few heads that wouldn't look out of place behind the wheel of a stolen Subaru Impreza, but mainly it was a crew of loved-up, hedonist, post-hippies out to get their groove on. This was a crowd that knew how to get immaculately wasted. Ace Ventura had the Neutronix folk heaving, the place was looking like an acid casualty's retina under UV lights, and the trippiness was catching. Jamie Jones was the main draw of the night, and probably of the weekend, and he pulled the biggest crowd. Top DJ in the world? He's no Larry Gogan, but he's all right.

In search of some respite from the beats, we managed to find a pasture full of nettles, which wasn't ideal, but did lead to the discovery that cool Fanta not only makes a wonderful mixer for vodka, it can also provide temporary relief from stings when it's too dark to find dock leaves. Very late in the night/early in the morning we visited some of the lads in their tent to make sure that they couldn't go to sleep; that's what friends are for. While about seven of us were in the tent, a stranger arrived in with a smiley head on him and sat down amongst us. After a couple of minutes, he asked us, 'Are youse my friends?' Now we didn't know the lad, but that didn't mean we couldn't be friends. When we expressed this, he got more confused and asked, 'Do I know yis?' Nah, but don't go, you're great craic. He was Rob, and he was awfully funny. He had been working at the festival as Artist Management, but was relieved of his post when he took his role a little too far and started socialising with the acts too. We liked Rob, and that he took his job that seriously. He had a great work ethic, and is a wonderful role model to young people everywhere.

We partied long and hard; it would have been a breach of contract not to. For the second time in as many weeks, I saw the sunrise and heard the dawn chorus strike up. Somebody had thoughtfully hung a large net-swing chair with a cushion from the branch of a huge tree at a secluded end of the site. Just before I made my way back to Wanderly Wagon, I swung back and forth in the chair listening to the birds singing and enjoying the arrival of the warmth of the day. If the rest of the summer continued to be anywhere close to how it had begun, it was promising be the best one yet. Just in case we hadn't laughed enough, on the way to bed, one of the lads and I passed three dodgy-looking young fellas strutting through the field. 'How'ye, lads?' says us. Nothing from the boys. When they were about fifty yards up the field, they shouted back at us, 'Pigs!' They thought we were undercover cops. This was funny enough considering the company I was in and the state of the two of us. It was funnier still when their shout attracted the ire and attention of a real garda, who thought that they were shouting at him. You can't beat going to sleep with a smile on your mush.

Festivals Attended in May

122. Festival of the Fires – Hill of Úisneach, Co. Westmeath
123. Vantastival – Bellurgan Park, Co. Louth
124. Camden Crawl – Dublin City
125. Dunderry Country Fair – Dunderry, Co. Meath
126. Waterford Festival of Light Opera – Waterford City
127. Bucket-Singing Championships – Dungarvan, Co. Waterford
128. Burren Slow Food Festival – Lisdoonvarna, Co. Clare
129. Drop Everything – *Inis Oírr*, Co. Galway
130. Dylan Thomas Festival – Ennistymon, Co. Clare
131. Ennistymon Book Fair – Ennistymon, Co. Clare
132. Ennistymon Horse Fair – Ennistymon, Co. Clare
133. Life Festival – Mullingar, Co. Westmeath
134. Dublin City Soul Festival – Dublin City

Other Recommended Festivals in May

Cup of Tae Festival – Ardara, Co. Donegal
Kilkenny Rhythm and Roots – Kilkenny, Co. Kilkenny
Bray Jazz Festival – Bray, Co. Wicklow
Festival of Fools – Belfast City
Fastnet Short Film Festival – Schull, Co. Cork

11 | *June – Buckfast 'n' Blues*

*H*aving just about recovered from the FOMO and travails of the May bank holiday weekend, it felt like the June edition had arrived a couple of weeks early. Completing multiple laps of the country must have had some time-zone implications that I wasn't grasping fully. The line-up of festivals for June's contribution to my bank holiday angst was just as intense. I set myself the challenge of getting to six festivals from Thursday to Monday. Somehow, I managed to get to seven – it's a much luckier number.

Thursday night was the opening of Cat Laughs in Kilkenny, a festival that I've been to many times. That cliché of laughter being the best medicine has a lot of truth in it, and as far as value for money and a good night out is concerned, a couple of hours watching top international comedians and pissing yourself (metaphorically) is hard to beat. As I was finding at other festivals, there was a high demand for tickets in Kilkenny even though money was tight. Once again, people were willing to stay in and brave a couple of Saturday nights with Brendan O'Connor for the promise of a pay-off down the line. It's quite a responsibility for festival organisers to bear, knowing that audiences make real sacrifices to take a punt on what they're offering, and that their festival and the experience it offers might be the thing that sustains some of their audience through some pretty bleak times. Thankfully, the majority of festival facilitators are very conscious of this, and no matter what the weather brings, the crew in Kilkenny have become masters at brightening June bank holiday weekends.

You have to get in a couple of weeks early to catch tickets for some of the best shows at Cat Laughs; they sell out pretty quickly. The surprising thing is that it's often the Irish comedians who sell out first, even though there are a string of incredibly talented international acts brought in for the weekend. Initially, I put it down to audiences being somewhat unadventurous and sticking with what they know and love, but I was delighted to discover it goes deeper than that. Ireland has such a talented pool of gifted comics that when they're lined up with the best in the world, they not only hold their own, they blaze a trail. From the gallery of international comedians I've seen at comedy festivals, arts festivals, theatre festivals and in comedy tents at rock 'n' roll circuses, David O'Doherty, Dara Ó Briain, Tommy Tiernan and Dylan Moran are the Jedi Masters.

Ó Briain can make audiences laugh without being nasty and without cursing; that's not easy. While listening to him onstage it feels like he's encouraging you to think about things and see them in a different light rather than going for cheap laughs, though he can pull those out too when required. He's a very clever, very funny man. Dylan Moran deals out existentialism, with generous dashes of surreal, bumbling genius, while David O'Doherty encourages audiences to gaze upon the world with the curious wonder of a 6-year-old (a particularly advanced and dirty-minded 6-year-old, mind you). Forget about Daft Punk's 'Get Lucky'; O'Doherty's 'I Know a Man Who Had a Wank on a Bike' was my feel-good hit of the summer. Tommy Tiernan burns up stages when he's on fire, relentlessly lashing the crowd with twisted scenarios that tap into the darkest recesses of our cultural and rural psyches. Tiernan is a dark prince of Irish comedy, and his fiendish glee in revealing deep truths hidden in Big Tom lyrics is surpassed only by the enthusiasm with which he can coax crowds to take up the Monaghan Cowboy's mantras. Tommy Tiernan is the anti-Gay Byrne. Hallelujah.

Thoroughly satisfied with my visit to Cat Laughs, I set the co-ordinates in Wanderly Wagon for west Kerry. Several pit stops are usually required on a spin like that, diesel and Meanies are the fuels needed, but I decided on an extra special treat in Killarney, stopping off to pay a visit to the wonderful olde worlde oasis that is Miss Courtney's Tea Rooms, for a cup of Earl Grey and a scone. In an unexpected twist of the tea leaves, I ended up at a biker rally with Sandra, the proprietor of the teahouse; she must be spiking the Darjeeling. I had visions of spending a quiet, spiritually nourishing moment, nestling the cup and scoffing the scone in genteel surroundings with doilies and silver cutlery – not quite how it turned out. Things got even odder when I met a crowd of Christian bikers who were over from the USA especially for Killarney Bike Fest. Riding through Ireland for Jesus – Born to be Mild!

Chatting to born-again bikers at Killarney Bike Fest was just an entrée for what was revving up later that evening. I found myself walking through Cahersiveen many hours later, rigged out in cowboy couture for the Wild West Ireland Festival. Walking down the main drag in Cahersiveen with spurs clinking, I couldn't help but feel that if I'd lived in the town and had spotted a tricked-out Tennessee tool traipsing along the main street like a reject from *Blazing Saddles*, I would have beaten the shit out of myself. The sad thing was that I actually had all the required gear sitting at home in the wardrobe (don't ask). Cahersiveen was transformed into a dodgy Dodge for the weekend. Thankfully, I wasn't the only tool who had Eastwooded up for the occasion. There was a clatter of cowboys and cowgirls down in the main square, and in the middle of them was weather girl Evelyn Cusack, who told us what to expect on the climate front for the weekend, right before she shot the pistol that got the party started. Yeehaw, as they say in west Kerry.

This excuse for a whole town to dress up like extras from *Oklahoma!* may seem a little strange, but seeing the smiles on faces and hearing the laughter of the good townsfolk suggested that it was an ingenious way for a community to have some old-fashioned fun. Only people who are dead inside don't enjoy playing dress-up. Between shootouts, I eventually cornered one of the organisers of the festival, a dodgy-looking character with a squint, who went by the name 'The Kid'. When I asked The Kid why they decided to have a Cowboy Festival, he replied, 'Well, tarnation, why the hell not!' punctuated by a spit that pinged as it hit the side of the spittoon. I wasn't brave enough to question the gunslinger any further.

The streets were lively that evening for the launch, and for the numerous shoot-outs that followed, but after sundown the good townsfolk were thin on the ground. A few headed to the local saloons, but most struck out home for the High Chaparral. Tumbleweed did not exactly roll along the streets later that night, but it certainly wasn't as lively or as entertaining as Glitter Gulch during the Gold Rush. Some pub-to-pub research was called for. Sauntering up to a counter in a pub that's full of auld fellas, who were oblivious to the festival, and who ended up looking at you like you had chickens dancing on your head, whilst in wild west garb, has a unique way of making you feel like a tit. As unsettling as the stares of quizzical disapproval were, the streets of Cahersiveen had a cinematic uneasiness to them that was even more disturbing.

Small speakers had been installed outside businesses all along the main drag of the town, the idea being that suitable cowboy music could be piped throughout the town to help with the atmosphere for the large-scale dress-up. The mood music became particularly effective as I strolled home along the lonely streets to my wagon just after closing time. The streets were deserted, the chink of my spurs echoing into the night and melding with the haunting sound of Ennio Morricone's 'Man with a Harmonica'. This was freaking me out a little bit. My left eye started to squint, and the trigger finger on my right hand started to twitch. It felt like Lee Van Cleef was going to step around a corner at any second with a primed Colt peacemaker in his paw.

The next morning I was still a bit jumpy, so I decided to get the hell out of Dodge, with a quick stop-off at Listowel Writers' Week before hitting the trail proper. Listowel has written the book when it comes to literary festivals: the annual get-together in Kerry is a highlight on the calendar of writers, readers, binders, publishers and discerning punters. It's been running for over forty years now, and the impressive national and international names that are attracted by the homely atmosphere of the small town event suggests that it is set to remain at the top of the class for years to come. When you arrive in Listowel, John B. Keane's statue has his hat off and waves a large hello, setting the atmosphere perfectly for the vibe of the festival. Festival regular Julian Gough was on hand to deliver a wonderfully entertaining and thought-provoking reading. Although comedians get us laughing at ourselves, authors who share their work and thoughts at the catalogue of literary festivals around the country tend to delve a little deeper and more widely. While on my travels I'd been lucky enough to hear Seamus Heaney, John Banville, Anne Enright, Paul Theroux, Roddy Doyle, Tim Severin and a catalogue of others read from their work. Between writers' festivals and book fairs, Wanderly Wagon's library was taking up more space than the wine cellar.

With a mixture of deep thought and high jinx to ponder, I began a very long spin from one end of the country to the other. I'd been threatening to hit the Rory Gallagher Weekend in Ballyshannon for years, but never quite managed to get there. It made sense this would be my year. This session is legendary, and as I rolled into town, there was an array of animated lunatics kicking up dust and ripping into it big style. In Cahersiveen they were dressing like cowboys; in Ballyshannon they were taking this shit seriously and walking the walk. This was the wild north-west.

It would have been easy to get distracted by the lunacy out on the streets, but the main attraction here for most of the huge crowds was the music. The racket being lashed out was blues rock, particularly the brand of that stomping electric-guitar-driven sound made popular by Rory Gallagher, a blues legend who was born in the Co. Donegal town. I'd been at a festival or two at this stage, but up to this point I'd never met as many foreigners who'd travelled to Ireland specifically to attend a festival. Hungary, Holland, Germany and Norway were just some of the crews I got talking to. The gang from Norway has been coming to Ballyshannon every year for this gig since 2004. They are fanatical about Rory, but it's the buzz in Ballyshannon that keeps them coming back. I don't know why I was surprised that the continental blues crew would travel to Ireland for a festival like this; Rory was always much more popular in mainland Europe than he was at home in Ireland. The French were well ahead of us in recognising his contribution to music, naming a street in Paris after him before the statue and square were dedicated to him in Cork, and even before the statue went up here in Ballyshannon.

This was the eleventh year of the festival, and for the first time a festival marquee was introduced, requiring punters to buy a ticket to gain entry, rather than the free gigs all around the town that had been the norm for the previous decade. I asked some of the Gallagher faithful what they thought about having to shell out €50 for a weekend pass for the gigs. They were as many different answers as there were head-a-balls in the town. One girl who's been coming for years said that she thought it was great, because when the big-name bands were in pubs in previous years, you often couldn't get in to see them or, when you could, the place was too packed. She liked the environment, and that the sound was spot on. You could see, hear, dance, drink, and the tent made the whole shindig showerproof. She was happy.

I met a guy from Tyrone who was indifferent; he saw the pros and cons. He didn't have the fifty quid to shell out for the ticket, but he knew that all the bands that played in the tent during the night would eventually play on one of the gig-rigs out on the streets of the town. His missus was much more caustic in her criticism of the move. She felt that it was becoming less about having a good time to the tunes and more about making a few bob. She had a point. Cans of beer (Tennent's?) at the tent were a fiver – Vantastival was still winning that rating system with their cans for €2.50. One of the ways the tent did work was that it gave the people who were there primarily for the music a chance to enjoy it without tripping over the lunacy that was afoot on the wild streets of Ballyshannon. This festival attracted just as many maniacs as it did musos.

Inside the tent, the crowd was giving the bands a great reception and going ape when they banged out of one of Rory's well-known tracks. Singing along and shaking their manes (most of them greying) was the most common method of appreciation. There were as many air guitars being whipped around in the tent as there were leather jackets on backs. The crowd was predominantly middle- to autumn-aged, denim-clad and long-haired, but they showed a youthful exuberance for the tunes that belied their years. Laundromat from Holland had the place rocking and the crowd loved them, giving a rapturous reception to every Gallagher song they lashed out. Johnny Gallagher was next, and he mixed up the set, playing a good selection of his own tunes as well as some of Rory's. Johnny and the lads are locals, and they got a suitable hometown welcome when they took to the stage, but it was well-deserved. Johnny pulled off a sound and mood that suited his grizzly black beard perfectly. When the lads eventually pulled 'Out on the Western Plains' out of the bag, the place went nuts.

Back out on the streets, there was more Buckfast being skulled here than I'd seen at any other festival. If you could buy shares in that shit around festival time, I'd be flogging everything I own to get a few bob together to invest in Cabernet de Crusty. The younger folk out on the roads were out of their bins and having a rare auld time of it. One of the young lads told me that he had no interest in going in to the tent; they were all far too old in there, and the craic was much better outside. He had a point. There was a bit of messiness, a few scuffles and one proper punch-up, where a lad ran the length of the very steep main street to hop on top of another fella and start pummelling the head off him. They were shouting something about a girl and inappropriate texting. I picked up an iPhone that flew through the air, and gave it back to the dude who owned it. After the scrap he may have needed to send lewd texts to someone's girlfriend later that night.

It was messy and it was wild, but it was awfully real, and, as such, enjoyable for its raucous honesty. If it all got too much, you could duck inside one of the pubs or just head back to the tent were the rockers seemed sheepish by comparison. The debauchery evident out in the open air wasn't really that surprising when you took into account the number of monkish wreck-the-hoose-juice bottles being swigged from. Buckfast is a high-octane and ferocious festival fuel.

I've always had a *grá* for Rory Gallagher's music. There are a few second-hand vinyl albums that get pulled out every now and again when the mood takes me, so it was great to finally get to Ballyshannon for this gig. The lunacy was just as enjoyable as the music; the crowd in Donegal do wild really well. If you're not into blues and rock, or going a bit doolally out on the street isn't your thing, you should probably stay away from Ballyshannon at Whit weekend. If you like kicking good times, throwing on a plaid shirt, a faded pair of jeans, shaking your head and going a bit wild, get thee to Donegal.

Whilst in the neighbourhood, I popped over for another quick visit to Ardara, the place that boasts that it is 'The Home of Festivals' on the sign that welcomes people to town. Their Melting Pot Festival sets out to promote diversity and multiculturalism in their community. Smack bang at the heart of the organising committee of this laudable event was my festival hero, drag artist and dairy farmer Martin McGuinness. Grub, exhibitions, a small parade, a brass band and a samba group were all in full effect when I arrived on Sunday. Only down the road from Ballyshannon, but a million miles away, Ardara had a really nice community vibe going on with this not-for-profit event. They also had The Bambir playing in one of the local pubs, a deadly band that I'd caught at a few festivals along the way. These Armenian boys know how to rock a party.

Where the Rory Gallagher Festival provided a beast of a bash, there was some beauty to be found in Dublin at Forbidden Fruit in the grounds of the Royal Hospital, Kilmainham. It was my next appointment. I was bewildered walking around the gig. In the name of all that's holy, where did all the beautiful people who populated this festival come from? After the beery brawlers of Ballyshannon, this was like stepping into a living musical edition of *Vogue*. It was outrageous! Even the fellas were gorgeous. Whoever programs this festival put together an uncommonly cool line-up that attracted hipsters with the most carefully messy hair and subcutaneous skinny jeans you have ever seen.

Interestingly, this festival was blazing a trail in the trend of offering a three-day festival that doesn't provide camping, herding the hipsters home after the last chord is struck. This model isn't as immersive, and doesn't create that same feeling of belonging to a temporary community, but it cuts costs significantly. The amount of security required, on-site services and twenty-four-hour monitoring of the animals is eliminated immediately. When the purse strings are a bit tighter, festivals like this keep the margins high for the companies promoting them. POD promotions are behind this one – the same people who brought us Electric Picnic. Longitude is a similar non-camping offering that has popped up recently in Marlay Park, this version shaped by MCD promotions. The interesting thing is that both Irish promotion companies have ties with Festival Republic, a UK-based company that was behind Glastonbury for many years. Festival Republic bought into Electric Picnic, POD's flagship festival, in 2009, after Electric Picnic had made some serious financial losses (in the region of €1.5m). MCD has a stake in Gaiety Investments, a company that co-owns Festival Republic. We're stratospheres away from the community vibe of Ardara here, and smack bang in the world of big business. Times may be tough, but all these corporations still feel that there's money to be made by facilitating good times in green spaces.

It's worth noting that Festival Republic was founded by Vince Power from Kilmacthomas in Co. Waterford in 2006, shortly after he and his business partners sold their stake in the Mean Fiddler promotion company for £38m. He started building the Mean Fiddler empire in London at the height of the economic recession of the 1980s. One of eleven children, he grew up in conditions that make *Angela's Ashes* look like *The Brady Bunch* (four of his siblings died as children, including his own twin). He left school at fifteen, and went to live with his aunt in England, working through several jobs in London until eventually opening his first club in 1982. Although he's no longer at the helm of Festival Republic, his former business partner Melvin Benn is, and these dudes have been cited as being responsible for pulling Glastonbury from the brink of going bust. Festival Republic now has a VERY large say in what happens on the Irish festival landscape. The sums of money involved in the world of the full-scale rock 'n' roll circus is mind-blowing, but even in times of recession, it seems people can scrape up a few bob to cut loose at a festival; these dudes are banking on it.

High finance aside, Forbidden Fruit was an enjoyable day out that was definitely enhanced by some amazing weather and the vibe that the sun brought with it. From talking to people who were there for the full three days, the previous day's gigs were enjoyable too, but lashing rain made it tough on the first two nights. It was definitely a step up from the one-day gig that kicked this festival off in its first year, and whoever was programming this thing did a great job, putting together a wholly hip line-up. I get nervous thinking about the amount of money involved in a gig like this, and the fact that it can all go tits up if the weather is bad. A roulette wheel would be a safer bet than an Irish summer, but these festival organisers still put their money down.

Wonderfully oblivious to the world of festival finance, I inadvertently invented a new cocktail for the occasion whilst decanting Buckfast into smaller plastic bottles to sneak into the gig. It seemed apt to be smuggling tonic wine into an event called Forbidden Fruit. One bottle was only half full, so, rather than wasting the space, I topped it up with ginger beer. It tasted amazing, so then I had to sneak in some extra ginger beer too. I christened the concoction 'The Foxy Monk'. Even after polishing off all the newly invented commotion lotion, I made it to the post-gig bash in the Button Factory. Le Galaxie were playing, and I'd love to tell you what they were like, but I have about as much of a notion of that as it seems Mick Wallace has chance of becoming *Ceann Comhairle* of *Dáil Éireann*. Just to underline my inability to provide any critique of anything after 10.00 p.m., the next day I was unkindly reminded of a disastrous Jägermeister Yiddish-type salute I tried to make in the early hours of the morning. 'Molotov!' shouts the eejit full of wreck-the-hoose juice. I think I meant to say mazel tov, but it is possible that they're interchangeable on the Gaza Strip.

I'd be lying to you if I tried to pretend that I was taking all these festivals in my stride – they were taking their toll.

I was doing some cycling and training occasionally to try and keep things on an even keel, but Easter had been tough, and it burnt me out a little. I also had a feeling that the chickenpox in December was a result of being run down. Over the June bank holiday weekend I'd cranked things up a couple of notches. I'd burned the candle at both ends, and took a blowtorch to the middle of it. I was delighted to find that the following weekend there were a few festivals that wouldn't require me to throw myself once more into the wild ravages of wanton debauchery. It was high time to pull myself up out of the gutter, dust myself off and raise my brow from below my toes to a middle or even upper position, and stay away from the wild sessions, just for a little bit. I was in danger of pulling a beer muscle.

At *Éigse* Arts Festival in Carlow, they'd erected a replica 1890s Wyoming barn built inside the Visual Centre for Contemporary Art. Not only was this a replica barn and performance space, its was also a roller skating rink. Perfect! Think *Back to the Future III* crossed with *Xanadu* and you're there. *Everything Can Be Done In Principle* was the title of an installation that invited the viewer to become an active part of the exhibit by skating round the barn and re-enacting a story from over 100 years ago from the frontiers of Wyoming. In the 1890s, such a structure of wood and cloth was actually built in Wyoming, and artist Brian Duggan wanted people to dress appropriately and skate round it, not only to populate the exhibit, but to also to get a sense of what it might have felt like.

This story might ring a bell with some of you. It was at the centre of Michael Cimino's 1980 film *Heaven's Gate*. The attention to detail in rebuilding the barn from the film was impressive. The stove and pipes immediately grab your attention, but it is the light in the place that really lent it an antique atmosphere. It was like being in a sepia photograph. The film created, and still creates, mixed emotions among cinema folk. Critically acclaimed retrospectively, mostly in Europe, for its artistic vision and commitment to a creative ideal, it was seen in Hollywood as the biggest commercial flop of all time, and it can still cause lively debate in some circles. As a primary school student, I had a teacher who used to rave about it, and he showed it to us in class. I think it may have been lost on us rowdy young fellas, but it made an impression, and getting a chance to skate around inside a film that I've known from childhood was initially an eerie experience.

It ended up being thoroughly enjoyable, even if I did have all the grace and poise of a pissed-up bullock on ice. Added to the pleasure of the experience was the fact that, for the second time in as many weeks, I got to dress up like a cowboy, with boot-skates instead of spurs on this occasion. I love festivals.

Next up on my weekend of high culture was the inaugural History Festival at Lisnavagh House, also in Co. Carlow. Yes, a history festival. The first thing to strike me about this shindig was the setting. It was pastoral and stunning in the stolen afternoon sunshine. A country manor with manicured lawns, lush gardens, mature, wooded surroundings, populated by ladies in floral summer dresses and dudes in trilbys and fedoras – this was plush. I wasn't sure what to expect, history not really being my bag. The most I can really tell you about history is that it has its own channel. It turns out, though, that there is a whole host of people for whom history is exactly their bag – they love a bit of it! This was like an Electric Picnic for anoraks … in a good way. Many of the talks and events were sold out. There were people sitting outside opened windows of the packed library of the main house so they could listen to some of the talks; there were no seats left inside.

There was also a marquee on the site for fringe talks and events, a pop-up bookshop, a bar, a tea tent and a stall selling pie and mash. This was a proper festival rig. Everything the discerning history buff needed for an afternoon out was here, including a quality line-up of speakers and events. Just strolling through the grounds I spotted Senator David Norris, Diarmaid Ferriter, Kevin Myers, Manchán Magan and Ruth Dudley-Edwards. The glitterati of the historical literati had turned out for the day.

Satirist and musician Paddy Cullivan chaired an event entitled 'Virtuous Villains – Five People who put the Hiss into History'. There were five speakers, who each put forward a description of a villain of their choosing from the annals, and the audience gave the historical bastards the thumbs up or down in true Roman style. Micheál Ó Siochrú gave a well-delivered, blistering and scathing account of our old buddy Ollie Cromwell. You'd think he'd be preaching to the converted with this one, but there were a couple of thumbs up for Ollie in the crowd. When the discussion was opened to the floor, there was heated exchange around the warted warrior and the accuracy of Micheál's assertions by a particularly trenchant supporter of Mr Cromwell.

I've struggled to find a delicate way of describing this Cromwellophile without being too jingoistic – let's just say that he'd be more partial to a crumpet than a crubeen. *Dtuigeann tú?* I was shocked with how much I enjoyed this talk, and hugely impressed by the bit of agro at the end of it. It was heartening to be amongst people who were passionate enough about something to actually get het up and argue about it. A little bit more of that on the festival trail would be awfully welcome, not as much of it as witnessed in Ballyshannon though.

Not content with culturing myself up a bit, I reckoned that I need some more physical stimulation. The PLAY Tag Rugby Festival was kicking off in Carlow, and I somehow managed to insinuate myself onto a team that was taking part in a fundraising game. I know as much about tag rugby as George Hook knows about skateboarding, and, coincidentally, either of us trying these respective activities would look equally ridiculous. You'd think that would have stopped me.

I arrived to find myself togging off with South African Rugby International and Leinster player Heinke van der Merwe on one side and New Zealander and TV pundit Brent Pope on the other side. No pressure so. Thankfully, tag rugby is a non-contact sport, where you have two Velcro strips on either side of your shorts to which a coloured strip of cloth is attached. If an opposing player rips the tag from you while you have the ball, you must stop and roll the ball back between your legs to a scrum-half, and then play resumes. It is like rugby, but without the crunching tackles, which was a comfort when you saw Heinke running at you. The teams are mixed, and I got some tips from Twitter telling me that on the tag field, women are your friends more than anywhere else in life; seemingly girls get more points for a try, so they are encouraged to score more often at these events. This sounded promising.

Playing the match was a whole load of fun, pure and simple. This game has been more successful in Ireland and Australia than in any other part of the world, and it's easy to see why we've taken to it: it's great craic, on and off the pitch. I didn't cover myself in glory, but I didn't make a total eejit out of myself either. It's not all about the fun, though; there is a competitive edge, and this festival did include a serious competition for tag teams who travelled to the event from all over the country. One of the attractions of the game is the mixed teams; there aren't too many competitive sports where you get to mix it up like you do with tag. Another big plus is the social side to the game. You have a like-minded crew who are out for some healthy fun and competition. When the sun goes down, they party as hard as they don't tackle. Unfortunately, I didn't score on the night ... or get any points on the pitch.

Still trying to stay on the dry, I decided that this would be the year I'd finally celebrate Bloomsday. The 16th of June is the day that James Joyce set Leopold Bloom traipsing around the streets of Dublin. It was also the date of his first 'stepping out' with sweetheart Nora Barnacle. An impressive anniversary present − way to go to make the rest of us look bad, Jimmy! I've been wrestling with *Ulysses* for years; my copy is dog-eared, not from constant rereading, but from moving house more times than Robbie Keane. Bloomsday falling on a Saturday during my festival quest seemed like the perfect opportunity to re-Joyce.

I arrived at Dalkey Book Festival on the bright Saturday morning to find that the picturesque pueblo was abuzz with the prosperous populace going about their daily, plus a few extra bookworms milling around for good measure. The Dalkey denizens are pretty well-heeled; it was the first time I'd felt the need to wipe my boots before getting out of the van. I ducked into a pub to use their facilities, and was greeted by the familiar sight of two auld fellas propping up the counter. It was only familiar to a point though − these two auld fellas had a bottle of white wine each. Only in Dalkey! Anywhere else in the country it would have been stout, McArdles or Smithwicks. I felt like asking the two lads if they could direct me to the people who had economically lost the run of themselves, but I resisted, even though I had a Ronnie Whelan they might know.

I was feeling a bit out of sorts until Joseph O'Connor began his wonderful interpretation of the rambunctious rapscallion Buck Mulligan. O'Connor was reading from *Ulysses*, and he confirmed what you will often hear said about the book and about Joyce's work in general: it really comes to life when read aloud. Joe O'Connor did a wonderful job, and his reading was deserving of the huge crowd that had gathered in the hall for this Bloomsday beano. O'Connor managed to breathe life into the text, and his love and understanding of the material was obvious. He brought a dynamic to the text, plumbing the depth of emotion and highlighting the sharp wit.

I was planning on getting to Taste Dublin Food Festival at some stage over the weekend, but it didn't happen. I got distracted by some wonderful company and by a text from a friend who was up on the skywalk on top of the stands in Croke Park. They informed me that a rehearsal Mass for the Eucharistic Congress closing Mass was in full swing on the pitch. Missing an opportunity to get an insight into the huge Catholic festival would have been sacrilegious. It also meant that I could get a taste of it without actually having to endure the epic Mass. Ideal!

The experience of being on the roof of Croke Park was enhanced by the surreal addition of The Three Priests doing their soundcheck (they're a middle-aged holy version of a boy band), and by bizarre messages on the big screens about gluten intolerance. As the three lads warbled away, a message came up on the big screens detailing how those who were gluten intolerant could get a sup of the 'Precious Blood' instead of chewing on the 'Sacred Host'. The message also asked other worshippers not to dip the 'Sacred Host' in the 'Precious Blood' lest it make it unsuitable for the bread-dodgers. Does this warning debunk the principle of transubstantiation? I hope it doesn't; I really want to believe that the miraculous can take place at GAA headquarters. Next to transubstantiation, Waterford lifting Liam McCarthy should be a minor miracle for senior hurlers.

Back out on the streets there were a host of Bloomsday enthusiasts in suitable garb living out the most enthusiastically re-enacted part of *Ulysses* ... the pub crawl. There were ladies in large hats, men with dicky bows, boater hats, parasols and characters singing outside Davy Byrne's. These weren't actors or street performers, just your average Joycean enthusiast having a blooming great day. I was trying to remain teetotal, but I'd be traipsing around town all day with Anne-Marie, Mayo girl turned Dublin native, and we agreed that not having a pint of stout in one of the pubs mentioned in *Ulysses* would have been even more of a crime than dipping your communion in the sacred blood. The pint was divine.

Overheard on the Luas leaving town that afternoon was a wonderful snatch of conversation, obviously inspired by the Holy Rollers milling around the city centre for the Eucharistic Congress:

Girl: 'What do you call them necklaces that they use for praying?'

Boy: 'Rosemary beads.'

It's easy enough take the piss out of the holy-Joes, but the truth is that the Catholic Church has been doing festivals for longer than The Frank and Walters have been playing festivals in Cork, and the religious revellers have it down to a fine art. Croke Park was packed out that Sunday for Mass (80,000 capacity), and people travelled from all over the world especially for it. The crowds around Dublin for the religious shindig got me thinking that I should maybe dip my toes into a spiritual spree again. I didn't have to wait very long to pull off my socks.

Grange Stone Circle on the banks of Lough Gur in Co. Limerick has been holding pagan parties of distinction since 3,000 BC. The largest stone circle in Ireland was recommended to me by a friend who knows about this kind of thing as the perfect place to catch some old-school Summer Solstice celebrations, and it turns out that she was spot on. I don't think there is any other festival as qualified to have someone to walk up to you and say, 'Ah, you should have been here for the first one. It was much better, man.'

I arrived at Lough Gur just before 4.30 a.m. to find three guys with cameras inside the stone circle. Never one to keep to myself, I strolled over to the lads to enquire what they were up to, as their cameras weren't pointing towards the east for sunrise. 'Taking pictures', they answered. A bit cagey, but I let it sit for a minute or two before delving deeper. 'Taking pictures of ghosts', they eventually revealed. The ghosts weren't playing ball with the photographers that morning, but the lads told me that they had been successful here in the past while focusing on one particular part of the circle. As the sun-worshippers began to arrive in bigger numbers, the ghost-hunters spirited themselves away. The more I was out and about, the more I was finding things that surprised me. Ghost-hunters, druids, pagans, environmentalists, a dancer, some fresh air, beautiful surroundings, and it wasn't yet 5.00 a.m. The next time I hear someone saying 'There's nothing to do', I'm going to gaffer-tape them to the front of my van.

One of the first members of the solstice crew to arrive was a lady who goes by the name of Meritaten RahaNamsai. 'Mer' is a Holder of Light, and she was there to perform a ritual that had something to do with Gaia, balance, Isis and the Paladies. I knew that, as Meritaten was telling me about the ceremony she was performing, I should have been writing it down. I can't remember the full gist of the thing, but if you want to find out exactly what the duties of a Holder of Light are, I suggest you trundle along to Lough Gur for the next solstice sunrise. If you do find out, any chance you'd write it down for me? It's awfully complicated.

I spent the previous day trying to figure out if that Wednesday was really the proper solstice, and then checking out what the weather was going to be doing and if it would suit the sunrise. With the power of the interweb and Met Éireann I was still unsure. How in the name of Gaia did the lads from 5,000 years ago figure all that shit out? Especially as the mobile coverage at Lough Gur isn't great! They either knew stuff we don't, or they were just on such a big goof that one of them was able to say, 'D'you know what? I could swear the sunrise hit that exact same spot 365.2 sunrises ago', and the lads hatched a bet. I'm going with the latter.

Also on hand was a clutch of Druids who didn't seem to be performing any ceremonies; they seemed to be on standby, ready to intercede should anything go wrong. Thankfully, it didn't. But you can never tell – maybe they were actually doing something important, but were just being subtle. It was a special morning in what is undoubtedly a special place. The solstice is an important time in a spot like this, but Grange Stone Circle is worth a visit at any time. Ireland's largest stone circle is impressive, not just in its scale, but also in its setting. There is something about the place that certainly makes it feel different from your standard field. If you are in the neighbourhood, take a spin down the road to visit the nearby passage grave that is also beside the lake.

This spot doesn't attract the same crowds as Newgrange, and that only adds to its charms – it has an eerie sense of peace about it. Mind you, I was there at 4.30 a.m.

The Summer Solstice is a signal that the crew of Body and Soul at Ballinlough Castle in Co. Westmeath has decided to take as their annual marker. For years, the Body and Soul folk provided all kinds of weird and wonderful sideshows to enhance the experience of punters attending Electric Picnic. Eventually B&S fledged, and has been running its own gig in the woods around the lake and in the walled gardens at the idyllic Ballinlough Castle ever since. Avril Stanley is the lady at the helm of this event, and she has drawn on her experience at Burning Man to feed this festival. It's not as driven by the main stage or headlining act as most other festivals; the crew here set out to give the punter an alternative festival experience. That said, there is a main stage and some headlining acts.

The line-up for this gig usually eschews the nostalgia-inducing 'banker' act or the commercial crowd-puller that you'll find at almost every other major weekend gig in the country. It works; this festival usually sells out. Body and Soul built its reputation on having interesting, engaging and fun distractions at the heart of Electric Picnic; it makes sense that these are the kind of things you could also expect to be going on in Ballinlough. There are hot tubs in the woods, tented jook-joints, trad-infested shacks, art installations, eerily lit glades, chill-out nets woven into baskets to kick back in, and lots of strange and engaging objects floating in the trees. All these weird and wonderful elements have music programmed in and around them too.

Most of the crowd coming to Body and Soul want to embrace the spirit of the event as fully as possible. This doesn't just mean dancing to bands or immersing themselves in the wondrous woods; it means dressing appropriately to fit with the theme of the weekend, attending talks at the 'Wonderlust' stage, getting their giggle on at laughter yoga, pedalling percussive bikes or donning some face furniture for Saturday's Masquerade Ball. It's that Burning Man ethos in action: you aren't just here to be entertained; you're here to become part of the event and create a temporary community. It certainly makes for a more enjoyable immersive experience, and points to festivals evolving into more than just a space for people to let their hair down – the festival can be a place of learning and discussion, something that bonds communities of like-minded people.

In a fluke, I met Nell McCafferty at the gig, and was delighted to chat with her over a fag and a can. Nell is a proper legend, best known as a civil rights campaigner, an outspoken feminist and hard-hitting journalist. For someone tipping 70, she's still one tough auld bird. I complimented her bright red Docs, and she started laughing. 'Would you believe that some wee scrap of a lad out there told me that a woman of my age shouldn't be wearing boots like these?' 'What did you do to him?' I asked, more than a little worried for the young fella. 'I told him a few home truths', she replied with a wicked grin on her face as she pulled on the smoke. I asked if the young lad had started crying. 'No, but he dropped his pint.' We both laughed at that. Not being able to hold his drink was the worst crime of all. She was at Body and Soul to cover it for a series of newspaper articles that were taking people outside their comfort zone and getting them to write about it. Nell was buzzing on Body and Soul. She loved it. She asked me, 'What is it about the woods?' and we discussed why mooching around the moodily lit forest was so appealing, not just to us, but to everyone who was there. I'm not sure if it's the sense of mystery, discovery or playfulness that gets awakened in us in a setting like that, but I do know that it's what the Body and Soul posse does best. It's why it has become such an integral part of Electric Picnic. That spirit of creativity, diversity, unconventionality and fun that is brought to the woods at Body and Soul is the heart of the affair. It doesn't really matter who is playing on the main stage, or where the main stage is; as long as the core of the thing is rooted with the trees, this festival has its special appeal intact.

I managed to stay mainly sober at Body and Soul, out of necessity really. I'd been on the road for nearly ten months at this stage. People had been asking me how I'd been managing, and I was never really sure what to tell them. I found that the best approach was to try not to think about it all too much, because if I started keeping track of mileage, over-indulgence and sleep deprivation, I'd probably end up feeling a lot worse. Sometimes, ignorance is bliss.

Over the course of those first ten months, I'd found that there are a few places in the country that lend themselves well to having hooleys. Donegal is definitely one of those places. The countryside is wild and rugged, and so are some of the heads knocking around in it. Ballyshannon was testament to that. It was probably inevitable that it would be there that I'd fall off the wagon ... with a bang.

I'd also noticed that Irish festival crowds are as hungry for fun and divilment as Keira Knightley is for a packet of Tayto. The upside of having a mad-for-it crowd is that bands get to feed off the energy of the loolaas jumping up and down in front of them. A good example of this was on display when the Delorentos played at Sea Sessions on a Friday night towards the end of June. The north-shore tent was packed, and the crowd was primed. They leaped around and lapped it up. The band joined in. It was great to see a bunch of musicians who really seemed to be enjoying playing and enjoying the atmosphere just as much as the crowd. Be wary of Irish festival-goers ... they're infectious.

This was the fifth year of the bash in Bundoran, and when it comes to sites for a festival, you'd have to go a long way to find one as good as this. It's right on the beach. Surfing, the sea and beach sports are an important part of the weekend, so being able to throw up the tents for the gigs right beside the beach is more than a little handy. The festival site is smack bang in the middle of the town too. The campsite is about a five-minute walk from the gig gate, but unfortunately it was waterlogged even before the first peg was banged in. I'm trying to steer away from talking too much about weather since there's nothing you can do about it, but if it has an impact on where you're going to be bedding down for the weekend, you do need to take notice. Thankfully, all but one very small stage was under canvas at the main site. Not only did the tents provide shelter, if the crowd was hopping, there was a bit of heat in there too. I know first-hand of one festival-goer who suffered The Coronas just for the heat of the crowd; the band left her cold though.

On Saturday, the wind and rain were blowing so hard that a secondary festival site (Surfers' Village) didn't run any of the fringe events scheduled. This festival had been growing year on year, and it wasn't accidental. In order to secure sponsorship, it helps if you can present figures that show that the festival has scope to increase its reach and numbers, giving investors bang for their buck. The Surfers' Village stage was an extension to the previous year's festival, and the hope was that it was a step towards Sea Sessions increasing its capacity. The money, time and booked acts pumped into the expansion was scuppered by the weather costing the organisers more than what two average industrial workers would earn in a year. These guys aren't big corporations backed by limited companies; they're a bunch of dudes who like surfing and gigs. One of the lads who started the festival told me that the whole thing was a weekend surfing session that just got wonderfully out of hand. I don't know how they deal with losses like that, but the festival lives on, and the lads keep praying for good weather. Luckily, they attract a good deal of sponsorship; the surfing and rock 'n' roll crowd is an attractive demographic.

One of the bands on the bill was a bunch of young fellas from Cavan called The Strypes. They tore into their set, not just with youthful enthusiasm, but also with equal amounts of skill, talent and precociousness. They radiated more energy than the sun did all weekend. Once you got used to the fact that the average age of the band was 16, you could concentrate on them just being really good, ageism aside. Parallels with the Beatles are obvious, but throw in a dash of the Animals with the frenetic energy of the Horrors/the Hives, and you're a bit closer to getting a handle on these fellas. If rocking out were a subject in the Leaving Cert, these boys would be elected.

The Happy Mondays were flat in comparison, reminding me of an Oompa Loompa on a zebra crossing – more than just a little pedestrian. If they had just a fraction of the vibrancy that The Strypes had displayed, we all could have sang along with 'Hallelujah' and meant it. They didn't click, and Shaun told us between songs that they hadn't all been together in years. They played like recent Ireland soccer squads, all well able in their own right, but lacking cohesiveness, dynamics, spark and creativity up front. They never looked like scoring, but it was a pleasant stroll down memory lane back to a much happier time in 1990, and we all got to dance and sing along a little. Pretty much like the Spain vs. Ireland game in Euro 2012.

Something that was becoming abundantly clear was that one of the most important ingredients for a good festival is the people who populate it, and this festival had more than its fair share of decent *daoine* knocking around. The heads I met and spent time with over the course of the gig made the weekend. The weather was shite, but the people had a sunny disposition in spite of it. A few days after Sea Sessions I got an email from Willy, a volunteer at the gig. He sent me directions to his house in case I needed a halting site on my spin around the country. It wasn't just the crowd and crew that were amiable. A girl at the festival told me that she had spent the previous night traipsing around Bundoran with The Hot 8 Brass Band, and their sax player had serenaded her all night. I witnessed Ollie, the drummer from Ham Sandwich, trying to help a girl he didn't know into her car after she locked her keys in it. Another fella told me he was at a lock-in with the lads from Jape, and even though he didn't know anything about the band, they were all really sound to him. Even the acts in Donegal were decent skins.

Unfortunately, I might not be as decent as most of the punters. I'm no scumbag, but I think I might have slight and occasional inclinations. As a result of writing about festivals, more blagging opportunities had been presenting themselves to me. I was at the side of the stage on Sunday night, hopped up on Buckfast, waiting for Happy Mondays to arrive, trying to hold it together enough to get a couple of photographs and struggling to maintain a serious festival correspondent façade, trying to blend in with the proper journalist type people. After the band started, I ducked out the front for a little dance, finishing off the last of the Foxy

Monk mix for the weekend. After the gig I was dry, so I ducked backstage to see what opportunities might present themselves. The Mondays were ensconced in their tour bus, leaving their beer and wine rider mostly untouched. It would have been criminal to just leave it there in the fridge and insult the hospitality of the Sea Sessions people who had put on such a wonderful weekend, wouldn't it? I thought so anyway, so I stole Shaun Ryder's rider.

Festivals Attended in June

135. Rory Gallagher Festival – Ballyshannon, Co. Donegal
136. Cat Laughs – Kilkenny, Co. Kilkenny
137. Killarney Bike Fest – Killarney, Co. Kerry
138. Wild West Festival – Cahersiveen, Co. Kerry
139. Listowel Writers' Week – Listowel, Co. Kerry
140. Melting Pot Festival – Ardara, Co. Donegal
141. Forbidden Fruit – Dublin City
142. *Éigse* Arts Festival – Carlow, Co. Carlow
143. History Festival of Ireland – Carlow, Co. Carlow
144. Immrama Travel Writers' Festival – Lismore, Co. Waterford
145. Live at the Marquee – Cork City
146. Tag Rugby Festival – Carlow, Co. Carlow
147. Dalkey Book Festival – Dalkey, Co. Dublin
148. Ecumenical Congress – Dublin City
149. Bloomsday – Dublin City
150. Summer Solstice – Lough Gur, Co. Limerick
151. Body and Soul – Ballinlough, Co. Westmeath

Other Recommended Festivals in June

Helium – Ballymahon, Co. Longford
Rosses Point Shanty and Seafaring Festival – Rosses Point, Co. Sligo
Spancilhill Show and Fair – Spancilhill, Co. Clare
Bloom in the Park – Dublin City

11 | *July – Little Fluffy Clouds and Diluted Orange*

So far, my quest had been more rewarding than a banker's bonus. Not only was I finding hordes of people who were striving to make their slice of the country a better place to live, I was also getting to visit and experience parts of the country that I never knew existed. Tang in Co. Westmeath is one of my favourite place names to date. I wouldn't go as far as saying there was a reawakening of my Irishness, but there was a renewed appreciation and connection to some of the things that make us a pretty darn wonderful and unique shower of feckers to hang out with. I'd been pushing my socialising skills to their limit, but I was ten months in, and hadn't really challenged any prejudices or preconceived notions that might be lurking under the hood of my jalopy of a psyche. I'd scratched the surface with some of the travellers I'd been meeting on the road, but it was time to dig deeper.

On 12 July, I headed to Enniskillen for the parades organised by the loyal Orange Lodge fraternity to commemorate the defeat of King James by William of Orange at the Battle of the Boyne in 1690. If that were all that was involved with the these parades, it would be harmless enough and easily handled, but the resonance and depth of these festivities goes beyond celebrating what happened between two permed-up dandies and their buddies in a field 320 years ago. Northern Nationalists will tell you that these parades are used to intimidate and incite their communities, with a dash of triumphalism thrown in for good measure. Loyalists will tell you that the parades are an opportunity for them to celebrate their culture and heritage. Whatever the parades are for now, they were never about brotherly love and inclusion.

Enniskillen is leading a drive to make the parades on the twelfth a bit more approachable, and maybe even something that might bring curious tourists across the border for a gawp: 'Diluted Orange' has the same basic principles, but watered down to make it more palatable. There were over 5,000 people parading on the day I landed in town, and crowds of 15,000 gathered along the streets to partake in the hoopla. For as far back as I can remember, the week of the twelfth was when northern tourists with Catholic or Nationalist leanings went south of the border for their holidays, to escape the parades, bonfires and mayhem that ensued. I think it's safe to say that there weren't very many Catholics among the 15,000 people lining the streets of Enniskillen. I was a bit apprehensive – not since hitting the Amateur Dramatic Festival in Bray had I been in a place where I didn't belong as much. I spotted one huge banner announcing the Temperance and Total Abstinence Lodge; they advocate 'Maintaining sobriety and good conduct'. I didn't even bother going near those lads; they had even more reasons to dislike me than the rest of their orange brethren.

I got stuck right in and started chatting to the variety of heads that were knocking about. The younger people there had no bother chatting to me, and even taking the piss a bit. One of the traditions of marching bands involved in these parades is to play tunes that detail slaughter and suppression of Catholics, just to wind them up as much as possible. I asked one of the young fellas from a fife and drum band if they played any songs that I'd like. 'Aye', says the young fella laughing, 'We play the theme from *The Great Escape*. We can play it as you're trying to get out of town.' Funny. It was when approaching the old timers that things got a little uncomfortable. Most people were willing to talk to me and answer whatever questions I had, including some of the county grandmasters; but there were a few auld fellas in bowlers and sashes who, when hearing my southern accent, just wouldn't talk to me. Their silence felt like it ran a little deeper than grumpy old man syndrome.

A lot of what was happening with the marching bands was pretty standard stuff, and if it wasn't for the banners, the sashes and the names and lyrics that accompanied some of the tunes, this could have been a St Patrick's Day parade in any town in Ireland. That was until the Enniskillen Fusiliers turned the corner. The first thing to hit you was the thump and thud of the drums, which was more of a stomp in steel toecap boots than it was a march. The band was made for getting people riled up, in one way or another. The profile of band members with this crew was slightly different too: shaved heads, white gloves and more tattoos than a Maori pow-wow. Tattoos don't really mean much nowadays – they've become a fashion accessory – but when they snake up the side of someone's neck and onto the back of their shaven skull, or detail three-letter acronyms and symbols for loyalist paramilitary organisations, you can safely hop, skip and jump to conclusions. These musicians would be more at home in a football riot than a concert hall, and I think it's safe to say that there weren't any Celtic supporters among them.

The Enniskillen crew were the only really menacing bunch in the parade. All the rest were middle of the road marching bands. Literally! For a celebration of Loyalist tradition, I was surprised not to see any Lambeg drums being played by any of the bands. There were bass drums with synthetic skins made by German, American and Chinese manufacturers, but none of the traditional hand-painted, animal-skinned monster drums that are surely an integral part of marching culture. Maybe I'll see them when I make a return trip to some of the less publicised marches. I got a taste for this thing, and found it really interesting to see exactly what goes on.

There was a little culture shock setting in as I was knocking around Enniskillen; the amount of flapping union flags was dizzying. I kept wanting to take people by the shoulders and try to explain to them that we were actually all on the island of Ireland, and that surely if they just looked at a map they'd all realise the mistake, put away the union flags and come out again on Paddy's Day, having learned 'Sean South' on the fifes for the occasion.

This whole thing on the twelfth is a Gordian knot, tied with unwieldy threads of socio-political, religious, familial and historical fibres. Houdini couldn't untie this yoke. I don't know how the Parades Commission is meant to cope. What I did notice though, and what gave me some comfort as I chatted to people, was the attitude of the younger people who were there on the day. They didn't seem too hung up on what was going on, and lots of them told me that they were just there to hang out with their friends and have a laugh; even the young fellas with their hair painted blue, with union flags draped over their shoulders. The fact that there was a southerner asking them questions didn't faze them at all. I took most heart from a young drummer. When I asked him what the twelfth meant to him, he replied without hesitation, 'It's a day off work.' Now there's a sentiment that can cross cultural divides. It's odd to get wisdom from a drummer though.

This was the flagship event for presenting the acceptable face of the Orange Order. It took me a few days to process it all and figure out how it made me feel, and it was actually whilst listening to a news report afterwards that it started to make some kind of sense to me. An item on the Irish national news focused on how much the parades in Northern Ireland cost taxpayers in terms of policing and criminal damage. I overheard a lady from Antrim complain that this was typical southern spin, and another effort to marginalise the Protestant communities by trying to turn people against the parades. She had a point; it was indeed a type of negative spin that we rarely hear applied to St Patrick's Day parades.

The event in Enniskillen had a PR machine pulling some of its strings in an effort to make it a tourist event, even though some of the old-school prejudices popped out from behind the façade from time to time to say, 'Wot about ya?' The Armalite has been replaced by the ballot box, and the new balaclava bandits are PR consultants who are repackaging bigotry as quaint cultural tradition. They are doing this on both sides of the border. They'll probably pull it off, too. A trip up north isn't complete any more without a tour of the murals on the gable end of the buildings in whatever city or town you find yourself in. Something with deep meaning and political significance has turned into a tourist attraction.

One of the most powerful images from Northern Ireland in recent years was Martin McGuinness and the Queen shaking hands: a PR coup for Sinn Féin. The new PR war is going to be an interesting one. Something that was highlighted by being in Enniskillen for this event was how little I know about what it must be like to live in

Northern Ireland, and what little right I have to have an opinion about what goes on up there. Enniskillen is only a thirty-minute trip over the border, but it felt like a different planet. I can't recommend highly enough getting a taste of the twelfth; it's an education, and it might help to break down a few more barriers, especially given the attitudes of some of the young people involved in the parades.

Something that cheered me up immensely while listening to multiple renditions of 'The Sash' was the fact that every banner and silken orange sash had the acronym 'LOL' on it. I took great pleasure in repeatedly asking some of the older and grumpier Orange folk if this stood for 'Laugh Out Loud'. They weren't impressed, and they tersely informed me that it stood for 'Loyal Orange Lodge'. I decided that if I had to listen to 'The Sash' all day, that this would be my little way of protesting; maybe one of them would see the funny side, and go, 'Oh, yeah! I never noticed that before, that's hilarious! Maybe we should get an LMAO or ROFL badge for next year.' Surprisingly, none of them did say that, but I'm determined to find someone that does eventually react in that way. I'll just have to keep asking.

After the trip north I needed some grounding and comfort. Christy Moore is red in the face from telling us, 'If it's music you want, you should go to Clare.' I took his advice, and headed to the Banner County for The Willy Clancy Festival, or 'Willy Week', as it's affectionately known in the locale. This is a summer school for students of all ages and nationalities to learn to play Irish traditional music, attend dance workshops, go to lectures, recitals, concerts and exhibitions, as well as a chance for a good few of them to get together informally to lash out tunes. There are a load of festivals that follow this model, and there may well have been a couple before this one, but Willie Week is the daddy, and the traddies have been gathering here for this craic for over forty years. The reason it's so successful is that it attracts some of the best musicians in the country, and most of them have been coming to Miltown Malbay since they were old enough to hold a whistle or strum a chord.

There is music all over the town, spilling out onto the street, sessions in doorways, hallways, backs of vans and in every pub you step into, and probably in phone boxes too, if you could find one. I was lucky enough to run into fellow Tramoron Jimmy O'Brien Moran, who was up in Miltown giving uilleann pipe classes for the week. Jimmy had a line on a couple of good sessions that were happening that night. For a small town, it's very easy to get sidetracked, and it certainly doesn't help when you're in a pub with Lynch's over the door, but the actual name of the pub is Friel's. Welcome to Ireland.

The session started gently enough in the back of The Central – a couple of light tunes and a singer or two. An auld chap with a fine beard at the counter leans in to me and says that we wouldn't get away with singing those auld, boring, maudlin songs as Munster men. He had a point. Colm was the bearded dude's name, and he was a bit of a character. It turns out that he travels around the country in a camper van going to festivals. Imagine that! We're either soulmates or, through some hallucinogenic property of dodgy porter and the hypnotic property of a polka, I met myself from thirty years in the future. Strange things can happen around the Burren.

Malka is a girl from Israel who travels to Ireland regularly for lessons to help her uilleann pipe playing. She was with a Japanese lad who also travelled over especially for Willie Week, and he actually makes pipes. There were more pipers here than at a plumbers' union meeting. Over the course of the evening I got chatting to a fiddler from Dublin, who was explaining to me with great difficulty (it transpires that we were both locked) that he doesn't really get to hear much music he enjoys at Willie Week. What now? 'First off', he explained, 'it's hard to find a good session with a musician playing that you want to hear. When you do, you rarely get to hear them on their own, or with only one other musician, so as to enjoy the subtleties and nuances of their playing.' At least, that's how I remember what he was telling me. 'So what's the point?' I asked him. He told me that on those rare occasions when a couple of stellar musicians' planets do align, it makes for a very special moment ... 'and anyway, in the meantime isn't it all great craic?' 'Agreed.' 'Will you have another?' 'I will!' There is probably a time and place for abstinence; this was neither. I imagined the Orange Men from the Temperance and Total Abstinence Lodge looking on with dour disapproval. This made the pint taste even sweeter.

The Street Performance World Championships had grabbed my attention for a couple of reasons. The main one was that the performers include some of the most weird, wonderful and talented freaks known to man, but it's also a free festival that runs in Dublin and Cork City centres. The fabulously talented freaks don't actually get paid for their performances; expenses are covered for the entrants, and they pass around the hat after every performance. The cash prize for the winners and the prospect of filling the cap while they're here surprisingly attracts some of the best street performers from around the globe. They tumble into in a park in Cork one week, and then cartwheel into Dublin the next.

The quality of the street performers in Merrion Square was top notch, and they had a patter to match their juggling and tumbling abilities. Most were mild-mannered in asking for money to be tossed in the hat, but quite a few did tell us that, if we put in paper money, we'd get a sticker or a signed postcard or a tattoo or something. They had marketing skills to match the sword-swallowing. As a form of payment for entertainment, this must be one of the oldest. You watch the performers do their thing, and then you give whatever you feel moved to contribute. This system of payment based on donation and worth was adopted by Radiohead when they released their *In Rainbows* album. The online interaction with the album could be monitored, and it turned out that 62 per cent of people paid only one cent to download the tracks, but 38 per cent of people paid an average of six dollars. From watching the crowd at the Street Performance World Championships, those figures don't seem too outlandish at all. The more entertaining and engaging the performance, the more money they made, and the percentages seemed a little above the Radiohead average. It also appeared that being able to make people laugh helped the payday. Thom may need to throw in a George Formby cover on the next album.

Lizard Man was one of my favourite turns; the dude is the quintessence of freak. Tattooed all over his body, he had sharpened teeth, a split tongue and a penchant for inflicting more pain on himself than James Blunt has inflicted on the music-loving public. He has green scales tattooed on EVERY inch of his body; there are Teflon implants creating ridges under his skin, vampire-like teeth and a long, forked tongue. The lad looked scary, but it turned out that he was a sound bloke; when he wasn't hammering nails into his head, that was. His ability to swallow swords while lifting kegs with his ears wasn't half as popular with the ladies as his ability to move either side of his forked tongue independently. He winked every time he did that.

From the generosity of flipping a few bob into a busker's hat, I was off to experience kindly acts of a different nature. My year coincided with the first edition of what was destined to become the Snow White of Irish festivals: Clonakilty's Random Acts of Kindness Festival. The town took a pretty hard hit with unprecedented flooding that happened during monsoon season (also known as the Irish summer). In an effort to celebrate the community spirit that was displayed during the town's hours of need, and also to give the place a shot of human sunshine, a few kind-hearted souls hit upon the idea of this festival. The idea was that there would be clatters of people roaming the town raining kindness down on people as they went about their daily business. I had only hopped out of Wanderly Wagon upon arriving in Clon when a chap by the name of Chris gave me an envelope. 'What's this?' I asked. 'It's a voucher. Happy Random Acts of Kindness Festival', says Chris, and he hopped down the road like a fella with a streak of Easter bunny in him. He had given me a voucher to have Wanderly Wagon washed. He was a car-wash bunny!

There were a number of scheduled events, as well as kindly roving randomers like Chris. One event was a speakers' corner, where people involved with community groups and folk who have ongoing work in the field of kindness and togetherness spoke about what they get up to in their day-to-day kindness. The president *of Macra na Feirme* was on hand to talk about what the young rural types turn their hand to. *Macra* was the crew who invited me to be an escort at the Queen of the Land Festival, and it turned out that they were pulling some of the strings at this festival. They're a great bunch, and it's not just about farming with this shower – a testament to this is the fact that a good deal of the crew behind the whole Random Acts of Kindness event are *Macra* members. A tip of the hat to ye, lads. Sean Kelly, former president of the GAA and a Member of the European Parliament, was also on hand to talk about volunteerism and its importance in the community. A whole range of interesting speakers were bigging up the positive vibes that were being sent all around the home of pudding. Clonakilty might have random acts of kindness as a festival, but it's made its name through the medium of black pudding.

Back out on the street, there was music, odd animal installations, vouchers, greetings and smiles all over the gaff. As well as the buskers, there were guerrilla guitaristas who were running into shops, singing happy ditties at the bewildered, smiling people in the shops, and then legging it off again. The first prolonged blast of sunshine in a few weeks was right on cue for the day that was in it. One of the kindly kin who'd set up a stall for the day was the Clonakilty Favour Exchange. The craic with this crew is that you register and donate a couple of hours of your time to them, and you may be called upon to do a favour for another member. You can also call on other members to do a favour for you. It's a bank of barter. I was really digging this and, after I'd dug it, someone came and weeded it, and then someone else planted some potatoes in it.

I'd become frustrated earlier in the week when I'd heard an economic commentator on the radio say that we needed to instill confidence in Ireland amongst those who deal in the Global Bond Market so we could 'get back in the game'. Back in the game? Jesus! It was such a joy to be immersed in a community that were all out on the streets and donating their time, vouchers, smiles, music and chat in an effort to make each other happier.

During this festival, Clonakilty in Co. Cork got pretty close to being a utopian State, and not just because they have orgasmic black pudding. From that week on, I made sure I'd borrowed more than enough audiobook CDs from my local library to ensure that I didn't have to listen to the radio while I did my rounds. Back in the game, my arse.

When the sun set that night in Clon, *An Teach Beag* was the site of a very intimate session with the wandering minstrel that I'd met in the tin-whistler's haunted castle, harper Anya, pulling some more strings. Either the country is really, really small, or there's some synchronicity to what happens out on the road at the festivals of Ireland. Probably a bit of both. Pat Speight told some yarns by the fireside, and a clatter of musicians made contributions that ebbed and flowed through the night. The atmosphere in this pub brought to life the idealised notion of a community hub that some rare pubs still manage to maintain – homely, snug, engaging and entertaining. When an elderly lady on the other side of the fireplace sang 'Hard Times Come Again No More', I was ready to call my whole festival quest to a halt. I may have peaked!

After the buzz in Clonakility, it felt like anything else that weekend would be a letdown, but the festival trail beckoned, so I popped into Cork City on my way home from Clon to get a taste of the Cork Food Festival. Outside the gates where you pay your admission fee were a lad and lass dealing out some tasty-looking salads. We were starving, so we strolled over to get a bit of grub from the salady folk. It was free. It seems as if these random acts of kindness were catching. Rocket Man works the markets around Co. Cork, and he was dishing out the free fodder to promote his wholesome and wholly scrumptious scran.

I've been trying to replicate his beetroot and sprout salad since, but I'm just not hitting it. It was a surprise to be greeted with some free grub, as I'm a little sceptical about the type of food festivals where you pay an entrance fee to get in, and then, once inside, you have to pay again for the food.

The entrance fee was twelve quid, and once you stepped through the gates all the food on sale seemed to be not just reasonable, but greatly reduced in price. It didn't feel as much of a rip-off as some other festivals that follow the same model, i.e. Taste of Dublin. The other thing that I find a bit uncomfortable at these shindigs is the food snobbery and overly fancy victuals on sale. I couldn't help but feel that champagne hawking was out of place and garish when we were all meant to be skint – but not totally skint yet, judging by the amount of it being sloshed out. The stalls weren't the only place you could pick up some food; I had some chips on my shoulder too. If people want champagne and fancy fodder, more power to them. I succumbed, and bought more mixed olive tapenade, and when I got home that night I dipped wheaten crackers deep into my secret shame.

Knocking around so many festivals in such a short period of time hadn't just shortened my life expectancy; it had managed to give me something akin to Peter Parker-like spider senses that still help me figure out if I'll dig a particular festival or not within minutes of stepping through the gate. There are a few physical pointers that help my FESP (Festival Extra-Sensory Perception). Dogs and dreadlocks are two of them. I'm not talking about a Damien Marley-playing Crufts kind of dog and dreads saturation; just a slightly above average sprinkling of Rastas and retrievers. I wouldn't consider myself a huge fan of either; standing next to a damp crusty who smells like a smoked rasher in a packet of brown Hula Hoops at a gig while a muddy terrier rides your leg is not ideal, but their presence points to something important.

If you're allowed to bring your dog into a gig, it probably means that the organisers are pretty chilled about all the other standard rules and regulations too. I would be willing to bet that any gig where you see a few dogs without leads means you're probably going to be allowed bring your own beer in too. Our Redheaded Rasta fraternity can beat bloodhounds when it comes to sniffing out serious sessions. The greater their number, the less commercial and more earthy the ethos, the less mainstream the entertainment and the more efficacious the range of procurable intoxicants. After I heard a bark, and caught a glimpse of matted mane or two, I had more than a Ronnie Whelan that KnockanStockan would produce the goods. I was so right.

This has to be one of the most idyllic settings for a gig in the country. As you travel through the Wicklow Mountains, spotting lakes en route, you're already chilling out by default, and preparing to tap into your inner freak-in-a-field mentality. The setting is ultra-rural, and it lends the event a charm that most other festivals, even the ones in fields, can't seem to foster. One of the reasons I think the rural roots are more exposed at this gig is that there is an air of unashamed wildness in the air when you arrive lakeside. The music, the installations, the well-being tents and all that other sideshow stuff are evident at this festival too, and obviously important for the overall experience, but it was the sense of unselfconscious feckless abandon wafting about the place that won me over. I really enjoyed Forbidden Fruit earlier in the summer in Kilmainham – the music was top shelf and the crowd was über-hip, but unfortunately an über-hip crowd rarely tear into enjoying themselves with the ferocity and wholehearted honesty that was on display here, and I have no doubt which kind of shindig I'd prefer to be at.

I'll be the first to admit that I knew only a smattering of the bands who were playing over the weekend, but that too is probably a good thing. As I was watching The Amazing Few whip the crowd up, I hit on what I thought was a pretty good analogy. The minor match before a senior championship game rarely gets much attention, and maybe pulls half the crowd that the senior game will, but often it's here you'll see some of the best skills, greatest heart, most honest endeavour and least cynicism. There are few things more satisfying while watching a senior hurling match than being able to answer the fella in the terrace beside you when he asks, 'Who's that young fella at half-back' by telling him about all the minor games you saw the young fella play, and better yet, the goal you saw him score at club level. You've adopted the mantle of a hard-core supporter. Festivals like KnockanStockan work in the same way.

Some of the bands at KnockanStockan aren't all-star material yet, but they did not lack passion, and it will be satisfying to watch some of them progress to senior level over the next few years. There were experienced, battle-tested warhorses on the bill too, all lined out to make for a solid squad that would be very hard to beat on a given All-Ireland Sunday. Did I take that analogy too far? Joe Brolly is shaking his head in disapproval.

I'd seen Jape and Ham Sandwich three times over the summer, Bressie and the Coronas I've managed to dodge, only bumping into them once or twice, but with so many festivals there was bound to be a *Groundhog Day* feeling rearing its head. KnockanStockan had a massive and original line-up that wasn't all amazing, but it didn't need to be, and with the amount of bands they had playing, it couldn't be. I saw a clatter of heads I'd never heard of before, and there were a good few of them I wouldn't mind hearing again. I'd love to tell you who some of the best bands I saw were, but I followed:

Irish Festival Rule No. 11: *Rip up your timetable and drift* (Buckfast helps this approach).

Are there more festivals popping up in the last few years than ever before? It certainly seems like that, but there have been gigs like this one chugging away in the background for years, working hard to get a foothold in a market that is becoming more competitive as people are picking and choosing how to spend their limited festival allowance with more care. KnockanStockan is approaching its tenth birthday, so it is no newcomer. In 2008, their minors and seniors helped them win the title of Best Small Festival, and it has been growing since. One of the ideas that the festival was founded on is giving musicians an opportunity to showcase their material, and having musicians involved in organising the event has kept this ethos alive. I'm always impressed that communities allow a crowd of lunatics to arrive on their doorstep, set up camp and party like a bunch of rutting wild goats for a weekend, before they head off, leaving a beleaguered battlefield of debauchery in their wake. The heads involved with this event must have a pretty good relationship with the townsfolk of Lacken, a beautiful and scenic village in the mountains, for them to allow the gig to continue. Donating a good few bob to community ventures over the last number of years hopefully isn't just to keep them sweet; it probably underlines the ethos behind this festival. Festivals need buckets of commercial savvy to keep them running, but it is nice not to feel like the money is the main motivator, and that is certainly true here. At €75 for a weekend ticket, and a slice off that going towards lay-bys in Lacken, no one is getting MCD, POD or Festival Republic type moolah here. Thank God!

Did you ever have a favourite pair of jeans? Had you a shoe whose loss of sole was long-lamented, or a T-shirt worn out from being worn out? Some things just fit right. It was about 7.00 a.m. on a Monday morning whilst bobbing in Blessington Lake in my underpants that I realised that KnockanStockan might just be the Irish festival that fits me best. About an hour later, when I witnessed someone eating a dried piece of cow-shite on a dare, there was no doubt about it. My judgement may have been skewed somewhat from sleep deprivation, but I intend testing the theory by attending this festival another few times.

Having once again thrown myself headlong into the festival experience, I was feeling like some essential organs had orchestrated an escape as I lay comatose in Wanderly Wagon. I didn't feel right. I was sicker than a large hospital; the phrase 'runny shite on a slate' comes to mind. I had 'The Fear', and was in dire need of cheering up; luckily, I knew somewhere that was offering suitable distraction. The scarecrow festival in Durrow, Co. Laois, had been pencilled in on the calendar at the very beginning of this festival caper. As shaken as I was, this was one I was looking forward to.

Up until the previous year, this shindig had been known as 'The Howya Festival' – a name that is among my festival favourites (Fair of Muff in Co. Cavan is my current favourite, sounding as it does like a wonderfully lewd Shakespearian compliment. Muff Festival in Co. Donegal is a very close second). The crow-worrying facet of the festival became more popular than the stranger-welcoming aspect, and the festival said see-ya to the howya. These festivities now focus fully on the feather-freakers. Imagine my delight and surprise when, two weeks earlier, a lovely lady by the name of Evelyn sent me an email and asked if I'd like to be a judge in Durrow's All-Ireland Scarecrow Championships. Too bloody right I would, Missus. If the festival trail kept cranking up the pleasure factor at this rate, it was likely I'd become addicted to life on the road.

I arrived in Durrow, and was given my paperwork to go and rate the rook rattlers ... all 115 of them! Yep, the town probably has more straw citizens during the festival week than normal townsfolk – well, to be honest, I'm not sure there are any normal citizens in Durrow. The last time I was there was for the High Nelly Rally. The inhabitants of the Co. Laois hamlet seem to have an advanced sense of fun and divilment.

The-bird worriers are distributed all around the town, in housing estates, garages, alcoves, dog kennels, boats, and even in the river. It was great to see people embracing the fun of the thing and firing scarecrows up in their gardens, and in any available alcove the town had to offer. There was a Lady Gaga at the front of one house, with red satin knickers, red patent boots and a net curtain as a blouse. Could have been her twin! One grandfather told me that the three scarecrows in the boat at the side of his house represented the three generations of his family that go fishing together for pike on the Shannon; he'd made them with his grandson. These scarecrows had better fishing gear than me. People put serious effort into making these avian aggravators and, although there is a competitive edge to the creations, it's the sense of fun that these straw creations bring to the town that is most striking. It's a simple idea, it's cheap, it's a great laugh, and it has captured the imagination of the people of Durrow and surrounding towns. Over 2,000 people visited the town on the Sunday of the festival to have a gawp at the straw swallow-scarers.

The sense of humour on display had a socio-political edge in places. Two Angela Merkels, two Seán Quinns, a clatter of politicians and a host of other characters got a good auld slagging. The banks were satirised in a number of the scarecrow tableaux, with one scarecrow dressed as a robber actually scaling the side of the town's Bank of Ireland with gun in hand. Emigration was evident too, with one scarecrow upside down in a hole that had a sign beside it that read: 'Scarecrow at Work – Digging to Australia'. Who knew that scarecrows could be a tool of socio-political commentary, protest and laughter while also putting the run on ravens? The Durrowers have this rural art form sussed.

It's not all fun and games, though – there is €3,000 in prize money up for grabs. Nothing to be sniffed at, Wurzel. The judging process is a serious business, with a number of selection panels and a formal voting process to adhere to. I am now incredibly familiar with Durrow, having literally walked the length and breadth of the town to view and rate all 115 crow-chasers. The winning entry was an amazing lion that was crafted completely from straw, its teeth and ferocious form surely proving to be the most effective warder-off of winged wildlife.

The scarecrows and atmosphere were just the tonic I needed, and I was feeling pretty happy with myself about how the quest was going. July had been epic. It's the busiest month on the Irish Festival Calendar and, as I trundled along the Sligo coast towards my next festival appointment, I managed to convince myself that nobody was enjoying the summer as much as Wanderly Wagon and me. I was wrong.

For a week, I'd been trying to track down one of the people from the Irish Cloud-Appreciation Society to have a chat with them about their annual festival. I was intrigued that there was a group of people passionate enough about clouds to start a society, and even more by the fact that every year they get together for talks, walks and workshops.

Sally was my contact, and every time I got a hold of her on the phone, she was on a beach, up a mountain or beside a lake. What a life this lady must lead, off gazing at clouds in beauty spots all over Ireland – I didn't know the half of it. The cloud-gazers were due to gather on Ben Bulben, and I tracked Sally down to a restaurant just inside the border of Donegal. Her enthusiasm for fluffy, floating, moisture carriers was infectious.

When I asked if she'd understand if some people found the Cloud-Appreciation Society somewhat odd, she parried the question by musing that a world in which you don't have time to stop for a moment and appreciate the beauty and wonder of a cloud would be odder still. She made a good point.

Chat complete, we strolled back to join her husband, who was still inside the restaurant. 'Back to work', she said, as we were walking up the road. 'Are you working in the restaurant?' I enquired. It turns out that Sally and her Husband John write the Bridgestone and McKenna guides, both well-respected publications detailing the best places to eat in Ireland. The McKennas travel the country eating the best food the island has to offer, and when that gets too much for them, they stop off in beauty spots to look at clouds. My aspirations for careers in set-dance calling and céilí drumming took a severe hammering.

Festivals Attended in July

152. Sea Sessions – Bundoran, Co. Donegal
153. Inisowen Clipper Festival – Inisowen, Co. Donegal
154. Cairde Arts Festival – Sligo, Co. Sligo
155. Irish American Festival – New Ross, Co. Wexford
156. Round the World Yacht Race – Galway City
157. Queen of the Sea – Youghal, Co. Cork
158. Orange Order Marches – Enniskillen, Co. Fermanagh
159. Earagail Arts Festival – Donegal, Co. Donegal
160. Junction Arts Festival – Clonmel, Co. Tipperary
161. 10 Days in Dublin – Dublin City
162. Willie Clancy Week – Miltown Malbay, Co. Clare
163. Galway Arts Festival – Galway City
164. Street Performance World Championships – Cork and Dublin
165. Cloud Appreciation Society Festival – Sligo, Co. Sligo
166. Random Acts of Kindness – Clonakilty, Co. Cork
167. Cork Food Festival – Cork city
168. Munster *Fleadh* – Dungarvan, Co. Waterford
169. KnockanStockan – Blessington, Co. Wicklow
170. Scarecrow Festival – Durrow, Co. Laois

Other Recommended Festivals in July

Kinsale Arts Week – Kinsale, Co. Cork
Swift Satire Festival – Trim, Co. Meath
Skibbereen Arts Festival – Skibbereen, Co. Cork
Groove Festival – Kilruddery House, Co. Wicklow
Riverside Jump – Enniscorthy, Co. Wexford
Ballyshannon Folk & Trad Music Festival – Ballyshannon, Co. Donegal

13 | *August – Falling Over the Line*

*A*ugust began with yet another bank holiday weekend, and this one was packing a hadouken Street Fighter triple-punch combo. Castlepalooza was happening in Co. Offaly, Lissard was grooving in Co. Cork, and Indiependence was hopping up and down in a field on the other side of the Rebel County. All three festivals had serious appeal, and I was actually playing at one of them, so the only thing for it was to hit all of them and batten down the hatches for what promised to be a tsunami of sessions.

Charleville Castle in Tullamore was the first port of call – yet another perfect setting for a carnival crew to pitch their tents. The grounds of the castle make an idyllic backdrop, and the campsite certainly isn't your average festival estate. Ensconced in the field were an enclave of Vikings, archers and medieval types drinking mead from beasts' horns. I'm still not sure if they were there for the festival or they just live there all year round – it was difficult to tell. With Charleville Castle on the skyline, it felt very Casterly Rock 'n' Roll. The Vikings had a friendly wolfhound by the name of Misty, but only friendly to a point. Misty lost the plot on Saturday morning when one camper insisted on singing 'Livin' La Vida Loca' at full throttle ad nauseum from his tent. Like the dressed-up beardy dudes carrying the Clan of Odin sigil, this dog had standards.

The craic in the campsite was an education. 'C'mere, man, is there any chance you'd brush my teeth for me?' croaked a cracked and jagged voice from a head that popped out of a tent after I stumbled over their guy rope, 'my mouth and throat feel like I've been smokin' turf rolled in sandpaper skins.' The morning before, the very same voice had been calling out to surrounding campers for valium, not to swallow, but to wrap in grass and use as earplugs in an effort to try and get some sleep. The briquette puffer's predicament was also felt keenly by near neighbours. The lads in the tent next door had spent the previous night brainstorming a billion-dollar business plan: www.wasponastring.com. As soon as they figure out how to keep the stinging feckers alive while they're delicately tethered to the tent they're protecting, they'll be all over *Dragons Den.* 'Speed is the most useless drug in the world' was another nugget the wasp-herders decided to share with all their near neighbours. 'I can't sleep, can't wank, can't have sex, can't get drunk and can't get stoned. All I can do is talk shite with a belly full of speed.' Welcome to The Moat campsite at Castlepalooza. After the speed symposium, the valium dude upgraded his search to opium suppositories.

This festival is nearly ten years old, and it has built up a loyal cohort of lunatics who storm the castle every year. The line-up for the gig wouldn't have your jaw hitting your converse, but it's usually solid, with a few gems glistening in there. Where the trip to Tullamore outshone the other two major festivals of the weekend was mileage for moolah. A weekend ticket with camping cost €50 if you bought it early enough, and cans of decent beer were about €2 when bought with tokens. As one enthusiastic reveller exclaimed, 'Sure you're saving money getting locked at this thing!' The perfect place for an Eddie Hobbs vs. David McWilliams mud wrestle. At one point I was shocked to be propositioned and invited back to a 'free gaff', i.e. empty tent, for some 'deep throat' and a wank. Unfortunately, it was by an awfully drunk, but awfully polite, young man named Ryan. If his mammy only knew! The crowd who populate this festival are an awfully nice bunch to spend a bit of time with, and very friendly ... especially Ryan.

Lissard Festival had a bit more pedigree and depth on paper when it came to the amassed minstrels; some were more for the chin-strokers than the buck-leppers though. Thankfully, the *bainisteoirs* weren't so po-faced as to ignore the dancing needs of the assembled feet. Toots and the Maytals on Sunday and Chic on Saturday were both more than a little old-school, but both capable of getting even Heather Mills to shake a leg.

There was a different age profile and demographic at this offering. The more seasoned crowd knew how to enjoy themselves fully and deeply, indulging in a more considered form of chaos than the cohort at Castlepalooza; these were experienced sessionistas. The whole affair had a relaxed and safe atmosphere that lent itself well to ravers of old who had brought the kids and dogs along for the weekend. The sideshows leaned heavily on gourmet grub, poetry and a healthy shot of Brechtian vibes. This felt like a festival in west Cork, and that's no bad thing, especially if you frolic in a field with some happy hedonists.

I've debated long and hard about whether I should share this honest and insightful story, reflective of how good Chic were at this festival and how much I may have thrown myself into being a tramp. By the time Chic took to the stage at Lissard, the Foxy Monk was all gone and we were on the second recce to sneak in a clatter of cans of Chateau du Clonmel from Wanderly Wagon. Nile and the Chic crew were ripping up the dance floor (when I say 'dance floor', I mean muddy mulch and sod), and I was getting my funk on big style and smiling like a tool. I eventually had to go and shake the dew off the lily, mounting the plastic, three-sided rocket urinal that you find at a lot of these festival gigs. I was still having a little bop when I whipped it out and, as a result, neglected to check the lie of the land before letting go. The urinal was a bit backed up, and when my stream hit the surface there was some splash back that caught me on the inner right thigh. It's bad when you inadvertently stain yourself with your own flow, but this splash back was the piss of several strangers – way worse. So I was faced with a dilemma. Should I choose plan A, and go back to the van and throw on a pair of clean jeans and miss roughly twelve minutes of Chic's set; or plan B: 'Fuck it, it'll dry while I'm dancing.' My choice to opt for plan B either points to how good Chic were, or it's how much I'd lost to the road. I'm still not sure, but reckon it was a bit of both.

It was Indiependence next, and what this gig lacked in headliners it made up for in head-the-balls. The mob down here needed a more than a little mentalness to help make merry in mud on a scale not seen since the trenches of the Somme. Walking across the site was like trying to negotiate a custard canal in a large pair of jelly jodhpurs and flippers. It turns out that a little loosener actually helped with plodding through the plop, just so long as you didn't over-medicate. It's all about balance in the fields of Mitchelstown.

I was playing with King Kong Company late on Sunday night, and negotiating the terrain while caddying congas at 3.00 a.m. felt more like a scene from a Dickensian workhouse than the Led Zeppelin-fuelled rock 'n' roll dreams of my youth. Too Many DJs had no such difficulty lugging their gear around: they arrived with four USB keys – now that's the future! It was fun though. I saw Monday's sunrise whilst sitting on the ground in the car park of an industrial estate in Mitchelstown; I'd probably be presenting *Xposé* now if the glamour of these adventures hadn't become so overly grotesque.

I spent Monday evening searching out a cure for trench foot, and trying to find a method of extracting mud from my sinuses and frontal lobe. Clocking up so much mileage wasn't just taking its toll on me; Wanderly Wagon was feeling the pressure too. The coolant had begun leaking from the radiator, and it got to a stage where I was putting as much Rad-fix into the engine as I was oil. I had stopped at a service station in Cashel with my head stuck in the engine when a dude came over and stuck his head right in beside mine. This isn't unusual behaviour for van brethren. When I had the vintage VW camper, people used to just pop in the side door for a gander. I was cooking some rashers one morning beside the sea in Dún Laoghaire when a garda landed in beside me for a cup of tea and a chat. I was stopped at traffic lights in Carlow when a traveller asked if I'd take him for a spin: his grandfather used to drive the same van.

The dude studied the engine with me for a while, and echoed my in-depth, technical and extensive expert diagnosis: 'Radiator's fucked.' 'Would you believe I have one in the back of my van?' he added chirpily. He actually did – the exact same radiator complete with fans, wires and intact connectors. We both knew that I wanted to buy it, but before I made an offer, we had a little dance to perform, chatting about vans, the state of certain roads, a little bit of hurling, and finally what the weather might do for the rest of the summer. 'How much do you want for the radiator?' I asked eventually. 'Fifty quid' was the surprising answer. It was a steal, no haggling required.

Unfortunately, after the epic month of July, and the tearing around the country at the beginning of August, lugging me around the country eventually proved too much for Wanderly Wagon. The engine threw a rod that went through the engine block, causing a bang and a quite dramatic little shot of flames. Wanderly Wagon was feeling sympathy pains. I'd joined the AA when beginning this caper, thinking it prudent, so as I travelled home with Wanderly on the back of a truck, I congratulated myself on signing up for roadside assistance, and considered joining the other club with the same acronym.

I scoured the Internet and found a suitable engine donor in Tullamore, but the dude was selling a dud that was rustier than Sheeba on a comeback tour. I eventually found the right engine in the wilds of Co. Tipperary on a dairy farm, which also had a large herd of VW vans in various states of dismantlement. A deal was struck, and Conor, who I'd met up in the mountains of Dingle, helped me load the engine into the back of his van, and we ambulanced the donor's organ back to Waterford for the transplant. Wanderly was off the road for at least a week, but I still needed to get around the country, so I put the back seats down in a Golf, inserted an inflatable mattress, a duvet and some pillows, and I was ready to start acting the goat again. Not a moment too soon – Puck Fair was kicking off in Killorglin.

A gig rig with a DJ belting out 'The Birdie Song' (if you're unfamiliar with this eighties version of 'The Macarena', be grateful), two girls with the biggest, blingiest ear-hoops imaginable, a rotund, sunburned traveller wearing only Farah slacks and slip-ons sprawled out atop his top-of-the-range rugs like a bright red bull seal, a goat so pungent you could smell him from forty feet below, a handful of bewildered tourists and a clatter of clients ready to ruck 'n' roll until the pubs closed their doors at 3.00 a.m. – welcome to Ireland's oldest licensed festival. They have a 400-year-old charter legitimising this session. It might not sound like a selection of scenes that would be well-received, but the rough-and-tumble nature of what was happening around the town fitted perfectly. Puck Fair is not a glamorous event; it's no gem in the crown of Discover Ireland's marketing campaign for Brand Ireland. There were no feta and chickpea pastry parcels for sale at the food stalls; thankfully, there was no olive tapenade either, there were no Prosecco peddlers lining the pavements, no airs or graces here; this was an earthy, balls-to-the-wall festival. It's not for the prissy or faint-hearted, but it's not dangerous or intimidating either. If you're up for a buzz and a shot of undiluted and unsterilised festivalling, this is the spot to grab the goat by the horns and wrestle the bastard all weekend long. This is not a boutique festival – thank Puck!

There aren't many other festivals in the country that can trace their origins back to 1613, when King James granted Kilorglin permission to party. Officially, we've had 400 years of Puck Fairs, but it's suspected that the goat has been an excuse for mayhem for much longer than that.

Every year a few lads head off up the hills, catch a wild goat, bring him back by the horns and, for the duration of the festival, he's the king of the town. In fairness, it could be argued that he does a better job as elected official for the weekend than either of the Healy-Raes have done; he smells a good deal fresher, and talks more sense too. On Friday there is a parade, followed by the Queen of Puck crowning the beast. The Queen of Puck is selected via a Lovely Girls competition earlier in the week (they're awfully fond of those things in Kerry). The Brits could take a leaf out of the book of this Kerry town. The King brings in tourists, similar to the Windsors, but at the end of the session it's possible to make a couple of *bodhráns*, a curry and a jumper out of the dethroned Czar. You'd never get that kind of mileage out of that old goat Philip when he kicks the bucket, although you could give it a lash for the craic. A *bodhrán* made out of the hide of the bold, baldy auld boy would fetch some bobs on eBay, and give a whole new lease of life to The Wolfe Tones, who were thankfully forced to decommission their instruments in 2005, although rumor has it that there is a ragtag unit of Continuity Wolfe Tones still at large in the country.

One of the most enjoyable things about Puck Fair was that it was as much, if not more, for the locals as it was for the blow-ins. As you literally rub shoulders with the clientele in Flavey's, it becomes clear that the vast majority of the crowd are local, and a clatter of them have returned home from far-flung places to be back in The Kingdom for King Puck's coronation. This festival isn't unique in this respect.

Many local festivals are not only a time to attract tourists to a place, but also a chance for those who had to leave an area to find work to come home and party unselfconsciously with those who know them best. Festivals like the Ballina Salmon Festival, or *Spraoi* in Waterford, are standout events on the social calendars of these places, and the perfect time for emigrants to return home, meet friends and party hard. When the town has a load of bunting and a band on the street to welcome you back is the perfect time to pop home for a visit.

Puck isn't all about the goat, the drinking and the sessioning. A horse fair that takes place at the start of the fair is a huge event in and of itself, and this blurs the boundaries between settled and Traveller culture once again. There is also a forest of stalls selling a kaleidoscope of kitsch circling the town, multiple stages banging out dodgy tunes for hours on end, parades, street entertainment, dancing and fireworks. At its heart, it's a community festival and, although the hordes who descend on the town probably leave the picturesque village in a worse state than if a herd of horned beasts had stampeded through it, the locals seem to take it in their stride, wishing each other a 'Happy Puck' amidst the madness. It's an exercise in old-school Irish festivalling. I'd recommend trying to go Puck yourself at least once. If acting the goat gets a bit much, Rossbeigh Beach is only fifteen minutes down the road, and you'd do well to find a better place to chill out anywhere in Ireland. I skipped the trip to the Kerry beach because I was bound for one of my favourite seaside spots in Duncannon, Co. Wexford.

Every year, sand sculptors take to the strand in Duncannon to take part in a seaside festival that makes use of all those buckets and spades that are sold during the summer. Besides being home to the Sand-Sculpting Festival, Duncannon has a special place in my heart; it's one of those very few beaches that you can drive onto. For just a little while, any time I park Wanderly Wagon on a beach like this, I have one of those homes I've always dreamed of, where on summer mornings, the tide comes right up and gently laps at my back door.

Even if you don't have a camper – the situation I was still in since Wanderly was laid up – being able to take the tent out of the boot and pitch it right beside the car is a bit of a luxury. When the sun shines down here, you wouldn't want to be anywhere else ... except maybe Inch Strand in Kerry, which is kind of similar, or Barleycove Beach at Mizen Head, or Roundstone in Connemara, or ... okay, I think you get the picture, we're blessed with a clatter of savage beaches. Waking up on the beach, in the sunshine, on a Sunday morning, and starting the day with a dip before breakfast is what summer should be all about. Lanzarote, me bollocks!

The professional bucket and spaders visit the Wexford seaside town earlier in the week, and have their creations prepared for people to visit when the assembled masses get to compete in the amateur sand-shovelling section. It's a competition, but it's fun. The entries range from your traditional sandcastle with moat, to cows and crocodiles. My favourite was a bottle of Guinness that used shells for the label and seaweed for the black stuff.

This is an ideal family festival that makes for a perfect day out, and it doesn't cost a bomb. Not only is there hours of fun to be had making stuff out of sand in a competition, but there were floating zorbs to run around in like an aquatic hamster, and proper wrestling with masked fellas pulling, dragging, jumping and lamping the bejangles out of each other – plenty of distractions for the most hyperactive of munchkins or ADHD adults.

Similarly to Kilorglin, the majority of people on the beach making castles were from Duncannon, but there were families from surrounding areas too. This festival isn't going to attract many foreign visitors, but that's not what it's built for. It's another simple idea, with some wholesome fun that energises a community and brings a few extra bodies into the town to join in the buzz. Crowning goats and building sandcastles are activities that hark back to bygone days, but both festivals show that it's still possible for old-time activities to provide good-time possibilities. With this in mind, I left the coast and headed inland for another antiquated pursuit at a steam threshing festival.

This was the second time I'd been to a vintage country fair in Co. Meath; they surely know how to throw a rocking rural reception in the Royal County. At the heart of this shindig is old-school steam threshing. This used to be a community activity where neighbours would call round and help each other to separate the grain from the straw. The steam and threshing machines were usually hired in for a few days of threshing and hard graft. It made sense for groups of neighbours to come together to hire the machines, use them communally and labour for one another. It was a keystone of rural community life. It also became an important social event, bringing friends and neighbours together in what was usually fine summer weather. It was tough work, but it had a festival atmosphere, and the hordes of people involved usually partied as hard as they worked when the sun went down and the large bottles of stout and instruments came out.

The combine harvester and increased mechanisation did away with the steam thresher and belt-driven elevators, but some people still fondly remember the old days spent threshing. It was honest graft, and getting everyone together was a great excuse for a party. It is not surprising, then, to find out that there are groups all over the country that maintain and wheel out these ancient machines to kick it one more time for the buzz and for old times' sake.

The folk in Moynalty have formed a club for this type of caper, and they get together to bring out the old machinery and immerse themselves in as much vintage romanticism as possible. There are tractors, cars, cottages, skillet pots, set-dancing, raffles, livestock competitions and many more activities that have been happening at country fairs for donkey's years. It might sound a little twee to some, but I find it very easy to be carried away by it all. There's a wholesome honesty and romanticism to the whole thing that sucks me in like a one-cent coin rattling up a Dyson. Give me a heaped plate of steaming colcannon, and an auld lad who's passionate about his rusting ancient Massey, and I'm happier than Jim Corr at a sci-fi convention. There's something safe and reassuring about auld lads and their love of tractors. It just feels right.

The public announcer at the festival had more than a little of *Father Ted* in his patter. I was waiting to hear an announcement about an incident in the tunnel of goats, but it never came. There were results for various raffles though, and thanks and praise to God for all the accidents that could have happened, but didn't. He went into detail about the accidents that might have happened. I had visions of children being maimed by threshers, and punters being attacked by rabid donkeys. Thank God is right! The whole day had a charm and cynic-slaying quality that is as rare as it is wonderful. This was some more of that good 'clane, chape fun' that I'd been running into all over the country. If there were any foreign tourists knocking around this joint, I couldn't spot them, and what a pity that is. The yanks would go nuts for this buzz. In a week that saw Discover Ireland support and lend their name to The Royal Dublin Horse Show, not steering a few foreigners towards the likes of Moynalty seems like a an awful shame and wasted opportunity. What visitor wouldn't want to stroke a prize-winning cock while being shown how to use an enamel potty and simultaneously fed pigs' feet? Then again, maybe the PR machine that churns out sterilised images of NAMA'd hotel resorts and perfectly manicured golf courses isn't needed in Moynalty. I've a

Ronnie Whelan that they'll survive, and happily continue to thresh the wheat regardless.

They might be there, but something told me you'd be hard pressed to find those responsible for our economic woes knocking around Moynalty. I might be wrong – it might be just that the atmosphere lent itself to harking back to the best parts of romanticized, innocent times, and I got tangled up in the visions of rose-tinted evenings in wheat fields. Even if that's what happened, there's nothing wrong with a little escapism every now and again, especially when it can be achieved without the use of intoxicants and for a minimal fee. I know that the likes of Moynalty Steam Threshing Festival might not be to everyone's jam jar of scald, and parts of it might even represent an Ireland that some wish was long-forgotten, but I couldn't help smiling like a fool as I skipped around the field humming 'I'm going home to Nobber'.

I was still kipping in the back of the Golf at this stage, but Wanderly Wagon was ready to be collected from the recovery ward, so I excitedly bounced down the road from Meath. My excitement was to be short-lived. In an ironic turn of events, I ended up being shipped to casualty myself. It was not through overindulgence, or the side effects of epic festivalling or socialising; it was while trying to be healthy that I did myself damage.

'So will you be going to your next festival in Wanderly Wheelchair this weekend?' read the text from a witty former friend when the news began to filter out that I'd been involved in a bit of rough and tumble. I felt like a tool, and more than a little guilty for wasting the time of the ambulance folk on something I shouldn't have really done.

While I was at home, I went out for a swim in a sea that wasn't too stormy, but was still kind of rough after some bad weather. I'd often been out in worse. The swim went off without a hitch, and it was invigorating being out in the swell. I'd finished, and was out of the water and back up on the platform built into the cliff side, when a wave came in over the rocks and washed across the platform. The sea decided that I hadn't finished my swim and, rather than letting me dive into the tide, it decided that the best way to get me back into the water was to wash me over the ledge onto some metal railings, some steps and across some rocks. The second swim wasn't as enjoyable.

I'd been romping around Ireland for more than eleven months, acting the maggot at every festival and freakish fête imaginable, and it was going for a fecking swim that saw me being loaded into the back of an ambulance. There's a lesson in there somewhere.

A busted nose, two black eyes, ligament and tissue damage in my right knee and in my foot, but the worst injury was a seriously fractured ego. An occasional camping buddy had brought his kids over to look at the stormy seas, arriving to have his evening brightened by the image of me and my busted nose being loaded into the back of an ambulance. Thanks for the photo, Gus.

There were only two weeks left in my quest, and it looked like I'd be limping over the finish line ... well, swinging over it on crutches. Thank God for painkillers!

More broken up than Katie Holmes and the little mad fella who jumps on couches, I still had three festivals a week to attend. I hopped up on the crutches and headed for Kill in Co. Waterford to attend the inaugural National Hen-Racing Championships. Racing hens at the back of a community centre in a rural part of Ireland is the kind of gathering that seems to pluck my feathers; it's possible I'd contracted some form of rural rubella after repeat visits to country fairs in Co. Meath, or maybe the chickenpox hadn't cleared up fully.

A flock of people had gathered, toting their feisty, feathered fliers in all manner of crates, boxes, cages and buckets. There were birds here of every shape, size, colour and level of experience, and there was even a pretty good variety of hens too. The competitors were registered, and assigned heats to establish a pecking order (expect some of the worst puns ever). Owners and trainers had to shell out a fiver for their birds to be registered, but this was a small price to pay for a shot at an All-Ireland title, and proceeds were going towards a defibrillator for the Community Centre – not as a first-aid precaution, but because it's the most efficient way to achieve the perfect boiled egg in one second flat. Clear! – *thump* – pass the toast.

The mood was more than a little flippant in the Olympic village. There was mention of hens being doped, training with Jamaican sprinters, Kentucky-fried losers and eggspert racers. The jokes were flying around the place like hens trying to escape a fox-infested coop. You could sense, though, that not that far beneath the good humour and hilarity lay a sense of pride, confidence and nervous energy. It was clear that a good deal of the crowd here were up for a laugh, but they wanted to win, and they believed that their chickens were destined to be something more than fast food.

Catherine, Paul and Johann had been training Thelma and Louise for months in preparation for the big day. Paul had perfected a series of calls that attracted the hens, and he had been practising these out in the back garden over the last few weeks. The lads even tried these techniques with the radio on, in an effort to create background noise that would be evident on the day, making sure that nothing would ruffle the racers' feathers. It was a sign of the times that this crew of coop-keepers weren't farmers, but town dwellers, who had joined the hordes of folk who had recently decided to grow some of their own grub and keep some hens for their daily eggs. They would have loved Moynalty.

The laughing and joking thinned out when race time arrived. The owners entered the enclosure with the sprinters, while the trainers went down to the finish line to try coax the racers home. You could have cut the tension with a knife. The referee told us that fowl play would not be tolerated, and that she wasn't afraid to give any bird that stepped out of line a roasting. She had her work cut out for her at times. One hen was starting fights with the other competitors and with the crowd. Paul has scars to prove it.

As the hens lined out for the first race, the owners placed them on the start line, and the referee shouted, 'On your mark. Set. Go!' the hens were released, and ... nothing! The birds ambled about, pecking the ground and nonchalantly clucking and checking out the crowd as their heads bobbed forwards in a full-frontal version of 'Walk Like an Egyptian'. It seems that one of the hardest things to train a hen to do is to run from point A to point B on demand. Eventually, one bird made a burst for the line, and the crowd erupted, only for the bird to turn around and head back the other way before crossing the line. This all just added to the general hilarity of the whole affair.

An afternoon watching hens kind-of-race each other is more fun than you might think, and it was nice to add some more photographs to my festival albumen (reaching with that one).

I was getting better on the crutches, and after a night buzzing around Dublin at the Down With Jazz Festival, it was off to Cong in Co. Mayo for some shenanigans at the

John Wayne Festival. I certainly wasn't going to be taking the piss out of how The Duke walked. Sixty years ago, the film *The Quiet Man* was shot in this picturesque corner of Mayo, and the village has been making hay out of it since. In fairness, the idyllic spot is worth a visit at any time of year. It's beautiful. The festival was a pretty standard small-town hooley with a gig-rig, some set-dancing and a duck race in the river. It was the setting that made it stand out from some others though; it's gorgeous around Cong. A goof under the weeping willows beside the river was ideal, charging the batteries and preparing for what was to come. I was finishing my year-long odyssey at Electric Picnic, the daddy of Hiberno-hedonist happenings.

One of the first things that this edition of Electric Picnic had going for it was the weather. After trudging through the mud at Indiependence, and having the bulb blown off us at Sea Sessions, it was nice to see smiling, happy campers flouncing about the pastures in their summer garb. Mingled with the smell of falafels and spilled beer was the light scent of Irish skin frying, and it did wonders for the soul. We deserved this. All summer we put the heads down and persevered with partying hard – this was our time in the sun, and when Max Romeo took to the stage on a glorious Sunday afternoon to lay down some reggae grooves, all was right in the world. Once more I felt that the Gods were smiling on my endeavour, and I cracked a smile too, knowing only too well that the heads who'd stayed up way past bedtime at the Rave in the Woods were more than likely cursing the same sunshine as they tried to catch a disco-nap in a boiling tent. You can't please all the people all the time, especially when disco biscuits and Buckfast are involved.

The difference the weather made to the disposition of the crowd can't be overestimated. We were ready to have a good time. There's always a huge mix of people and age groups at this gig, probably more than any other festival in a field I'd been at since my travels began. There were more kids and a wider span of age groups and demographics in this field than you'd get queuing to give Marty Whelan a puck in the jaw. It seemed as if there might actually be something here to keep most of them happy, most of the time. The kids are always well looked after by programmed events in the Body and Soul area, and even Heineken pitched in, offering the kids prizes for returning twenty empty cups. Having the children advertise the beer behemoth may have been morally questionable, but everyone involved seemed happy. Bless.

The Mindfield area prides itself on offering some mental stimulation. Here, you can buy Prosecco in stemmed glasses. Anne Enright was on hand to fire the imagination, Joe Duffy was grilling John Banville, and David McSavage was loitering with a set of nipple clamps. While all that was going on, the Trinity Orchestra started the morning out at the main stage with some Pink Floyd and the hard-core sessionistas were down in Trenchtown skinning up for breakfast and quaffing the first slugs of Buckfast to kick-start the day. On the wooded paths, the most hard-core contingent was finally making a burst for bed, shuffling along the woodland paths, pinballing off the trees and asking the freshly pressed family folk if they knew where Jimi Hendrix was.

A strange mix of heads from differing social stratospheres coexisted quite happily in the same space, each pursuing their own particular interests without caring what the rest of the Body Picnique was up to. Many times over the weekend I was put in mind of lyrics from Pulp's 'Sorted for E's and Whizz': 'Is this the way they say the future's meant to feel, or just 20,000 people standing in a field?' From early on, this was shaping up to be a memorable one. Cormac's Big Band kicked it off in style, and Donal Dineen gave thanks and praise to the massive crowd gathered down in Body and Soul in the wee small hours of the morning. I ran into Donal again hours later, when one of the lads, a bit the worse for wear, thought he was Donal Lunny and started singing Planxty tunes at him. Being a gentleman, Donal neither corrected nor objected.

This was the perfect way to finish my festival quest. I bumped into old and new friends, discovering that one of the advantages of being on crutches was that people reckoned it was hard for you to get to the bar, so they offered to get you pints. Score! Shauna turned up with her super soaker and distributed pressurised Buckfast direct from gun to gob – fair play to her. By 3.00 a.m. on the first night, my busted knee wasn't hurting me as much any more, and ligaments seemed stitched together – possibly a miracle. By the time I hit the *leaba*, after 7.00 a.m., I hardly needed the second crutch at all. I was expecting severe payback the next day, but whatever cocktail of intoxicants I hit upon, it did the job, and I stuck to one crutch on day two. I stayed up until exactly the same time on the second night, and tried to recreate the same pattern of consumption, just to be on the safe side.

Choosing a path through Electric Picnic is never easy. Should you head up to Natasha's for a healthy brunch and skip down to Mindfield with a wheatgrass smoothie to cast an ear over some thought-provoking chat? There's a gospel choir over here, there's an S&M freak in rubber over there, a young fella trying to eat a Kellog's Nutrigrain through his ear telling you about last night's conquests in front of you, and disco bunnies in the woods peddling pills. There are as many routes through Electric Picnic as there are bachelor farmers in Lisdoonvarna on a September weekend.

Restaurateurs gushed about the Theatre of Food, buzzers suggested avoiding the blue ghosts, a medical student was selling vodka jelly shots, and a respectable businesswoman threw seaweed at a midget down at the Salty Dog stage at 5.00 a.m. There was something here for everyone. Even though the word 'boutique' is still bandied about, thankfully there were a couple of scumbags knocking about the place, lending some needed edge and colour.

I was down in the woods at all hours of the morning when a big Eastern-European lad on crutches hopped up to me, and through our common complaint we started chewing the fat. 'How d'it happen?' I asked. 'Two guys held me down and a third guy broke my leg in three places with a hammer.' 'Sweet Jaysus! Why did they do that?' 'I stab one of them with screwdriver.' Of course, I had to ask what any reasonable person would ask in that situation. He'd used a Phillips-head.

Two pretty girlies came up to us feeling all motherly and asking us if we were okay. As soon as your man told them the story, they legged it. I would have been out of there too if he wasn't so hard to shake. He was pretty handy on those fecking crutches. I'd been at many Electric Picnics, getting gloriously wasted at the very first one, and missing most of the acts I'd gone to see. I knew that I felt just as comfortable in the woods at 5.00 a.m. as I would in the Mindfield at 5.00 p.m., but it was always in the woods where I laughed more lustily.

A couple of friends of mine brought their kids to the festival, and the whole crew of them loved it. The only drawback was that they had the misfortune to make their home beside some boisterous *buachaillí* who were determined to show how true to life Ross O'Carroll Kelly's characters can be, even in festivalling twenty-somethings. Catherine, Allie and the three kids weren't keeping the same hours as their neighbours, and when the lads next door came home and fired up the stereo after 4.00 a.m., the girls had to ask a few times if they wouldn't mind keeping the noise down. The boys were quite nasty in return with some comments, and they actually turned up the stereo, laughing at their drunken bravado. Had this been Oxegen, shouting, scrawbing and scuffles might have ensued, but this was a much more refined affair; all this happening in the VIP camping area, the young lads had connections with the top brass.

The girls called down to the van the next day, and were telling me about their sleepless night when one of them spotted my en-suite. I had got into the habit of keeping an empty Innocent juice bottle in the van in case I needed to shed the tear for Parnell in the middle of the night. Those particular juice bottles are the perfect shape and capacity. (What? There's no point introducing glamour at this late stage in proceedings.) Catherine asked if they could have my now-full en-suite facility to take away with them. It saved me emptying it, so I let them take it away, a little confused.

The girls went back to the tent, waited until the coast was clear that afternoon, and it was then they snuck into their noisy neighbours' tents, where they proceeded to mix my piss with the lads' Captain Morgan. Spicy! That night they lay back to enjoy their *Fried Green Tomatoes* moment. Hell hath no fury, dude. A saline salient lesson: sure it never did Madonna or Gandhi any harm and, to be honest, after the night I'd had, my piss was probably more potent than the lads' rum.

One of the events that seemed to catch the spirit of the whole weekend for me was Mr Motivator leading aerobics

sessions in front of massive crowds who were on a dance
floor that generated electricity. Here was fella in his sixties,
wearing a ridiculous leotard, a dude who was kitsch even
in the early nineties, jumping up and down and punching
the air, and the crowd loved it. There were hundreds of
people packed into the tent, and they went all the way from
little kiddies up to Motivator's contemporaries. Drunken
louts, hyper kids, hipsters, ecceed-up youfs and yummy
mummies, all smiling like tools, doing exactly what the
looper in the leotard told them. It shouldn't have, but it
worked, and it made people smile ... a lot! You can't argue
with that. Genius.

It was a suitably epic weekend. Electric Picnic was the
perfect way to finish my quest, going out with a bang and
a bit. Monday night saw the most extreme bout of post-
festival blues I'd ever suffered. It felt like there had been
a death in the family, and I was the corpse. To paraphrase
Jarvis Cocker, it felt like I may have left an important part
of my brain somewhere in a field in Co. Laois.

That was it, I was done. Three festivals every week for a
whole year. Finito! There would be no three festivals for
me the following week. What would I do with myself next
weekend? I decided I'd only go to two. Bog-Snorkelling
and Harvest Time Blues in Monaghan. Did you think I'd
be able to stop?

Festivals Attended in August

171. Castlepalooza – Tullamore, Co. Offaly
172. Lissard – Bantry, Co. Cork
173. Indiependence – Mitchelstown, Co. Cork
174. Puck Fair – Killorglin, Co. Kerry
175. Sand-Sculpting Festival – Duncannon, Co. Wexford
176. Moynalty Steam Threshing Festival – Moynalty, Co. Meath
177. Kilkenny Arts Festival – Kilkenny, Co. Kilkenny
178. Hen-Racing Championships – Kill, Co. Waterford
179. Summerfest – New Ross, Co. Wexford
180. John Wayne Festival – Cong, Co. Mayo
181. Tall Ships Festival – Dublin City
182. Down with Jazz – Dublin City
183. Electric Picnic – Stradbally, Co. Laois

Other Recommended Festivals in August

Spraoi Festival – Waterford City
Big House Festival – Cellbridge, Co. Kildare
Birr Vintage Week and Arts Festival – Birr, Co. Offaly
Booleigh Ska Festival – Booleigh, Co. Kildare

14 | *Full of Gemütlichkeit*

This festival quest saw me clock up 183 festivals in twelve months. The numbers pleased me, as did surviving and completing the whole year's travels. What was even more satisfying and rewarding than crossing the line or hitting a target was the journey itself. At Castlepalooza I parked my van alongside Martin's – he's the fella responsible for putting together the Trenchtown area at Electric Picnic and Body and Soul. We aligned our vans very closely, so that the sliding doors were facing each other and we could kick back in our respective comfort zones and chew the festival fat into the wee small hours. 'Martin, would you believe that people keep asking me if I don't get tired going to all of these festivals?' Martin chuckled and replied, 'If only they knew.' Hopefully, you've got some idea now.

I'm still surprised at the amount of things that are happening all over Ireland every weekend, and at the effervescence with which the inhabitants of our towns, villages and cities are fizzing and popping.

The Germans have a word of which I've become very fond: *Gemütlichkeit*. In the early days of my festival odyssey, I rolled up to the gate of a festival called *Rock an Oírr* in west Co. Waterford. At the security checkpoint, a burly dude in a luminous vest approached the van and made that defunct but still recognisable gesture to roll down the window. I readied some tried and trusted blags for dealing with such bouncer *buachaills*, but he caught me on the hop. 'Open your mouth and say "aww",' he instructed, and, startled by the odd request, I obliged. He produced a super-soaker and proceeded to spray a jet of beer directly into my gob. I had an immense sense of *Gemütlichkeit*.

I was lucky enough to duck up to Derry for a gander at what was happening at the *Fleadh Cheoil na* hÉireann, the first *Fleadh* held north of the border. The buzz in the Derry air was palpable. Businesses had their windows painted, temporary stages and bars popped up in the most unlikely places, the PSNI felt more like holiday reps than the law, continental markets, bunting and banners, friendly natives, wall-to-wall trad and T-shirts that overcame that old political hot potato of the city's name by having 'LegenDerry' emblazoned across the chest. There was heaps of *Gemütlichkeit* corralled within the city's walls.

Hitting so many festivals every week, there are always some familiar faces knocking around. One of these faces belongs to a dude called Cheeves. You can usually find this fella after sunset by following the trail of balloons that light the night with their internal LEDs. Cheeves brings hundreds of balloons and tiny LED lights with him to festivals, handing out the bouncy night-lights to strangers for free. The LEDs only cost ten cents, so for a tenner a night he inflates and lights up a hundredweight of joy. Cheeves is a *Gemütlichkeit* generator.

Joanna fills her pockets with glittery stars when she heads off to a festival, and as she waits in the queue for the jacks, she takes them out and sticks them on the faces of those waiting with her. She told me that it makes the wait seem shorter, and makes everyone around her smile. *Gemütlichkeit!*

Sian and Dave are very easy to spot once the sun goes down at some of our biggest festivals in fields. This married couple put their wedding gear on most nights, but their clothes have been fitted with hundreds of twinkly and shiny lights. If you give one of them a hug, the lights will flash and change colour. These guys brighten the night at every festival they attend. Like so many other people I met over the year, they are full of *Gemütlichkeit*.

As I kicked back in the van, chatting to Martin at Castlepalooza, he excitedly told me about plans for an installation/drive-in that would be screening Jamaican flicks in Trenchtown at that year's Electric Picnic, and about some of the savage acts who'd be dropping beats and booming out some sub-bass on stage. Martin explained how it's getting tougher to put the whole show together without making a loss. I asked why in the name of God himself the crew works so hard putting the thing together if they're not making a few bob out of it. 'Seeing people's expressions and how much they enjoy the thing.' A marvelous masala of *Gemütlichkeit*, *cairdiúlacht* and *irie na* hÉireann.

We might be short of a few bob, but our reserves of *Gemütlichkeit* are as healthy as ever. I'd decided to head off on the road, looking for a side of Ireland that not only hadn't lost the run of itself, but was working hard to promote everything that was good about the places where they lived. Meeting all those people and experiencing the festivals they organised rekindled the most positive aspects of the country within me. It's been the oddest and best decision I've ever made. The quest turned out better than I could ever have imagined.

There were other things that happened outside the festival experiences, which made me feel like I was actually a jammy bastard.

Winning the All-Ireland Conker Championships was a fluke, and awfully funny, but the next morning I was on-air with Hector on 2FM talking about my festival quest. Hector and his producer Alan kept in touch, and I've been on with them for a chat from time to time since. When I won the Bucket-Singing Championship, I ended up on-air with John Murray on RTÉ Radio 1, embarrassingly giving a demonstration of the ancient art live on the show. I became a regular contributor to the show with a weekly festival diary, and I contribute content to the programme from time to time.

After a few months on the road, I sent the editor of 'The Ticket' in *The Irish Times* an email, and she somehow decided to give me a weekly column. Being printed in the national press every week opened so many doors, and got me into places in which I had no business being at all. No matter how risqué and colorful the content got, Anthea still let me put it in the paper. She rocks.

Interest in my journey kept gathering momentum as I trundled around the country, and there were several more interviews on radio and television, but there were a few things that happened that stood out and saw me having another couple of 'moments'.

The Young Scientist and Technology Exhibition is an institution and a wonderful event that I can't praise highly enough. The last time I attended, it was the usual invigorating and enlightening experience that I've come to expect and love. As I left the RDS, I noticed some press cuttings pinned to a display, and I stopped for a look. In the middle of them, highlighted with luminous green marker, was a piece I'd written in that week's paper about the event. I was taken aback. I was shocked and confused; it hadn't really dawned on me that other people, besides my mother, might be reading what I was writing. I felt kind of humbled to have the thing that I banged out at home on my laptop pinned to a notice board at the Young Scientist and Technology Exhibition. There was either some kind of mistake, or this shit was getting serious.

On a St. Patrick's Day recce, I ended up in Duncannon, Co. Wexford, for Ireland's only parade on a beach. The tractor-porn on display was magnificent. But by far and away my favourite element of this parade, and possibly of any parade anywhere ever, was Duncannon's Parish Priest, Father Nolan, in a tricolour wig and shamrock Elton John shades, aboard one of the best vintage tractors you're ever likely to see or hear chugging along. He was rocking that tractor chic. I took clatters of pictures of Father Nolan and his wonderful machine, and wrote about it the following week. Some months afterwards I got an email from a dude in Duncannon, who told me that when the kids of the town made their communion that year, they had received a copy of the piece I'd written and one of my photographs, and put it in a frame and presented it to Father Nolan. The bastards made me well up; it was just too darn sweet.

I wasn't used to all this kindness, especially as I wanted to maintain something close to a rock 'n' roll image of life on the road. This stuff was turning me mushy, and worse was still to come. I'd been invited to give a talk on my journey and discuss the Irish festival landscape in general by the Association of Irish Festivals and Events, an umbrella group whose members include most of the sessions I'd been attending all year. The talk went really well, even the parts about amateur drama festivals, so I decided that I deserved a pint in the hotel bar. I was dug into some enjoyable chats about festivals when we were asked to adjourn to the ballroom for a bit of a to-do with the Minister for State Tourism and Sport. The minister was on hand to pass out some award or other. I wasn't really paying attention, but then I heard my name called out, and people started clapping. The people who organise the festivals I'd been leeching off for the previous year were giving me an award, after they did all the blooming work! I was mortified, and had another 'moment'. Even after I ended up in a wrestling ring in the hotel lobby at 4.00 a.m. that night/morning, they've invited me back to speak again. It's nuts!

It has reached a point now where I sometimes get offered work by PR agencies representing corporate clients to go to festivals for them, taking photographs, offering festival advice and writing about the experience. Let me just clarify that: people are now willing to pay me to go to festivals. The wonderful irony of my year-long quest is that I may now be in danger of losing the run of myself. The cost of houses shows signs of bottoming out, austerity is being rolled back and the light at the end of the tunnel may be about to be reignited. Am I ready to go back to the bank with cap in hand and to try to sort out a mortgage? Fuck that!

I bought another camper van.

Safe travels, don't die.